KT-423-888

Working for Women?
Gendered Work and Welfare Policies
in Twentieth-Century Britain

Celia Briar

UCL
PRESS

© Celia Briar, 1997

This book is copyright under the Berne Covention.
No reproduction without permission.
All rights reserved.

First published in 1997 by UCL Press

UCL Press Limited
1 Gunpowder Square
London EC4A 3DE
UK

and

1900 Frost Road, Suite 101
Bristol
Pennsylvania 19007-1598
USA

The name University College London (UCL) is a registered
trade mark Used by UCL Press with the consent of the owner.

British Library Cataloguing-in-Publication Data
A Catalogue record for this book is available from the British
Library

**Library of Congress Cataloging-in-Publication Data are
available**

All efforts have been made to trace the copyright holder of
the illustrations used on the front cover. These were photo-
graphed by P. G. Hennell and were reproduced in J. B.
Priestley's *British Women Go to War* (Collins, c.1942).

ISBNs: 1-85728-784-3 (HB)
        1-85728-785-1 (PB)

Typeset in 10/12 pt Times
by Best-set Typesetter Ltd., Hong Kong

Printed by SRP Ltd, Exeter.

THE
NORTHERN COLLEGE
LIBRARY CANCELLED
BARNSLEY

CN 331·4
=
AN 58771

Working for Women?

Northern College
Library

NC00172

Contents

Contents

Preface

My interest in factors affecting women's employment has arisen first out of the personal, but for women very common experience of a meandering career path. After leaving school in the mid-1960s, apart from taking two years out following the birth of my first child, courses of study and short periods of unemployment, I was employed in a series of typical 'women's jobs'. I worked in hotels and bars, a library, a hairdressing salon, a university bookshop, the office of a brewery, an unemployment benefit office and the shop floor of a factory which had once been a cotton-weaving mill.

Second, my experience of social policy has also been personal as well as academic. I was attracted to return to full-time education in the late 1970s by new and relevant-sounding social studies degrees at my nearest polytechnic; but it was the availability of student grants and a policy of welcoming mature students with childcare responsibilities that made it possible for me to take up the opportunity. Nine years later I re-emerged into the paid workforce with a degree, a divorce, a PhD, teaching experience and my second child. By this time, however, the labour market situation had altered radically. Government-induced high unemployment and rampant 'qualifications inflation' meant that individuals re-entering the paid workforce had little chance of finding a secure full-time job. Employers and the government assumed that part-time temporary employment (and pay) was perfectly adequate for mothers. For the next two years I maintained my family by holding part-time lecturing positions simultaneously in three different towns. In 1988 I accepted an offer of a full-time tenured university lecturing position in New Zealand, where at that time policies of 'deregulating' the labour market were less advanced than in Britain.

This book draws upon my PhD thesis, which was completed at Sheffield University in 1986. In 1995 I was able to spend nine months back in England to revise, update, add three new chapters and publish it. I owe a great deal to the people, groups and organizations that have helped and encouraged me in various ways., My PhD supervisor, Alan Walker, and Hilary Rose first suggested that I publish it. The members of the Lancaster Women's Studies Research group, especially Sylvia Walby, Janet Finch, Penny Summerfield and Jane Mark Lawson provided support, advice and inspiration during the thesis-writing stage of the project. Gordon Johnston did more childcare and housework than the average father; and my two sons Liam and Michael, both much younger then, provided diversions, motivation and a sense of perspective.

I am grateful to my employer, Massey University, for giving me paid sabbatical leave in which to write this book, and the Departments of Women's Studies and North West Regional Sudies at Lancaster University for hosting me during the writing process. I should especially like to thank Penny Summerfield and Elizabeth Roberts for making me welcome and for reading part of the book in draft form, and Irene Bruegel, Diane Perrons, Deirdre Beddoe, Dulcie Groves, Gail Braybon, Jane Millar, Mary Nash and Christine Cheyne who also read and commented on draft chapters. Lydia Martens engaged in some useful conversations and let me read her unpublished work. My mother, Audrey Harland, kindly collected relevant press cuttings, and she and Jean Withington often listened to my ideas at length over coffee. Any errors or omissions are entirely my own.

I found the staff at Lancaster and Sheffield University libraries, the Equal Opportunities Commission and the National Library, Wellington, New Zealand, all very helpful. Thanks to Mary and Roy Nash for lending me J. B. Priestley's *British Women Go to War* (Collins, *c*.1942) from which the cover illustrations were taken. Finally, I particularly appreciated Alison Chapman and Fiona Kinghorn at Taylor & Francis keeping me in touch and on track by e-mail on my return to New Zealand.

Chapter 1

Introduction

Social and Economic Policies: Working for Women?

Why do women work so hard and yet remain so much poorer than men? And why, at the end of the twentieth century, have the interventions of governments still not changed this basic fact? This book examines the ways in which women's patterns of paid and unpaid work have been mediated by past and present social and economic policies, and whether these might conceivably change in the future. As the title, *Working for Women?*, implies, it is questionable whether most twentieth-century British governments have improved the position of working women relative to working men. Indeed, *Working for Women?* highlights a series of processes and strategies through which politicians of all major political parties (even when claiming to promote equality) have subverted feminist demands for improved economic rewards for women in paid employment and unpaid work. The evidence suggests that despite some feminist victories, patriarchal forces have combined to dominate government policy-making throughout the century.

The main interests influencing government policies in twentieth-century Britain have been those of employers and, to a considerable but lesser extent, those of working men. Although employers and trade unions are normally characterized as having conflicting aspirations, there is a good deal of evidence in this book and elsewhere of collusion between them about the position of working women. Many of the important policy agreements referred to in this book have been 'tripartite': that is, they have been made between government, employers and trade unions, but have usually not included women's organizations. Most often, although not always, these arrangements have been detrimental to working women's interests. It is important to question why this alliance has existed, and whether this is inevitably always going to be so.

However, the book also argues that different alliances could be formed at the level of the State, which would improve the material position of all low-income groups. This is important, because State policies have greater potential to improve the economic situation of women and other marginalized groups than the unrestricted market. The book therefore ends by exploring how the patriarchal welfare State might become a 'woman friendly' State, which new principles could inform policy-making and which policies could work for women.

The Scope of the Book

There is now a considerable body of feminist writing which has documented women's varied experiences in paid and unpaid work, past and present (see, for example, Roberts, 1984, 1995; Braybon and Summerfield, 1987). Many precise forms of discrimination against women, in various kinds of workplaces, have also been described in detail.[1] However, most writers have devoted little attention to the effects of the State's social policies on working women.[2] *Working for Women?*, by contrast, concentrates mainly on the policies of the State, which have profoundly influenced women's pay, conditions and experience in paid and unpaid work. *Working for Women?* takes an overview of government policies affecting women's relative economic position in Britain between 1905 and 1995. It traces shifts and continuities through periods of boom and slump and two world wars. Other useful feminist historical works which are referred to in this text have dealt with social policies affecting working women in shorter timeframes and hence in greater detail.[3] A long timeframe, as in this book, is also useful, however, as it allows patterns in policy-making to emerge more clearly.

By contrast, mainstream social policy texts have on the whole tended to devote very little attention to employment policies, and especially to their impact on working women. Some still omit to mention women at all.[4] Feminist social policy writers have, not surprisingly, made the largest contribution to an understanding of the effects of social policies upon working women.[5] There is also a small but growing international feminist literature on women and economic policy which concentrates firmly on working women and the state.[6] Even social and economic policy texts which look at the relationship between working women and the State tend to look at recent history, rather than at longer historical patterns. Finally, *Working for Women?* is unusual in proposing alternatives. The problem of working women's poverty seems so large and yet so institutionalized that it appears difficult to find any solution which would be effective for most working women but would still be considered 'reasonable' by employers and most politicians.[7] Yet if solutions are not found, most women will remain poor. In a number of respects, therefore, *Working for Women?* fills a gap in the existing literature.

Working for Women? is, nevertheless, not intended to be a comprehensive account of social and economic policies affecting women's material wellbeing. To do so would have taken several volumes. For example, it does not deal in detail with taxation policies or retirement pensions. More attention is given to policies affecting women's paid employment than unpaid work. Policies affecting working-class women receive somewhat more attention than those affecting middle-class women. However, the book does focus on patterns of recruitment of women into paid work and demobilization out of paid employment, the unequal treatment of unemployed women, equal pay and opportunities policies, government-sponsored training and the principles governing the nature and extent of State child care; and, in a later chapter, it also examines the gendered impact of the deregulation of the labour market. It should hopefully be useful to students of women's studies, social policy, economics and history as well as to the interested general reader.

Women, Paid Employment, Unpaid Work and Government Policy

Work consists of all activities which people carry out in order to live (Lewenhak, 1988, p. 15). In pre-industrial times most work was unwaged (Pahl, 1992, p. 132). By contrast, the majority of people in modern societies do not have access to an independent livelihood, for example from the land. Most are dependent on a wage from paid employment (which has come to be treated by policy-makers as if it was the only form of work), on a State benefit or on another person. However, an equally striking feature of the organization of work is the way it is divided by gender. There have been 'men's jobs' and 'women's jobs' since before industrialization, although many occupations that were formerly female-dominated have been taken over by men and vice versa. The enduring difference between 'men's work' and 'women's work' is that occupations that are seen as men's at any particular time are usually valued more highly (Bradley, 1989).

Government accounting systems in countries such as Britain do not count unpaid work, most of which is performed by women (Waring, 1988); and women working outside the paid workforce are still officially described as 'economically inactive' (*Employment Gazette*, 1995). Even some feminist writers describe women who are out of paid employment as 'not working' (Dex, Walters and Alden, 1993). Housework, though essential, is hidden, private, isolated, trivialized and unpaid: it exists outside what is still often considered to be the world of production, and it is normally by the goodwill of a wage-earner that the housewife receives all or part of her economic support. By contrast, paid employment, though often producing inessential or even harmful items, and frequently debilitating and boring for the employee, is dignified with the title of 'work', and waged workers have been regarded as 'independent', even though they are in fact dependent on a wage.

In modern economic systems, money is the main measure of value. A large part of women's work is unpaid and therefore unvalued. Work is also the means by which people create their social identity. If the work of a group of people is unvalued or undervalued, those people are also deprived of status and power. By describing a woman with preschool children, who may be working 100 hours a week, as 'economically inactive', we are effectively making her, as well as her work, invisible. In this book I distinguish between paid employment and unpaid labour, but describe both as work. Virtually all women work.

How should we assess whether social and economic policies have benefited working women? The extent to which women's share of direct income has increased between 1905 and 1995 and the proportion of women capable of supporting themselves and any dependents are the main criteria used in this book. Although women have largely obtained formal political equality during the twentieth century, and have entered paid work in larger numbers, economic independence and freedom from poverty have continued to elude women, especially wives and mothers (Lewis and Piachaud, 1992). This is a worldwide phenomenon: however, the extent of women's economic dependency has been particularly striking in countries such as Britain, the United States and Australia, compared with nations such as Sweden (Hobson, 1990; Bryson, 1992). These differences are associated with significant divergences in social policy. Scandinavian social policy has been consistently characterized by stronger equal-pay legislation, more State nursery provision and more generous child benefits and paid parental leave than the English-speaking nations (Adams and Winston, 1980; Ruggie, 1984; Hernes, 1987, p. 15). Nonetheless, even the more 'progressive' welfare States remain gendered, in that their policies still reproduce income disparities between women and men, and caring is still done primarily unpaid in the home, mainly by women (Leira, 1993).

The employment and family policies of the State, particularly in the English-speaking world, tend to be implicit rather than overt. Normally the impression is given that most of the conditions in the paid workforce, including inequalities based on gender, ethnicity and class, are the result of agreements freely made between employers and employees. Nevertheless, governments in twentieth-century Britain have at times directly exercised enormous powers over working men and women and even over employers. During the Second World War women and men were conscripted and could be directed into the most dangerous types of paid work; and leaving such employment, or persistent absence, was an imprisonable offence. Even in peacetime, government social and economic policies have a major impact on the number and types of jobs available, over how different types of work are valued and over who has preferential access to the positions with the best pay and prospects within the paid workforce. Similarly, the equally hidden family policies of the State have had a huge impact on power relations within households and over who does the bulk of the unpaid work. The State's role in maintaining inequalities at work has nevertheless been largely hidden, especially since the 1970s. Exposing the gendered social and economic policies of twentieth-century British governments is a central task of *Working for Women?* Equally, however, it is argued here that the State has enormous power which could potentially be used to bring about greater economic equality for women.

Working Women and the State in the Late-nineteenth Century

Much of the policy framework which is described in *Working for Women?* was already established by the late-nineteenth century. A series of government reports from the 1840s illustrated policy-makers' concern that girls should learn to become good housewives rather than regular employees.[8] In particular, inspectors of mines and factories judged girls and women according to their sexual conduct rather than their capacity for hard work (Walby, 1986, pp. 115–16). Wives' economic dependence came to be seen by policy-makers as normal and desirable and the concept of the family wage was accepted, irrespective of whether workmen actually earned enough to support a family. Lower pay for women was legal and the general rule.

During the nineteenth century women's opportunities for remunerative employment narrowed, as many traditional areas of 'women's work' were moved to factory production and came to be performed by men. The main opportunity left open to women was domestic service (Schreiner, 1918; Pinchbeck, 1981; Walby, 1986, pp. 94–5). Women were excluded by working men from most trade unions and thus from a wide range of skilled occupations, thus keeping men's wages higher than they would otherwise have been (Walby, 1986, p. 92 and Appendix 1). No State action was taken to prevent these restrictive practices against them, even though unions themselves were at times illegal. A series of pieces of 'protective' legislation from the 1840s onwards limited the hours of paid factory work of women and children and banned women from working underground in coal mines. It became more difficult for working-class women to obtain a living from paid employment. Opportunities for middle- and upper-class unmarried women to obtain a dignified livelihood through their own labour were also restricted.

There were exceptions, however. For example, during the early-nineteenth century, in cotton-weaving, because of the initial reluctance of hand-loom weavers to give up their independence and enter the factories, some employers took the opportunity to employ women and children instead of an exclusively male workforce, although males were still employed in the best paid and most senior positions. Working-class women in the Burnley/ Nelson area retained their position in cotton-weaving until after the Second World War.

Although access to a livelihood from paid work was becoming more the exception than the rule, it was high on the agenda of feminists in the second half of the nineteenth century. The Campaign to Promote Women's Employment was founded in 1859; and women became more active in trade unions: this included forming their own Women's Protective and Provident League in 1874. By the first decade of the twentieth century feminists were making demands for women's equal right to an independent livelihod through paid employment.[9]

Contents of Chapters 2–10

Chapters 2–7 examine a series of twentieth-century employment policies towards women. The focus of Chapter 2 is on government responses to feminist demands for women's 'right to work' and for women's unemployment to be treated as a serious issue during the decade before the outbreak of the First World War. Following a campaign by the Women's Industrial Council, women were included in the 1905 Unemployed Workmen Act and some women were provided with work – although not on the same scale or under the same terms as men, nor was the value of their work assessed according to the same criteria. During this period a number of the principles that governed policies about women's paid and unpaid work were challenged, partially revised and ultimately reaffirmed, laying the foundations for policy later in the century. Women's unemployment did not come to be seen as a problem requiring intervention by the State, and arguably it still has not. Married women were not classed as 'independent' but were expected to be dependent on husbands and obtain their keep through their unwaged household labour. Single women were also expected to obtain their living through domestic labour, but for low pay in the homes of either the well-to-do or in their family home. Whereas men's 'morality' was judged by policy-makers in terms of whether they were good regular workmen, women were judged in terms of whether they were thrifty, sober, obedient and faithful actual or potential wives. During this period the State was ambivalent about the position of widows, however, and much of the debate around women's 'right to work' centred on this group. By the end of the decade, policy-makers had settled on a view that 'good' widows were to qualify for a State benefit and that the State would act as surrogate husband and provider; whereas waged labour was appropriate only to mothers who were 'fallen'.

Chapter 3 examines government recruitment policies during the First World War and the idea and process of 'substitution' of women for men in the paid workforce. The chapter describes the process by which, following a slow and reluctant start by government, women were drawn into the lower ranks of 'men's jobs'. It examines the ways in which women were brought into 'men's jobs' as 'subsitutes for men', but always treated *as women* in terms of wages, conditions and job security, notwithstanding some of the tensions that existed because of the reluctance to allow women to do 'men's jobs' which undercut the drive for increased production. Finally the process of demobilization is recorded. At the end of the First World War this involved a rapid removal of women from 'men's jobs', as the result of pressure from both employers and trade unions. Certain questions are highlighted by this chapter: for example, why, given that women rapidly and efficiently learned to 'substitute' for men, did gender differentiation in the workplace remain so marked? And why were employers prepared to allow the exclusion of low-paid, productive and exploitable women workers at the end of the war?

Chapter 4, by contrast, documents a series of policies affecting working women during the period of high unemployment between the wars. It charts the drive by governments of this period, including Labour, to remove women, especially married women, from jobs that provided an independent livelihood and to reaffirm women as low-paid or unpaid domestic workers. Specifically it examines the removal of women from 'men's jobs' between 1919 and 1928; the 'marriage bar', the use of benefits regulations to persuade women to re-enter domestic service, including the domestic service training schemes, the refusal to provide work schemes for unemployed women, and the denial of benefits to unemployed women, through the Not Genuinely Seeking Work Clause and the Anomolies Regulations. Again the evidence shows that trade unions and employers had very similar polices where the employment of women was concerned, and that these were largely supported by government measures.

Chapter 5 focuses specifically on the processes by which, despite a huge increase in demand for labour during the Second World War, the wartime government managed to maintain hierarchical gender divisions virtually intact during and after the war. During both world wars there was a marked decrease of horizontal gender divisions in paid work, as women moved into the wider range of jobs normally dominated by men; but vertical gender divisions in employment were carefully maintained. This chapter looks particularly at patterns of government recruitment and training of war workers, and the ways in which these helped to maintain gender distinctions even when women were doing vitually the full range of 'men's jobs'. The chapter also describes the 'welfare' policies for women workers (childcare, time off for shopping, the encouragement of works canteens and British Restaurants) which made it somewhat easier for women to combine paid work and housework during the war, without actually relieving women of the responsibility for unpaid domestic work and caring. Finally the chapter examines the intricate process of demobilization and the transfer of women back into lower paid 'women's jobs' during the last stages of the war, and the policies and principles which were to inform social policies towards working women in the postwar era.

The postwar boom, up until 1970, has been described by contemporary policy-makers as one in which women were emancipated, gained the 'right to work' and equality of opportunity in employment. Women's participation in paid employment, particularly that of married women, increased and the 'marriage bar' was officially ended after the war. However, as Chapter 6 shows, the policies of governments helped to ensure that women in Britain did not participate in equal numbers or on the same terms as men. Although women labour force participation rates rose, and women were described during this period as having a 'dual role', it is clear on closer examination that women's domestic role was still central, at least where white and British-born women were concerned. Opportunities for women in paid employment were overwhelmingly in low-paid 'women' jobs', and there was a growth in part-time employment which could be fitted around women's domestic responsibilities. Governments in Britain delayed equal pay legislation for as long as they were able, and then introduced narrow and relatively ineffective laws. The recruitment and training strategies of postwar governments, as well as childcare policy, also reinforced women's disadvantaged position in the paid workforce, so that most women did not gain economic independence through their paid work. At the same time, most welfare benefits were denied to married women. In these ways, the creation of the 'dual role' meant that women's secondary position in paid work and their primary responsibility for unpaid domestic work was reinforced.

Chapter 7 examines the contradictions between equal opportunities policies and the move to a more flexible labour market. It explains why, despite the 1975 Sex Discrimination Act (and its subsequent amendments) and the United Nations Decade for Women which also began in 1975, over two decades later women still occupy a marginal position in the paid labour force and continue to take most responsibility for unpaid household work. It does this by examining other policies affecting women's paid and unpaid work during the same period, and the ways in which these undermined the stated intentions of the 1975 Act. These included childcare policy, parental leave policy legislation, deinstitutionalization and 'community care', benefit regulations which were kept outside the legal scope of the Sex Discrimination Act, the type of training and the scale of provision of work for unemployed women, and especially the expansion of temporary part-time employment. It assesses the extent to which working women have benefited in economic terms from the policies decribed in the ealier chapters. It argues that women's poverty and economic insecurity is still a major problem, and that government policies have not made the kinds of changes in women's working lives that most feminists would have hoped for.

Chapter 8 acts as a 'bridging' chapter to see whether, looking at the whole period 1905–1995, employment policies have served to improve the position of working women. It does this mainly by assessing whether women's relative material position has improved markedly since 1905. It shows that despite women's rising labour force participation rates, this has not been accompanied by economic independence or equal status – or even the prospect of these. It also attempts to see which of the policies that have been implemented so far appear to have been most beneficial to working women, which have been least effective and which have been positively harmful.

Chapter 9 asks whether, since State policy has throughout the twentieth century been to a considerable extent responsible for women's subordinate social and financial status, it is now realistic to expect British governments to enact reforms to conteract women's poverty and economic dependence. It argues that although State action has been disappointing to feminists, there appear to be no viable alternatives; and that the challenge is to create a combination of forces which could bring about such a policy transformation. The chapter asks: What kinds of principles and economic policies could win the active support of both women and men? What kinds of safeguards would women require to ensure that their interests are not overlooked again?

Chapter 10 looks at the kinds of specific policies which would fit with the principles discussed in the previous chapter. It suggests that in addition to an expansion of the policies described in Chapter 8 as having worked, there are others which, with enough popular support, could be introduced and which would improve women's *and most men's* financial position and quality of life. It proposes three interconnected additional policies. These are a universal basic income, a shorter working week and a guaranteed minimum hourly wage. These would not by themselves guarantee women full social equality or citizenship. However, by lifting women out of poverty and providing economic security they would nevertheless provide women with greater and more genuine freedom and choice.

Notes

1. Considerable similarities in these patterns exist throughout the English-speaking world. British examples include Harriet Bradley (1989) *Men's Work, Women's Work*; Cynthia Cockburn (1991) *In the Way of Women* as well as her earlier works such as *Machinery of Dominance* (1985); Angela Coyle and Jane Skinnner (Eds) (1988) *Women and Work: Positive Action for Change*; Rosemary Crompton and Kay Sanderson (1990) *Gendered Jobs and Social Change* and Lisa Adkins (1995) *Gendered Work: Sexuality, Family and the Labour Market*. Examples from the United States include Reskin and Roos (1990) *Job Queues, Gender Queues*; and, from Australia, Ann Game and Rosemary Pringle's (1984) *Gender at Work*.
2. Exceptions include Sylvia Walby (1986) *Patriarchy at Work*.
3. Especially useful are Gail Braybon (1981) *Women Workers in the First World War*; Deirdre Beddoe (1989) *Back to Home and Duty* and Penny Summerfield (1984) *Women Workers in the Second World War*.
4. For example, Michael Sullivan (1992) *The Politics of Social Policy* makes no mention of women. This was commonplace before the feminist writings of the 1980s; and Titmuss was exceptional in that he did mention women.
5. For example, Gillian Pascall (1986) has a chapter on women and work; but on the whole they have concentrated more upon women's poverty and State 'welfare' than on policies directly affecting women's paid work: Elizabeth Wilson (1977) *Women and the Welfare State*; Clare Ungerson (Ed.) (1985) *Women and Social Policy*; Cora Baldock and Bettina Cass (Eds) (1988) *Women, Social Welfare and the State*.
6. For example, Rhondda Sharp and Ray Broomhill (1988) *Short Changed: Women and Economic Policies*; Prue Hyman (1994) *Women and Economics*; Marilyn Waring (1989) *If Women Counted*.
7. 'Employers object to women's desire to have their cake and eat it, to reproduce and go on earning . . . This desire is considered unrealistic, but the only way to be realistic in the world of work is to be a man.' Evelyne Sullerot, quoted in Carolyn Teich Adams and Cathryn Teich Winston

(1980) *Mothers at Work: Public Policies in the United States, Sweden and China.*
8. As Elizabeth Wilson pointed out in *Women and the Welfare State* (1977), the state has always been closely connected with the development of the family, and has acted to reinforce it in an assortment of ways.
9. Olive Schreiner, 1918 p. 283. Women's representation in trade unions grew from 6.5 per cent in 1901 to 10.6 per cent in 1911.

Chapter 2

Women's 'Right to Work' and the State, 1905–1914

Before 1905, in all-male government circles, employment policies were being developed which catered for a proportion of unemployed working-class men, but which omitted any specific reference to women. Feminist campaigns for unemployed women's inclusion resulted in the creation of a limited number of places for women under the 1905 Unemployed Workmen Act. Although the attempts of the 'right to work' movement in the decade before the First World War was to force the State to accept responsibility for creating paid employment for unemployed men have been documented (Brown, 1971), the fact that there was a women's 'right to work' movement at this time has been mentioned only in passing (Harris, 1972). This omission is serious, because it obscures the fact that unemployment and income maintenance policy in this period was devised to manage and control a male workforce, and the ways in which women were treated very differently. The debates surrounding women's 'right to work' before the First World War highlight the way in which feminist demands for the right to paid employment with the potential for economic independence for women were regarded by leading policy-makers as highly threatening.

Women's Inclusion in the 1905 Unemployed Workmen Act

There was no reason to suppose that women would be included under the Unemployed Workmen Act. Neither the 1886 Chamberlain Circular nor the 1904 London Unemployed Fund had contained any provision for unemployed women (*Women's Industrial News*, March 1905). Schemes were targeted at the male workforce, particularly skilled tradesmen, whose unemployment had been seen as responsible for riots and disturbances.[1] Women's exclusion from paid employment and consequent dependence on men was by contrast seen as a stabilizing factor, by having a steadying influence on male workers (Lewis, 1983). During this period, therefore, policy-makers tended to see women's employment rather than their unemployment as a social problem.

Further, the extension of the franchise to a large section of working men (and not women) led to the election to Parliament of a number of men from trade-union backgrounds who strongly opposed married women's employment.[2] During this period the Trades Union Council pressed for a 'family wage for men' and the extension of 'protective' legislation to limit women's paid employment.[3] This was partly because married men benefited from the domestic comforts provided by wives who stayed at home; but it appears to have been mainly because men could command higher wages if they did not have women's competition in paid employment. The trade unionist Tom Mann, for example, strongly objected to the employment of mothers, claiming that 'their employment nearly always has a prejudicial effect on the wages of the male worker'.[4]

However, support for limiting the paid employment of wives and mothers also came from members of the employing class, including some whose family fortunes owed much to the employment of married women.[5] This may have partly stemmed from dislike of the fact that working-class women who had economic independence, particularly those living in areas where women's full-time emplyment was the norm, such as Burnley and Nelson, were relatively active in the women's suffrage movement and the Independent Labour Party (Liddington and Norris, 1978).

Men's unemployment had come to be regarded as a problem requiring government action during the mid-1880s, but before 1904 women's unemployment was 'little considered or discussed'.[6] There was a prevalent view that 'there need never be any unemployed women if they were not perversely indifferent to the charms of domestic service'.[7] The 1901 Census described 6,046,435 married and widowed women, including widows in receipt of poor law relief (*Women's Industrial News*, December 1907, Mrs Macrosty), as 'unoccupied or without special occupation'[8] but no official figures existed on women's unemployment. Although it was known that especially at times of recession, the 'women's trades' became severely crowded, as the wives of unemployed men competed with single women for the available employment,[9] the shortage of official statistics made it relatively easy to ignore women's unemployment.

It is hardly surprising, therefore, that initially the Unemployed Workmen Act contained no provision for unemployed women.[10] However, in May 1905 an announcement was made in Parliament that women were, after all, to be included under the Act.[11] This followed a series of actions by the Women's Industrial Council, at a time when the women's movement was particularly active.

In 1904, noting that thousands of men had been provided with work in London under the provisions of Walter Long's London Unemployed Fund, the Women's Industrial Council had resolved to campaign for the inclusion of women and girls in public works schemes.[12] They conducted a survey in London on women's unemployment, and then wrote twice to each local authority in London asking what was being done or planned to assist unemployed women. Receiving 'no satisfactory answer', in December 1904 they sent memoranda to the central and local committees administering Long's scheme, requesting that unemployed women be invited to apply for places on the schemes and that they be provided with 'suitable' employment such as bee keeping, fruit growing, upholstery and poultry keeping. However, by the time a deputation of the Council was met by the Central Committee, all available funds had been spent on the men's schemes[13] and the committee still seemed to believe that all unemployed women could be catered for by entering domestic service (Abbott, 1907, p. 518).

Nevertheless, the Women's Industrial Council had succeeded in bringing women's demands for public works to the attention of men in authority (*Women's Industrial News*, March 1905). Further, the Council was only one voice in the women's movement of the time, whose keynote, according to Olive Schreiner, was: 'Give us labour and the training that fits for labour' (*ibid.*). Women had been pressing for increased employment opportunities since the second half of the nineteenth century, for example, through the Campaign to Promote Women's Employment, founded in 1859; and in 1874 had formed their own union, the Women's Protective and Provident League, which was active during the prewar period. Women's membership of unions, though lower than men's, rose rapidly between 1901 and 1911, from 6.5 per cent of total membership to 10.6 per cent (Schreiner, 1918, p. 283). Morover, leaders of the suffrage movement were acutely aware that women's lack of political representation made it easier for policy-makers to neglect their economic needs (Tawney, 1910, p. 131).

On 12 May 1905, Mrs Pankhurst, angered at the way a Bill for women's suffrage had been 'talked out' in the House of Commons amid great hilarity, wrote to Arthur Balfour, the Prime Minister, threatening that the Women's Social and Political Union (WSPU) would oppose the Conservatives at the forthcoming general election (Pankhurst, 1911). On 29 May the new President of the Local Government Board, Gerald Balfour, brother of the Prime Minister, unexpectedly announced that women would, after all, be included in the Unemployed Workmen Act.[14] He used the provisions of the 1889 Interpretation Act to rule that the term 'unemployed workman' would include females (*ibid.*), although the Interpretations Regulations were not normally used to women's advantage (Sachs and Hoff Wilson, 1979, pp. 22–38).

However, this was followed by an attempt by the government to abandon the Unemployed Workmen Bill, although apparently not simply because of its inclusion of women. The Independent Labour Party had hailed the Bill as a sign that the State had accepted the principle of the 'right to work'.[15] The adoption of this principle would have transferred to the State from the individual the responsibility for procuring sufficient paid employment. The ILP saw in the acceptance of the 'right to work' the potential for State management of the level of demand in the economy, the elimination of cyclical unemployment[16] and a peaceful route to State socialism. They also believed in the 'right to work' of women 'dependent on their own earnings'. It was a principle which both Liberals and Conservatives were most anxious to avoid. Popular pressure for the Bill's revival led to rioting in Manchester on 31 July 1905. The following day it was announced there would be a Royal Commission on the Poor

Laws, and that the Unemployed Workmen Act would be passed by the government on a three-year experimental basis.[17]

No work schemes for unemployed women were provided during the first few months after the passage of the Act, and so the Women's Industrial Council kept up their pressure. In November 1905 a procession of 3,000 unemployed women marched to Whitehall and a deputation met Gerald Balfour (Macdonald, 1912, p. 152). The women's action received sympathetic reporting the next day in *The Times*.[18] As a result of these representations it was decided at the first meeting of the Central Unemployed Body, which administered the Act in London, to form a women's work committee (Macdonald, 1912, p. 153) and this first met on 10 February 1906 (Abbott, 1907, p. 519). At this stage although notices had been issued inviting women to apply for places on the schemes, only 388 women had done so in London (Abbott, 1907, p. 520), presumably because no work had yet been provided.

By the time the women's workrooms had begun to operate in April 1905, the men's schemes has been working for nine months. Nevertheless, the inclusion of women had survived a change in government as well as the selection of John Burns – noted for his hostility to both women's employment and the unemployed – as President of the Local Government Board. At this stage in his career, however, Burns bowed to public opinion, saying that 'women suffered in patience, and for that reason they ought to be more sympathetic to them'.[19] Largely as a result of feminist organizing, women's unemployment had been forced to the attention of all-male politicians and some remedial action was being taken by the new government.

The Scale of Provision of Work for Unemployed Women

During the first year of the operation of the Unemployed Workmen Act only three schemes for unemployed women were established. All were sewing rooms and all were in London, at Poplar, Camberwell and St Pancras. Between April 1906 and June 1907, out of 802 women considered 'eligible', 308 were found work. Normally employment was provided for 16 weeks, although in cases of exceptional need this was extended to 24 weeks (Beveridge, 1909, p. 181). Provision for males, by contrast, was on a far larger scale. Seventy-nine distress committees were creating employment for men; and in 1905–6 they provided a total of about 40,000 places,[20] while 18,000 jobs were also created by smaller local authorities still operating under the recommendations of the Chamberlain circular.[21] Nevertheless, the Prime Minister,[22] the President of the Local Government Board[23] and William Beveridge (1909, p. 181) all claimed that the proportion of women assisted was higher than that of men. They chose to regard the small number of women applicants not as a result of the eligibility criteria for places, but as indicative of the extent of unemployment among women. They thus attempted to convey the impression that female unemployment was a problem of tiny proportions, which had been largely solved by government intervention.

In the meantime, Independent Labour Party Members in Parliament were using question time in the House of Commons to ask for extension of the women's workrooms schemes.[24] In fact there were no legal restrictions preventing local authorities from providing work for unemployed women.[25] However, there was a general reluctance to divert existing funds away from job creation for men; and John Burns refused to allocate additional funding to assist unemployed women.[26]

The women's Industrial Council also attempted to persuade Burns to expand the number of schemes for unemployed women. In March 1907 a deputation handed him a memorandum deploring the small number of places for unemployed women (*Women's Industrial News*, March 1907). Receiving no satisfactory response, they then circularized 1,700 authorities dealing with the unemployed, asking about their plans for catering for women under the Unemployed Workmen Act (*Women's Industrial News*, 1908, p. 6). It is difficult to be certain that this strategy was effective, but nevertheless by the end of 1907 a women's sewing room had been opened in Liverpool, and two in Manchester (*Women's Industrial News*, 1907, pp. 700 and 703). A women's workroom also opened in Glasgow in 1909, but soon closed, apparently because of problems concerning the 'eligibility' of the applicants.

During 1906–7 the Unemployed Workmen Act catered for around 37,000 men (Beveridge, 1909, p. 179) somewhat fewer than during the previous year. It was suffering from bad publicity and a shortage of charitable funds (on which it partly depended); and was due to expire the following year. However, in 1908 the Labour Party presented its 'Right to Work' Bill, which would have given local authorities a statutory obligation to provide work for all the unemployed. Its defeat provoked a series of huge demonstrations and the Local Government Board responded with a series of palliative measures, all aimed at the male unemployed. The number of places for men was increased to 85,000;[27] the government provided a further £100,000 towards the working of the Act, and charitable contributions rose from £7,800 in the previous year to £31,000.[28] Further, a Cabinet committee set up to deal with the problem of unemployment in October 1908 voted 24,000 extra places in the army, 8,000 in the post office at Christmas and extra work in naval dockyards.[29]

However, provision of work for unemployed women did not rise in proportion. The largest number of places for women, 334, was in London, while Manchester catered for 236 (but rejected 2,047), and in Liverpool 87 women were given work, compared with just 24 in Glasgow (Tawney, 1910, p. 133). The total number of unemployed women provided with work under the Act in 1909 therefore was 681: it was tiny in comparison with the number of places provided for unemployed men.

Eligibility Criteria for Places on Work Schemes

The 1905 Unemployed Workmen Act was originally envisaged as a means of contributing to 'national efficiency' by saving regular and skilled workmen from pauperism and the workhouse, rather than as a form of poor relief (Beveridge, 1909, p. 185). The selection of regular rather than casual workers was initially intended to apply equally to women. A circular issued in connection with the opening of the registries for women said that the Act included 'temporarily unemployed women who are usually self-supporting' and excluded women who were 'only in a normal state of underemployment or underpaid employment' (Abbott, 1907, p. 251). However, the actual administration of the women's scheme produced the opposite effect, and 'the spirit of relief works was forced upon it persistently' (Macdonald, 1912, p. 153; Tawney, 1910, p. 138).

There were broad similarities in the 'eligibility' criteria for places between the towns which set up unemployed women's workrooms, but also some significant differences. In London the labour exchanges which were created as part of the Unemployed Workmen Act would register women only if they could prove they were the sole 'breadwinner' of the family, and if they were not domestic servants (Harris, 1972, p. 201). The majority of those who were seen as 'normally self-supporting' were childless and single; but this meant they were then regarded as suitable for domestic service. Women with able-bodied husbands were specifically excluded (Tawney, 1910, p. 135). This meant that only widows and women whose husbands were too sick to work were eligible to register for places on the schemes. The average age of the women who were selected was between 45 and 50. Most were regarded as 'simply fitted for charring work'; many arrived at the workrooms in a state of semi-starvation, and most were thought unlikely to obtain work afterwards, because of the lack of demand for plain needlework.[30] In one of the London workrooms, 41 of the 52 women were widows, and 42 were aged over 40 (Abbott, 1907, p. 525). In Liverpool, the workrooms also gave priority to widows as a matter of policy (Tawney, 1910, p. 136). It was only in Manchester that the two workrooms allowed for the employment of women with unemployed husbands (*ibid.*), probably because of the greater general acceptance of the importance of women's financial contribution to households in industrial Lancashire. In most of the women's workrooms, therefore, because of the priority given to the classification of women according to marital status, the principle of giving work to women 'normally in paid employment' was subverted in favour of 'relief' principles: that is, taking in women not to preserve their skills as workers but because they were semi-destitute through the lack of a male 'breadwinner'.

The selection of applicants for the men's schemes also departed from the intention of the Act, which had been to act as a bridge over the 'abyss of chronic pauperism' for some 5 per cent of men 'exceptionally displaced' (Beveridge, 1909, p. 185). Instead, despite official disapproval,[31] the schemes catered mainly for 'low skilled and irregular workmen, whose distress was neither exceptional nor temporary' (Beveridge 1909, p. 187). *Only* married men (or men with other dependents) were catered for under the Act.[32] Nevertheless, the regulations governing the men's schemes represented an attempt to move from the 'relief' principle to 'national efficiency' in their selection of applicants, whereas the women's workrooms did not. For example, men who had been in receipt of poor relief during the previous 12 months were barred from receiving work,[33] whereas for the women, having been dependent on poor relief during the past year was a *requirement* for admission to the workrooms.[34] Many of the successful women applicants had previously not worked for pay at all, or had earned only tiny sums, (Beveridge, 1909, p. 181) and the vast majority seen as 'eligible' had been casual or underemployed workers (Abbott, 1907, p. 524).

There were thus greater attempts made by the leading politicians and adminstrators (although these were not always successful) to encourage the 'independent' male worker: the man who was usually in regular paid employment and not dependent on the State. The priority given to married men also reinforced men's obligation to maintain a family. Men were classed first according to their record in the labour market, and only secondarily according to their family responsibilities, which were seen as providing income rather than care. Women were classed primarily according to their marital status rather than their employment record and constructed as men's dependents – and so denied a place if they had a man in the house, even an adult son seen as capable of supporting them.[35] Only when a woman had dependents and no man seen as able to keep her would the state treat her as provider.

The eligibility criteria for the women's workrooms demonstrate a strong governmental resistance to viewing women as unemployed. Single women, including childless widows, were not provided with public works because of the availability of work in domestic service – widely regarded as a training for marriage. Once married, women were treated as the responsibility of their husbands rather than the State, irrespective of men's ability or willingness to support them. Only widows with children were regarded as having a legitimate claim for State-provided paid employment. This was because although widows of 'good character' were usually given outdoor relief,[36] the practice in most localities by the first decade of the twentieth century was to require widows to earn at least part of their income in the labour market.[37] However, this became an ambiguous and contested area throughout the prewar period. Feminists attempted to strengthen claims for women's 'right to work' by beginning with 'women dependent on their own earnings', particularly widows with children, for whose employment there was at least some central and local government support and considerable public sympathy.

Women and Public Works: Wages and Conditions

The principles and regulations which governed wages and conditions on places provided under the Unemployed Workmen Act were designed for a male workforce. In general the wages paid for work provided under the 1905 Act were set by two opposing principles: that of keeping pay high enough to maintain the 'physical efficiency' of recipients and their dependents, but also of 'less eligibility', which entailed keeping job creation wages below the lowest prevailing rates in ordinary employment.[38] The aim was to ensure that workmen provided with temporary employment under the Act would be both able and willing to accept ordinary employment in their own trades when the opportunity arose. Thus, on the men's schemes, workers received about £1.00 per week (Beveridge, 1909, p. 16). Skilled tradesmen, for whom the Act was chiefly intended, would have earned 42s–45s per week in their usual employment, and even unskilled labourers would normally have earned 23s–25s for a week's work.[39] It was, however, just possible, as Maude Pember Reeves (1913) pointed out, for a family to live on £1.00 per week.

However, on the women's workroom schemes it was not possible to maintain 'less eligibility' without paying wages which were below subsistence level, because of the low levels of pay in women's ordinary employment. Women in industry usually earned only 6s or 7s for a week's work, or even less, for very long hours, in the 'sweated trades';[40] while 10s was said to be a 'good wage' for a woman.[41] These pay rates were considerably below the 14s 6d–15s calculated to be necessary to maintain a single woman in 'reasonable decency'[43] and clearly inadequate for a woman with dependents. The women assisted under the 1905 Act were among the poorest of all (Beveridge, 1909, p. 181), which may partly explain why 'less eligibility' was largely abandoned for these women.

In the London women's workrooms wages were paid which, although small in terms of maintaining a family, were said to be a good deal higher than those which any women, apart from the most skilled workers, could earn in London (Beveridge, 1909, p. 181). Each woman was paid 10s per week for herself, 2s per week for the first child, 1s 6d for the second and 1s for each subsequent child under 14 who was not earning, up to a maximum of 17s 6d per week (Tawney, 1910, p. 136). Deductions were made for any child who was employed (Abbott, 1907, p. 523). The women also received a daily dinner, valued at 6d and fares to and from work in excess of 2d per day (Tawney, 1910, p. 136). If the value of the dinners is added, a London widow with five young children would have been in the highly unusual situation of receiving the same as the men employed under the Act.

In other cities the women fared less well. The Manchester workrooms paid piecework rates which allowed the women to earn between 7s and 14s per week; and from 1908 they also received a free midday meal from the local education authority (Tawney, 1910, p. 136). Although lower than the wages paid in the London workrooms, the pay was still said to be higher than that normally received by the women attending the Manchester workrooms. In Liverpool, the women only took home 5s per week once the cost of their midday meal had been deducted, and there were no allowances for dependents.[43] According to Eleanor Rathbone this was symptomatic of general low wages in Liverpool.[44] However, contemporary sources do not indicate that women's wages were significantly lower in Liverpool than in Manchester.[45] Performing plain needlework by hand (Abbott, 1907, p. 528) in the workrooms was also considerably easier than the very heavy domestic work to which many of the women would have been accustomed (Abbott, 1907, p. 525). By contrast, the work on the men's schemes involved hard physical labour, which some skilled men, such as watchmakers, could have found extremely demanding. Concern was expressed that men's work should not be so heavy as to affect their future employability in their usual trade (Beveridge, 1909, p. 156 and 185).

The women's almost equal pay and better conditions were offset by longer hours of work, which were between 48 and 50 hours per week (Beveridge, 1909, p. 188; Tawney, 1910, p. 136). These would have been problematic for widows with sole responsibility for young children. Men employed under the 1905 Act, by contrast, worked 40 hours or less per week (Beveridge, 1909, p. 191). This was a continuation of a custom which had emerged in the 1890s which allowed public works schemes to pay 'less eligible' weekly rates to unemployed men without undermining trade union agreements on hourly labouring rates of pay.[46]

Conditions on public works for men were made relatively unattractive, through policy-makers' concerns that men should not come to prefer these temporary schemes to their normal employment; but this was not the case on the women's schemes, nor was it seen as a problem. Although in most of the workrooms the women enjoyed better pay and conditions than in their usual work, no concern was expressed that women's incentives to move on to paid employment would be undermined. This appears to have been based on a strong resistance to seeing women, even widows, as having a proper place in the labour market. The chairman of the Women's Work Committee of the Central Unemployed Body, James Ramsay Macdonald, argued in retrospect that the virtue of the workrooms was that:

> hundreds of women who were breadwinners were taught tidiness, were taught to mend and darn, and a new standard of comfort and domestic efficiency was made possible to them. That, in addition to the mere temporary money help to those who were employed, was part of the original intention (Macdonald, 1912, p. 153).

Thus, widows, the only group of women regarded by policy-makers as genuinely unemployed and eligible for public works, were being trained to devote themselves to unpaid domestic work at home, where they would be obliged to claim poor law relief. This was the very antithesis of the main principle governing the 1905 Unemployed Workmen Act, which aimed to get unemployed workers back into paid employment. It illustrates the way the Act was geared towards men, while women were regarded as an anomaly.

In part, the differential treatment of unemployed women was forced on policy-makers by the reality of women's low pay in the labour market. It would have been impossible to retain the principle of 'less eligibility' on any State public works scheme when its workers had already been living in extreme poverty and had no prospects of work paying a living wage after the scheme ended. Therefore most of the women employed on the workrooms schemes were provided, for a short period, with relatively good pay and conditions – and the women's movement certainly did not decry this. However, the women were then seen as objects of pity, dependent on poor relief, rather than as unemployed people being prepared for economic independence through employment. That being the case, they were given domestic training. This was far from the aims of the Women's Industrial Council.

Public Works for Women: Politics and Administration

The women's work scheme was acknowledged as an experiment and as a testing ground of whether widows – and perhaps eventually all women – should be seen as having a right to paid employment and thus counted as unemployed when looking for work. For this reason the workrooms became not only a focus for political debate but also a target of attempts to discredit them. From the beginning, the administration of the women's schemes was beset by problems, stemming largely from obstacles placed in their way (Macdonald, 1912, p. 153). John Burns, as president of the Local Government Board, was strategically positioned to make his opposition to the schemes carry weight: he made it almost impossible for those administering the workrooms to carry out their job effectively.[47]

Considerable restrictions were placed on the operation of the London workrooms, which for some time were not allowed to sell their products – alledgedly in case they 'distorted' the ordinary markets – or even to give away any of the goods as gifts.[48] When this ban was lifted, allegations followed in the press that it was impossible to sell the items made in the workrooms because they were too expensively produced (Morning Post, July 22, 1908). Burns attacked the workrooms in Parliament on the grounds of their running costs,[49] even though he had hampered their attempts sell products to help cover costs. The workrooms had in fact never been intended to show a profit,[50] although when they were allowed to sell garments the women's workrooms' recoupment rates were very favourable.[51] The women's work programme was also significantly cheaper to run than the men's schemes.[52] Inconsistent and often erroneous though Burns' criticisms were, they nevertheless enabled him to refuse to grant additional funds for the expansion of this very tiny scheme.[53]

Despite problems besetting the schemes, the Women's Industrial Council chose to regard the women's workrooms as a successful experiment (Women's Industrial News, March 1907) and published comments on the 'improved physical efficiency' of the women as a result of their regular income and the daily hot meal.[54] Margaret Macdonald of the Women's Industrial Council and

Women's Labour League, who was also the wife of James Ramsay Macdonald, trod a careful path in her submission to the 1909 Royal Commission on the Poor Laws which said that 'the training in good work that some of these women have received has been as valuable as the actual money wages in time of need' (Macdonald, 1912, p. 153).

Nonetheless, as Burns confidently predicted,[55] the 1909 Poor Law Commission's Majority Report omitted to even mention the women's workrooms scheme. The Minority Report mentioned them just once, dismissively:

> It is in vain that the Central Unemployed Body have sought to meet needs by the opening of workrooms where the women are employed in making garments. It is no gain to set these mothers to work at the most 'sweated' of trades in which there is a chronic over-supply of labour. They are but taking the work out of other women's hands.[56]

From 1909 it became obvious that the women's workrooms system was not to be expanded to form the basis of future policies catering for unemployed women. Rather they were regarded by policy-makers as residual models of a failed experiment and were at times under threat of closure. In March 1909 the Local Government Board refused to grant £1,200 to carry the women's workrooms through the summer, even though £2,500 from the Exchequer grant for the Unemployed Workmen Act was returned to the Treasury unspent the following month. On that occasion the money required was raised from charitable donations, allowing the workrooms to remain open.[57] However, in 1911 the workrooms did close for the summer as a result of Burns' refusal to grant the necessary funding. Burns claimed that the closure of the workrooms would 'test' women's desire for paid employment:[58] a remarkable piece of hypocrisy, given both Burns' views on female breadwinners and the known lack of available employment.

The workrooms nevertheless did reopen and were still operating at the start of the First World War when, following the dislocation of many staple 'women's trades', the system was considerably expanded. Between the outbreak of war and January 1915, 9,000 women passed through the 'Queen Mary's Workrooms' at wages of 10s per week (Braybon, 1981, p. 44). However, once the workrooms closed in March 1915 they were never opened again.

Viewpoints about Women's 'Right to Work'

The women's workrooms scheme was remarkable for its time, given that women were not included again in public works schemes for the unemployed until the 1970s. Its very existence was a tribute to feminist organizing. Yet clearly the opposition to women's 'right to work' in this period was also overwhelming.

Part of the discrediting of the women's workrooms came from a more general drive to avoid the adoption of the principle of the right to work for all the unemployed, particularly in 1908–9 when the 'Right to Work' movement was particularly active. The 1909 Royal Commission on the Poor Laws condemned the Unemployed Workmen Act in almost all respects, but particularly for assisting intermittently employed male workers and making them dependent on the provision of employment by the State.[59]

However, a considerable amount of opposition was directed specifically at the notion of women's right to work. It was widely believed that the employment of wives would undermine men's position in the family. Burns, for example, thought the State should be:

> very careful in providing state or municipal work for women that they were not providing opportunities for loafing husbands and sons to exploit their wives, sisters and mothers, to the permanent demoralisation of the workman and the permanent undoing of the wife and children.[60]

Many policy-makers distrusted and disliked the domestic role-reversal arrangements which occurred in districts such as Dundee and parts of Lancashire where there was regular employment for women but not men.[61] However, in the context of a discussion of the women's workrooms, Burns also revealed a strong concern about the possibility of women's competition with men in the labour market:

> I believe and I will maintain that if we go on allowing married women
> increasingly to work in factories, doing the chief portion of the hard
> industrial work which ought to fall upon the male breadwinner, the
> tendency will be still further to increase the ranks of the male
> unemployed.[62]

Given that the workrooms were normally only open to enable widows to do traditional low-paid 'women's work', policy-makers' fears of married women becoming heads of households and taking men's places in the workforce might appear to have been excessive. Further, although the women's movement had been attempting to expand women's opportunities in paid employment there was a lack of unity over the question of married women's right to work. Within the leadership of the Women's Industrial Council, Clementina Black believed that employment gave even women who were obliged to work for pay a 'partial feeling of freedom and independence' (Black, 1915, p. 4); children would be better cared for by professionals, but that 'even an unemployed husband will keep toddling children from being run over, tumbling downstairs or setting themselves on fire' (Black, 1915, p. 4). Some Women's Industrial Council supporters also believed that women's economic dependency 'put them in the power of their husbands'.[63] By contrast, another Women's Industrial Council leader, Margaret Macdonald, claimed that the organization 'did not and never had sought to aid women whose work served to aid their lazy husbands'.[64] The Women's Labour League, of which Margaret Macdonald was a member, supported the Labour Party's 'Right to Work' Bills of 1908 onwards as a 'charter of leisure and comfort for wives'.[65] Policy-makers' opposition to women's increasing participation in paid work could not be overcome by women's organizations which were divided or equivocal about the right of all women to an independent livelihood.

Women and the 'Right to Work' 1909–1914

Despite the efforts and initial sucesses of the Women's Industrial Council in drawing attention to the nature and extent of women's unemployment,[66] by 1909 the attitudes of policy-makers had hardened into a refusal to acknowledge that the problem existed. The Poor Law Commissioners reported in 1909 that women's unemployment was a 'negligible factor';[67] Beveridge claimed that the women in the workrooms had not been unemployed in their own right, but had been reduced to poverty by the death, sickness or unemployment of their husbands (Beveridge, 1909, p. 181). Even 'unsupported' women could not be viewed as unemployed, it was implied, because they were still men's responsibility and thus had no right to earn their own living.

One consequence of this was that new schemes to assist the unemployed after 1909, such as the 1909 Development Act, did not include women. A second result was a growing refusal to regard even widows as a legitimate part of the labour force. The 1909 Royal Commission on the Poor Laws (Minority Report) took the view that when a man died or became incapable of supporting his family, the State rather than the wife should take up the role of the breadwinner:

> It seems to us clear that, if only for the sake of the interest which the community has in the children, there should be adequate provision made from public funds, *conditional on a woman's abstaining from industrial work* and devoting herself to the children.[68] (emphasis added)

Although widows' pensions were not introduced until 1925, relatively generous allowances were given before 1909 to widows who abstained from paid employment in some localities such as Glasgow, on an experimental basis.[69] Since some 10 per cent of recipients were said to have 'fallen into drink and immorality' it was recommended by the 1909 Royal Commission on the Poor Laws (Majority Report) that such a benefit should be given only in 'deserving' cases; while for the 'undeserving', who were bad housekeepers and mothers or who had illegitimate children, the benefit was to be withdrawn, and work for wages was seen as a 'positive safeguard'.[70]

It can be seen therefore that after the discrediting of the women's workrooms scheme, employment policies towards women, and particularly mothers, were precisely the opposite of policies towards workmen. Priority of access to paid work was to be given to the 'best' of the men according to the moral values of the labour market: those who were regular rather than casual workers. For women, work for pay was to be a punishment for behaviour which was immoral according to the values of the marriage market. Thus, women's economic independence and the right to work was recast as an undesirable and stigmatized state.[71]

Conclusions

During the late-nineteenth century, working-class male unemployment had been forced by working-class organizations to the attention of the State. At the same time, feminists were demanding more and wider employment opportunities for women; and between 1901 and 1911 women's official labour force participation rates were increasing.[72] However, politicians remained reluctant to see women as unemployed in their own right and excluded women from public works programmes. There was strong resistance on the part of policy-makers to see married women as 'independent' workers, and particular concern that partnered women should not become breadwinners on a larger scale than before. Campaigns by women's groups and sections of the labour movement in 1904–5 succeeded in obtaining small-scale provision of women's workrooms targeted at a minority of women job-seekers: widows with children. Work was provided under terms and conditions which treated the women as dependents of the State (paupers) rather than temporarily unemployed independent workers. 'Less eligibility', usually seen as a central organizing principle in employment policy, was largely abandoned where these women (and some married men) were concerned.

It was obviously advantageous to the women on the schemes to be provided with an income by the State which was higher than they could normally earn. During their time in the workrooms, these widows' material wellbeing improved significantly. However, the cost was that women continued to be seen as marginal in relation to the paid workforce. Further, before the programme could be expanded it was systematically discredited by policy-makers who obviously feared a potential loss of power by men in the home and the workplace through any expansion in women's economic independence. As a result, even widows were divested of part of their limited right (and obligation) to work outside the home for pay, and there was a growing tendency, which developed further between the wars, for employed wives, widows and mothers to be portrayed as deviant.

The decade before the First World War was also rife with class-based struggle, of which the popular 'Right to Work' movement was one example. Many working men in unions opposed women's right to work as detrimental to their own interests, however; and even the Independent Labour Party did not campaign for married women's right to paid employment. Yet it is clear that the sexual division of labour in the home and the labour force was also being protected by leading policy-makers, many of whom were employers. There can have been no financial incentive to employers (unlike working men) derived from the exclusion of low-paid women from competition with working men in the regular paid labour force. However, the incentive for employers probably lay in working women's economic dependence on their husbands, which undoubtedly helped to maintain social order by giving men greater privileges but also financial responsiblities as a result of their breadwinner position within the family. With such an alliance between a large section of working men and employers, it is not surprising that the battle for women's right to work was lost.

Notes

Note: unless otherwise stated, *Hansard* refers to House of Commons Parliamentary debates.

1. During the winter of 1902–4 there had been campaigns by the unemployed of besieging the offices of the Boards of Guardians in all major cities, according to Walter Long, President of the Local Government Board between 1900 and 1905 and 1915–16: in his evidence to the 1909 Royal Commission on the Poor Laws, Q.78466.
2. For example, John Burns, who was President of the Local Government Board for much of this period, strongly opposed married women's employment, claiming that it led to high infant-mortality rates, and citing the high rates of both women's employment and infant mortality in Burnley, compared with the lower rates of both in Battersea. In fact writers argue that there was no firm evidence in this period to link women's employment, including Clara Collett in 'The Extent and Effects of the Industrial Employment of Women', *Journal of the Royal Statistical Society*, June 1898; *Women's Industrial News*, October 1917; Doris Nield Chew (1982) *Ada Nield Chew: the Life and Writings of a Working Woman*, p. 212. Rather, a third variable, housing quality, appears to have had a more definite impact on infant mortality rates.
3. For example, during this period the Scottish TUC supported an attempt to remove all women working above ground at coal mines except cleaners. See *Women's Industrial News*, September 1911; and *Hansard*, Vol. 29, cols 1128 and 1352.
4. Royal Commission on Labour, Minutes of Evidence 1893–4, Q.4447; Jane Lewis (1984) *Women in England 1870–1950*, p. 175.
5. For example Lord Shuttleworth of Burnley argued that mothers' employment and lack of 'intelligent mothering' was contributing to the physical deterioration of the race (House of Lords Debates, 4th series, Vol. 149, cols 1311, 1325 and 1328–30).

6. Jeanette Tawney, 'Women and unemployment', *Economic Review*, 1910, p. 131. Jeanette Tawney, wife of R. H. Tawney, was also the sister of William Beveridge, and is described by Beveridge's biographer Jose Harris (1977, p. 68) as his greatest friend and confidante. However, following Beveridge's dismissive account of the women's workrooms schemes in *Unemployment: A Problem of Industry* (1909 edition) she published this article defending the workrooms.

7. Edith Abbott, 'Municipal employment of unemployed women in London', *Journal of Political Economy*, November 1907, p. 516. There is, however, some evidence that women of mixed racial origin were unable to secure employment as domestic servants (Ramdin (1987) *The Making of the Black Working Class in Britain*).

8. British Parliamentary Papers: summary tables on occupation based on the Census of 1901, Session 1902–3. It is significant that women were classified more according to marriage than occupation. See also Leonore Davidoff (1976) 'The rationalisation of housework', in D. L. Barker and S. Allen (Eds) *Dependence and Exploitation in Work and Marriage*', p. 139.

9. Royal Commission on the Poor Laws, 1909, Minority Report, p. 605. These trades included dressmaking, millinery, cardboard box making, tailoring, artificial flower making, waterproof clothing manufacture, Christmas cracker making and the fur trade.

10. *Women's Industrial News*, December 1907: Mrs H. J. Tennant of the Central Unemployed Body.

11. *Hansard*, 4th series, Vol. 147, cols 81–2.

12. *Women's Industrial News*, March 1905: M. E. Macdonald.

13. *Ibid*.

14. *Hansard*, 4th series, Vol. 147, cols 81–2.

15. *Hansard*, Vol. 150, col. 992; Harris, 1972, p. 162 and 164.

16. *Hansard*, Vol. 169, col. 993.

17. *Hansard*, Vol. 150, col. 1348.

18. *The Times*, 7 November 1905, reported: 'Mr Balfour had a very difficult and painful task yesterday in meeting a deputation of the unemployed, reinforced by a procession of women whose pinched faces bore testimony to their privation.' The same article by contrast vilified unemployed men: 'in every great town, and especially in London, there is a great population of wastrels whose profession it is to be unemployed, whose repugnance to steady work is invincible.'

19. *Hansard*, Vol. 161 col. 432.

20. Beveridge (1909), p. 179. According to Beveridge, there were 110,000 male applicants for places, of whom 37 per cent were accepted.

21. *Hansard*, Vol. 161, col. 421: report by John Burns.

22. *Hansard*, Vol. 198, col. 2151: Mr Asquith.

23. *Hansard*, Vol. 161, col. 462: John Burns.

24. In fact additional funds were supplied for the working of the Unemployed

Workmen Act following riots in July 1906, but this money was returned unspent to the Exchequer at the end of the financial year.

25. These MPs included James Kier Hardie, James Ramsay Macdonald, George Lansbury, Will Crookes, Pete Curran, Will Thorne, Thomas O'Grady, J. R. Clynes and George Barnes. House of Commons, *Hansard*, 4th series, Vol. 176, col. 856; Vol. 181, col. 1148; Vol. 194, col. 1614; 5th Series, Vol. 1, col. 107 and 1220; Vol. 6, col. 1157; Vol. 17, col. 1451; Vol. 26, cols 15–16.

26. *Hansard*, 5th Series, Vol. 14, col. 1614: John Burns.

27. *Hansard*, 5th Series, Vol. 6, col. 1191.

28. *Ibid.*

29. K. D. Brown, 'The Labour Party and the unemployment question 1906–1910', *The Historical Journal*, **XIV** (3), 1971, p. 611.

30. *Women's Industrial News*, December 1907: Miss Smith, Superintendent of Women's Workrooms.

31. A major intention of the 1905 Act was to get away from the 'poor relief' principles which had pervaded the earlier schemes, and which were abhorred by leading policy-makers. An act of compassion by a local authority in giving all unemployed married men one day's work before Christmas, to ensure that their families all had some food on Christmas Day was described as 'a charitable dole which could not possibly do any good'. *Hansard*, 4th series, Vol. 147, col. 1122: Gerald Balfour.

32. Beveridge, 1909, p. 170. The distress committees had to be satisfied that a male applicant had a wife, child or other dependent.

33. Regulations (Organization for the Unemployed) Art. 2 91.2, Statutory Rules and Orders 1905, 1071.

34. *Women's Industrial News*, 1907, p. 700: Miss Smith.

35. Abbott, 1907, p. 522. Policy-makers did not see women, other than widows, as having economic dependents. This does not mean, however, that other women did not have family members whom they supported financially. According to D. E. Smith (1915) *Wage Earning Women and their Families*, about half of single women had family members for whose maintenance they were fully or partially responsible. B. S. Rowntree and F. Stuart (1921) put this figure lower, at about 12 per cent.

36. Karl de Schweinitz *England's Road to Social Security* (1961), p. 132. A widow of 'good character' was defined according to the moral principles of the marriage market, as one who had no illegitimate children.

37. Royal Commission on the Poor Laws, 1909. From 1871 the Local Government Board advised that outdoor relief should not be given to childless widows or those with only one child.

38. Unemployed Workmen Act Regulations Art.V (i)(f)(g); House of Commons, *Hansard*, Vol. 147, col. 1116; Beveridge 1909 p. 163.

39. *Ibid.*, p. 186. See also Maude Pember Reeves (1913) *Round About a Pound a Week*.

40. R. Mudie-Smith (1980) *Sweated Industries*. However, E. Cadbury, C. M. Matheson, and G. Shann (1906) *Women's Work and Wages*, put women's average earnings in the non-textile industries as 12s 6d. per week.
41. Royal Commission on the Poor Laws, 1909, Minority Report, p. 607.
42. J. J. Mallon (1915) in Hutchins, p. 227.
43. Tawney, 1910 p. 136. The weekly value of the meals was 1s 3d.
44. Eleanor Rathbone, speaking at a conference on the 'Needs of working women dependent on their own earnings', reported in *Women's Industrial News*, 1907, p. 700.
45. See S. Newcombe Fox on women's wages in Liverpool, in Clementina Black (Ed.) (1915) *Married Women's Work*. The statistics were gathered in 1910–11.
46. Select Committee on Distress from Want of Employment, 1986, p. ix.
47. *Women's Industrial News*, 1908, p. 6: Mrs H. J. Tennant of the Central Unemployed Body.
48. *Hansard*, 4th series, Vol. 193 col. 1551; James Ramsay Macdonald, 1912, p. 153.
49. House of Commons, *Hansard*, 5th series, Vol. 1, col. 144: John Burns: 'Women's workrooms, to which I had been sypathetically considerate, have not that charm and attractiveness which they had three years ago. On three women's workrooms, employing less than 800 people in the last three years, £16,000 has been spent, and less than £6,000 secured by the sale of the products.'
50. *Women's Industrial News*, December 1907: James Ramsay Macdonald.
51. Tawney, 1919, p. 137, showed that the total recoupment rate for the women's schemes was 45.5 per cent, 'which compares favourably with other relief schemes of a similar character'.
52. *Hansard*, 5th series, Vol. 1, col. 1447: James Ramsay Macdonald. It was stated that the women's workrooms cost only 14s 6d per week per head to run, compared with between 20s and 40s per head on the men's schemes.
53. *Ibid.*, col. 144: John Burns.
54. *Women's Industrial News*, December 1907: Miss Smith.
55. *Hansard*, 5th series, Vol. 1, col. 144.
56. Royal Commission on the Poor Laws, 1909 Minority Report, p. 609.
57. *Hansard*, 5th series, Vol. 6, col. 1189.
58. *Hansard*, 5th series, Vol. 26, cols 15–16.
59. Royal Commission on the Poor Laws 1909, Majority Report, pp. 502–3; Beveridge, 1909, p. 187.
60. *Hansard*, 4th series, Vol. 193, col. 1522: John Burns.
61. Royal Commission on the Poor Laws, 1909, Majority Report, pp. 202 and 415 spoke of the 'disastrous effects' of men's economic dependence on women in regions where this occurred.
62. *Hansard*, 5th series, Vol. 1, col. 1340: John Burns.
63. *Women's Industrial News*, December 1907: Mrs Greenwood.

64. *Women's Industrial News*, 1908, p. 89.
65. Mrs J. R. Macdonald and Mrs Player *Wage Earning Mothers*. p. 15; Lewis, 1984, p. 51.
66. *Women's Industrial News*, September 1906.
67. Royal Commission on the Poor Laws, 1909, Minority Report, p. 607.
68. Royal Commission on the Poor Laws, Majority Report, p. 202. These allowances were up to 18s per week.
69. *Ibid.*
70. *Ibid.*
71. Elizabeth Roberts(1984). Roberts, E. (1988) *Women's Work, 1840–1940* points out that here has been a certain amount of disagreement among historians as to whether working-class women excluded from employment opportunities wanted paid work and saw it as a potential means to emancipation (Tilly and Scott, 1978; Walby, 1986) or whether many married women obliged to do a 'double shift' would have preferred to have been able to afford to stay at home (Lewis, 1984). However, most working women did not have a genuine choice, since they were barred from better paid jobs and often could not afford to turn down poorly paid work.
72. Between 1901 and 1911 both the percentage of women recorded as working for pay and the percentage of the employed population that was female rose slightly: C. Hakim (1979) *Occupational Segregation*.

Chapter 3

Women as 'Substitutes for Men' in Recruitment Policy, 1914–1918

Upon the womanhood of this country most largely rests the privilege of creating and maintaining a wholesome family life and of developing the higher influences of social life. In modern times, however, many of the ideals of womanhood have found outward expression in industry, and in recent years hundreds and thousands of women have secured employment within the factory system.[1]

Women are already doing the work of men and doing it wholly admirably ... men will have to look to their laurels after the war if they are going to return to avocations which women have now adopted in their place.[2]

During the First World War the substitution of women workers for men in industry was actively promoted by the State. Outwardly this appeared to be a vast change, which contrasted markedly with prewar policies. However, this did not mean that women workers doing 'men's jobs' came to be treated interchangeably with men. There continued to be separate employment policies towards women throughout the war, whether they were employed in women's work or men's work. The recruitment of women into men's jobs and the income maintenance policies of the State gave many women financial independence from men for the first time. However, in contrast to the claims made by some historians,[3] it is argued here that such gains were deliberately made strictly temporary for most women; even though, as the quotations above suggest, while the war lasted women were led to believe otherwise.

State Recruitment Policy and the Processes of 'Substitution'

The sudden outbreak of war in August 1914 brought with it no immediate increase in the demand for women's labour. Instead the effect of the war was at first to dislocate many traditional women's trades; and women in the boot and shoe trade, jewelery, herring curing and the 'luxury trades' were made redundant in large numbers (Hutchins, 1915, p. 242). The industry affected most severely was cotton: a large traditional employer of women;[4] and women's employment generally did not regain its prewar levels until April 1915 (Andrews, 1918, p. 1).

Greater attempts were made by the State in the first months of war to create employment for unemployed women than in the prewar period, although once again employment was in traditional women's work. Government contracts were given specifically to firms employing women for sewing military uniforms and the central committee on Women's Employment was given State assistance in setting up extra workrooms where women were trained in sewing, cooking and service, at wages of 10s for a 40-hour week.[5]

Despite unemployment, leading politicians forsaw an increasing demand for women workers early in the war. However, there was widespread reluctance among employers, trade unionists and politicians to encourage a large-scale substitution of women for men during the first year of war. Many politicians said that women would not be capable of doing the same work as men or working the same number of hours;[6] that women had no useful skills to offer and were reluctant to see women 'diverted from their ordinary domestic occupations' or 'deserting their children'.[7] Many occupations, such as window dressing, which involved climbing ladders, and working in butchers' shops were widely thought to be beyond women's capabilities at this stage, although the Women's Industrial Council pointed out that women window cleaners and butchers' wives were already doing such work.[8] Early in the war politicians chiefly envisaged the substitution of women for men on a very limited scale, as in, for example, women relearning past traditional women's skills by becoming milkmaids and dairymaids.[9]

However, by the summer of 1915, concern was being expressed at the way in which Germany was perceived as taking a lead in substituting women workers for men and releasing more males for the armed forces.[10] An additional concern at this point was the fact that, as a legacy of prewar employment policy towards women, little statistical information about the numbers of women in the working population was available: and the results of the 1911 census were not yet published. The President of the Board of Trade estimated that out of a female population of 15,650,788 of working age 'probably about 5,600,000 between the ages of 15 and 65 are occupied'.[11]

In March 1915, without consulting any of the women's organizations such as the Women's Industrial Council (Hutchins, 1915, p. 253) an appeal was made in the press asking women to register themselves for emergency war work at their local labour exchange. The object of the appeal was merely to discover 'what reserve forces of women's labour, trained or untrained, can be made available, if required to meet the needs of the present emergency'.[12] A further appeal to women to come forward was made in July by David Lloyd George.[13] Large numbers of women responded: as early as 15 April, 47,000 women had placed their names on the special war service registers.[14] This was not simply because women thought it their patriotic duty to preserve the prosperity of the country – 'the ultimate military asset'[15] – or because of Emmeline and Christabel Pankhurst's wish that the capabilities of women be

58771

fully utilized (Marwick, 1977, p. 28), although these played a part; but to a great extent because many women were still unemployed and seeking work. However, employers were giving priority to the employment of men and many resisted employing women. In mid-April only 440 of the women volunteering had been found employment[16] and still as few as 5,511 by September 1915.[17] It became clear that women were offended at the attempt to use them in an enumeration exercise without giving them employment. One male MP noted:

> There is a very widespread idea, and it is not altogether unjustified, that they are being treated at this time of national crisis with a little contempt . . . and that they are only to be accepted here and there as mere makeshifts where men are not available.[18]

Politicians had no wish to alienate women's support. One of the government's first moves at the onset of war had been to release militant suffragettes and trade unionists from prison as part of a policy of creating national unity (Marwick, 1977, p. 28); moreover the extent to which women's labour might be needed was still unknown. Consequently, attempts were made to placate women's organizations. Women were included in the National Registration Act of 1915,[19] despite vociferous opposition from many MPs, on the grounds that women had assured Walter Long that:

> women would not only resent being excluded but would look upon it as a serious rebuff, and wholly unjustifiable in the face of the splendid service they had rendered already in the prosecution of the war.[20]

In spring 1915, the Ministry of Munitions donated £ 3,000 towards the expenses of a demonstration in favour of work for women organized by Mrs Pankhurst,[21] a move criticized by several Labour and trade unionist MPs. It was defended by Lloyd George on the grounds that it had enabled the government to recruit women into munitions factories and spare men for the army,[22] since by this time the processes of dilution of skilled labour and the substitution of women for men had been forced on employers by acute labour shortages. However, placatory policies did not extend to giving women's organizations any decision-making power over the processes of substitution and dilution, which were of far greater material importance than financing demonstrations and the inclusion of women in an Act which was never utilized in relation to them.

In a variety of ways, government recruitment policies maintained women's subordinate status in the paid workforce despite the growing labour shortage. First, women were placed at the back of the queue for recruitment into most forms of war work. For example, in the four weeks to 12 November 1915, 118,451 women and 41,412 men were registered unemployed, but only 29,327 women and 58,306 men were found work by labour exchanges.[23] The practice in occupations such as clerical work was first of all to employ all men above military age: then women already trained and unemployed (who were extremely few in number); boys under military age, who became 'worth their weight in gold';[24] soldiers and sailors invalided out and finally women without experience of men's work – the majority of women.[25] Only in agriculture was it proposed (by the President of the Board of Agriculture) that women be employed in preference to boys;[26] but this was the lowest paid of all men's occupations, there were few women with experience of this kind of work, and the WIC described it as 'cruelty' to recruit townswomen into farming.[27] Nevertheless, despite wages even lower than the lowest paid male agricultural worker, many women failed to secure work on the land in 1915 because of the prejudices of employers.[28]

As the labour shortage became more acute, the lines of demarcation between men's work and women's work were progressively redrawn (Hutchins, 1915, p. 252) but were never significantly eroded. Men's trade unions resisted the entry of women into skilled work.[29] However, this meant that there was a shortage of skilled labour. In February 1915 the government appointed a committee on Production in Engineering and Shipbuilding which, the same month, secured the Shells and Fuses Agreement, which allowed women to do the work of semi-skilled men.[30] Vertical sex segregation at work was maintained partly by the promotion of semi-skilled men to skilled jobs, and partly by processes of dilution in which existing men's jobs were altered and broken down, and adapted to a less trained workforce: it has been estimated that only some 17 per cent of female substitutes for men were allowed to do the whole of a man's job (Lewis, 1984, p. 181). In March 1915 the Treasury Agreement was made between government, employers and representatives of 33 principal unions, and further agreements were made on dilution for the duration of the war, but the National Federation of Women Workers, with 20,000 members, several branches of which were already in munitions work, was not invited (Drake, 1917, p. 18; Andrews, 1918, p. 59). Some male unions, notably on Clydeside (Lewis, 1984, p. 181), and in transport (Marwick, 1977, p. 48) resisted the entry of women to the end of the war.

There were obvious economic incentives to employers of substituting lower paid women workers for men: however, many employers were slow to do so. During the second winter of the war a large amount of plant was standing comparatively idle and manufacturers were complaining that the necessary labour could not be recruited.[31] Early in 1916, therefore, an appeal signed by the Home Secretary and the President of the Board of Trade was sent to employers asking them to employ women, either in direct substitution for men or by sub-division and rearrangement of the work. The appeal stated that:

> We are confident that the women of the country will respond to any call that may be made, but the first step rests with the employers – to reorganise the work and then give the call . . . There is one source, and one only from which the shortage can be made good, and that is

from the great body of women who are at present unoccupied, or engaged in work not of an essential character. Many of these women have already worked in factories and have already had an industrial training: they form an asset of immense importance to the country at the present time.[32]

In order to encourage employers to take on more women, the government produced pamphlets and an illustrated monthly magazine called *Dilution Bulletin*, in which women were depicted at work on machines demanding varying degrees of skill, as well as on tool setting and tool making: jobs for which men were paid up to £12 per week.[33] An information bureau on the substitution of women for men was also established by the Board of Trade at the Victoria and Albert Museum in London to show the kinds of work which women were successfully undertaking.[34] A good deal of publicity was given by the wartime coalition government to the speed and success with which women had taken over men's jobs in industry, and it was claimed that in some cases women dilutes had more than doubled the previous output of trained male mechanics[35] and had learned skills in 5–6 weeks which had previously been done by males who had served apprenticeships of 5–7 years.[36]

In addition to being given every encouragement to recruit low-paid women, employers were being given an opportunity to break the power of skilled male workers permanently. This was not only because of the labour shortage but also because of wartime restrictions on industrial action by workers and the high degree of employer representation in the State; for example, some 90 'men of first-class business experience' worked at the Ministry of Munitions alone during the period when Lloyd George was its minister (Wrigley, 1982, p. 42). Nevertheless, the vast majority of employers chose to retain an hierarchical sexual division of labour: men usually occupied the most skilled, best-paid and most powerful positions and women were seldom in a position of authority over men. This enabled employers to maintain a peaceful working relationship with skilled men.

Only in the very new factories, employing more than 95 per cent female labour, was it commonplace for women to be put on the most skilled jobs – and even there many of the jobs were broken down. Even in occupations where the men's trade unions were relatively weak, such as clerical and shop work, employers chose not to promote women but rather to replace enlisted men with younger men and fill the places of the younger men with women.[37] The Women's Industrial Council commented on employers' willingness to promote office boys, who were liable to enlist in the forces as soon as they were old enough, while refusing to promote women on the grounds that they would 'only go off and get married'.[38] Most employers in the retail trade would not promote women to heads of departments or managers, especially where they would be in authority over men, except occasionally if a woman was regarded as being of a higher social class than the men.[39]

State employment policy did not specifically oppose the employment of women in positions of authority over men: in fact, in a rare instance where three women were appointed as overlookers in a men's department in an explosives factory, and their local MP complained in the House of Commons of resentment by the workmen, the Parliamentary Secretary to the Admiralty defended the employment of the women on the grounds that it was far more common for men to supervise women.[40] However, patriarchal practices among employers and trade unionists ensured that for the most part the 'problem' did not arise. Government policies of encouraging employers to substitute women for unskilled and semi-skilled men made 'steady progress' from spring 1916 onwards, however.[41]

Few efforts were needed by the government to encourage women into most men's jobs: generally speaking women flocked into occupations such as munitions and aircraft manufacture because of the relatively high pay. However, from late 1915 onwards campaigns were conducted by the State to recruit women into agricultural work and also into traditional women's trades such as cotton weaving. In November 1915 the Board of Trade and the Board of Agriculture set up an interdepartmental committee 'to consider utilising to the full the reserve of women's labour'. This appointed local advisory committees on women's organizations such as the women's Cooperative Guild and the YWCA.[42] Their exact functions varied from area to area, but were all concerned with facilitating the increased employment of women: in Todmorden, a house-to-house canvas found enough women textile workers to restart 400 looms in the cotton industry; the Bristol Committee persuaded unemployed women to train in men's work in the boot and shoe trade, while in other areas suitable lodgings and transport were organized for women workers. The same two departments, having campaigned to overcome the prejudice of farmers against the employment of women since spring 1915, also set up Women's County War Agricultural Committees, of which there were 63 by December 1916. These were given considerable discretion in the ways in which they recruited women into farm work and were expected to use their knowledge of the localities in which they worked.[43]

Women were also increasingly recruited into the auxiliary forces as the war progressed. In the early stages of the war, women in the Volunteer Aid Detachments were taken to France as nurses on pay of £20–30 per year (Marwick, 1977, p. 84). Early in 1917 recruitment began for the Women's Army Auxilliary Corps where, once again, women were employed chiefly on women's work of nursing, cooking, domestic work and clerical duties (Marwick, 1977, p. 90). Only in early 1918, with the formation of the Women's Royal Navy Service, were women employed on work with machines on a more significant scale (Marwick, 1977, p. 93). Once again the demand for women's labour had created additional new employment opportunities, but demarcation lines between women's and men's roles were kept in place. For the most part women continued to occupy auxilliary and support roles in relation to men.

This is not to deny that the government's recruitment programme had a major effect on the lives of working women during the First World War. By 1917, women were accepting the offers of work away from home made by the labour exchanges at the rate of 4,000 to 5,000 per month (Andrews, 1918, p. 72). Many women were doing work they could not have imagined even attempting before the war: a Women's Forestry Corps had been formed (Marwick, 1977, p. 84); the staff of the Ministry of Munitions by late-1918 was composed of 61 per cent women employees (Wrigley, 1982, p. 42) and in 1917 there was a total of 1,392,000 women in men's jobs in industry, commerce and agriculture (Andrews, 1918, p. 40). One of the chief benefits to women was that the range of available options in employment increased considerably.

Nevertheless, it is clear that changes only took place within prescribed limits. Women fell foul of employers' and union agreements of 'last in and first out', and were confined to the lower paid and lower status positions within workplaces. Employers did not use the power at their disposal to dilute the positions for which there were still men available. The government, similarly, pressed for the increased employment of women only as the supply of men diminished, and also assisted the maintenance of women's subordinate and supportive role in industry and the armed forces.

Women Workers and Wages Policy

During the First World War the question of equal pay for women workers was a live political issue. Some of the gender lines of support for and opposition to equal pay were oddly drawn, with some male trade unionists favouring equal pay for women and some feminists opposing it.

The feminists who opposed equal pay for women included Clementina Black and Eleanor Rathbone, both of whom were aware of the temporary nature of women's war work and believed that it would injure women's employment opportunities at the end of the war if they were paid as much as men.[44] Some commentators have suggested that these women were motivated by a belief that women were inferior workers (Lewis, 1984, p. 203), but it seems more likely that they were simply aware of the reality of discrimination against women by employers, and believed that employment on lower pay was preferable to unemployment or confinement to very low paid women's jobs.[45] Some feminists were sufficiently angered by the Treasury Agreement which stated that women should vacate men's jobs at the end of the war, and over which women had not been consulted, to support women undercutting men in paid work (Drake, 1917, pp. 82–4).

Nevertheless feminist opposition to equal pay seems to have been confined to a minority of women. The Women's Industrial Council did not advocate undercutting men at the end of the war.[46] Feminists such as Millicent Garrett Fawcett (1918, pp. 1–3) thought that the fact that women were proving themselves to be at least equal and often superior workers provided a case for equal pay, and should be enough to guarantee women a permanent place in industry. Sylvia Pankhurst and the East London Federation of Suffragettes campaigned strenuously for equal pay during the war, and pointed out some huge discrepancies between men's and women's pay. These included the cases of the aeroplace works in Hendon, where women received 3d and men 10d for the same work; and the Vickers Munitions factory in Sheffield, where women received 8s–14s per week, whereas the minimum wage for an unskilled male labourer was £1 6s 6d.[47] Many women's organizations including the women's cooperative assciations, women's labour union and the suffrage societies, campaigned along with the ILP for a minimum wage for women over 18 of £1 per week.[48]

Men in unions continued to demand equal pay for women since this had been adopted as official TUC policy since the 1890s. However, it was widely believed by working men that continued low pay for women would result in the permanent displacement of men from industry by women after the war. As one trade unionist MP put it:

> the temptation of employers to dismiss skilled men and take on women to do the work at lower rates of wage will become more and more . . . the matter affects women, but it affects skilled men even more, because the men's conditions may easily be damaged by unfair forms of competition.[49]

However, men's unions did not pursue equal pay for women at all vigorously, and achieved few results in terms of raising women's pay. Despite the commitment of trade unions at a national level to the principle of equal pay for women, in practice at local and shop-floor levels unions did little to overcome the hostility of many working men. Male workers' reluctance to admit that women were capable of doing equal work, and resistance to seeing wives and daughters receive the same rates of pay as husbands and fathers, sometimes found expression in sabotaging women's machines[50] or causing women to lose pay, by refusing to mend a machine.[51] It may also be that another reason why trade unionists were relatively unwilling to pit their relatively slender resources against employers and the State in favour of equal pay for women was that men's jobs appeared relatively secure as a result of the Treasury Agreement and Shells and Fuses Agreement.

Employers were completely opposed to equal pay for women. This might appear to be easily explained, since it was more profitable to pay women low wages. At an early stage in the war most employers showed a strong preference for recruiting untrained women and as a result the government provided few training courses. Trained women would have been able to command better pay.[52] In 1915 many employers would only hire women if they could be paid very low wages and it was said that 'the patriotic feelings of the women were shamefully exploited' (Hutchins, 1915, p. 254). Instances were cited of women being paid 'sweated' rates, for example as little as 16s per week for a 53-hour week in a munitions factory.[53] Women (and men) employed in government-controlled factories were not allowed to leave without a Leaving Certificate, which meant that if they did so they were barred from munitions work in any other establishment for six weeks. While they remained, however, women were often paid extraordinarily low wages. For instance, a mica driller from Chester with a family to support was paid only 10s per week;[54] and three women from Cardiff, charged before a Munitions Tribunal for absenting themselves from work without leave, had been receiving only 8s per week.[55] However, the profit motive does not explain why employers during the war readily gave much larger pay rises to men.[56]

Nevertheless, although employers were the most powerful group in influencing government policy, the combined pressure of women's organizations and trade unions secured some limited guarantees on equal pay as 'the price of dilution' (Lewis, 1984, p. 203). Under the Shells and Fuses Agreement early in 1915 it was agreed that women performing the work of semi-skilled men would receive the same rate of pay as men (Braybon, 1981, p. 52). However, this only referred to piecework rates.[57] This extremely limited notion of 'equal pay' was used until the end of the war and was recommended at the end of the war by the War Cabinet Committee on Women's Employment.[58] Under such a system it was easy for employers to avoid paying women as much as men, either by putting them on timework or, more commonly, putting them on a hybrid system of timework and piecework. Following circulars L1 and L2 to government-controlled factories, women taking over the whole job of fully skilled tradesmen were to be given the same timerates as men from 1915 (Lewis, 1984, p. 181), but employers arranged production so that less than one woman in 1,000 fell into this category (Drake, 1917, pp. 17 and 35).

The government, as the manager of controlled establishments and the civil service, as well as the armed forces, became a larger employer during the war, but soon earned a reputation as one of the worst-paying employers of women. In clerical work, despite a recommendation in 1915 by the Clerical and Commercial Appointments Committee that 'the scale of wages should, as far as conditions permit, be based upon the wages paid to men who have been engaged in similar duties' (Cmd 8110, 1915), the Treasury had issued a circular letter fixing the rates of pay of female clerks and typists in government departments at a lower rate than that of men doing the same work with same degree of efficiency.[59] In 1916, women employed by the government on clerical work frequently only earned £1 per week, when the men whom they had replaced had earned £2.[60]

The government was also lax in its enforcement of the few regulations and recommendations protecting women's pay. Even when government circulars made firm recommendations, such as the provision within circulars L1 and L2 that all adult women on 'men's work' be paid at least £1 per week,[61] these did not carry the force of law (Braybon, 1981, p. 54). The pay levels of women on women's jobs were initially not protected and officials seldom checked employers' classifications of jobs.[62] When the Munitions of War Act appointed tribunals to fix women's wages in individual cases, these were not mandatory either. The government's limited interventions nevertheless had some impact on women's wages (Drake, 1917, p. 33), especially after July 1916, when a legal minimum wage of 5d per hour, or £1 per week was established for a 48-hour week in government-controlled establishments.[63] However, the value of this was offset by rising prices, which meant that by 1916 the pound was worth only 12s at prewar prices.[64]

The State also facillitated unequal pay rises during the war. In April 1917 the Committee on Production, which contained no women members, increased the wages of men and boys in munitions factories but not those of women and girls. Following complaints, the Ministry of Munitions raised women's and girls' wages by a smaller amount.[65] Larger pay increases for men were made again early in 1918.[66] The Ministry of Munitions was nevertheless unrepentent:

> We face our critics without apology, and we shall find, I believe, in the rates of pay . . . (that) the Labour Department of the Ministry of Munitions has made an enduring contribution of high value towards our industrial methods.[67]

Other orders were also made regulating women's wages; yet women's pay remained at least one-third below that of men and women in the women's trades were particularly poorly paid.[68] The Trade Boards, which had been set up before the war to control wages in the 'sweated trades', continued their work, but they consistently fixed women's wages below those of men and increases barely kept up with the cost of living (Andrews, 1918, p. 101). The Women's Industrial Council reported in 1917 that poverty among women remained a severe problem and that: 'There are few women's employments that, even in the height of the trade boom, pay more than sufficient to keep a girl of 18 decently according to the standard of life of her class.[69] Although some trades, such as dressmaking and millinary, improved hours and conditions in an attempt to lure women back during the labour shortage (Andrews, 1918, p. 40), pay remained a problem: the adult rate of pay was often as low as 12s–15s per week on timework.[70]

The government tended to recommend higher wages to women in 'exceptional circumstances', such as dangerous and unhealthy processes in the government-controlled factories and work which was 'especially laborious'.[71] In agriculture, women received particularly low pay during the first two years of the war, usually earning only 12s–15s for a seven-day week,[72] which was below subsistence level.[73] However, once low pay was identified by the Ministry of Labour as a cause of the shortage of women workers on the land,[74] the government considered a minimum wage for agricultural workers[75] and a Wages Board set up in 1917 set men's pay at 25s per week[76] and women's at 18s, although women were paying as much as 15s per week for their accommodation.[77]

Although there was a general rise in women's wages during the war (Cmd

135, 1919, p. 174), this has often been exaggerated. Some, but by no means all wartime women workers obtained pay which took them above subsistence level. The improvements in pay that did occur were chiefly among those who moved into men's jobs (Andrews, 1918, p. 40). Further, many women were brought out of poverty by the government's separation allowances for the wives and children of servicemen and which continued to be paid if women had earnings from employment (Rathbone, 1917, p. 56). However, many women continued to be financially dependent on their families even during the war. The Ministry of Labour was hampered in its attempts to transfer women workers to other areas by the fact that 'in many cases the wages offered were too low to support a woman living in a strange town'.[78] Even in munitions work, high wages for women were exceptional,[79] and the Cabinet Committee on Women in Industry admitted that munitions work was 'not a gold mine'.[80] Although the labour shortage might have been expected to drive wages up, the system of Leaving Certificates which prevented the women from moving into better paid employment held wages down close to the minimum in many cases.

As a result of government policies which kept women's wages low and the high quality and productivity of women's work, industry, both State-run and private, benefited enormously. As Winston Churchill, then Minister of Munitions, told the House of Commons in 1918:

> aided by the proper development of industrial organisation, and by the increasing standardisation of production, not only have these enormous outputs been achieved by women, but the cost has gone down and the quality has gone up to an almost incredible extent.[81]

Policies Affecting Women's Hours, Conditions and Welfare

Policies restricting women's hours of paid employment had existed in Britain since the 1840s. At the onset of the war the restrictions included the prohibition of night work, limits on the length of a woman's working day and prohibition against women's participation in types of work classified as hazardous to health and the 'maternal function'. During the nineteenth century, legislation had been passed ostensibly to 'protect' women, mainly in the better paid areas of employment such as mining and factory work, although there had been no similar attempts to protect women from excessive hours and poor conditions of unpaid labour in the home (Walby, 1986). During the First World War, however, restrictions on women's hours of employment were considerably relaxed, and the emphasis of State employment policy moved towards women's 'welfare' in the workplace.

During the first two years of the war, prohibition of night work ceased for women and exemptions from the conditions in the Factory Acts relating to women's hours of work were easy to obtain. Infringements by employers carried negligible penalties, because of the 'essential nature of the work'. A case was cited of Greenwood and Batley of Leeds, who were given probation for employing a woman and a girl continuously for 36 hours and 24.5 hours respectively, whereupon the girl had met with an accident.[82] In 1916 it was common for women and girls to work 70 hours per week, and up to 100 hours per week was not unusual (Andrews, 1918, p. 116). In the early stages of the war, women were working a seven-day week, because the government had not trained enough weekend relief workers to keep the factories running.[83] Although the government issued a circular in September 1915, requesting that women be given a weekly rest, this was not made compulsory until 12 months later.[84]

There were widespread concern that women's health would not stand the strain of long hours of work over a sustained period of time, and in September 1915, the Health of Munitions Workers Committee was appointed to investigate (Drake, 1917, p. 28). The Committee issued a series of memoranda and reports in 1916. These were widely read and influential and provided evidence which appealed to all the interested parties involved. In an early report they recommended that women should not work above 60 hours per week[85] but in a later report they said that 60 hours was too much (Cd 8511, 1917). Night work was said to cause deterioration of women's health and disruption of home life.[86] This was welcomed by many male unionists, ostensibly because long hours were 'disastrous from the standpoint of health and motherhood',[87] but also because it was believed that if women proved they could work long hours in paid work without ill effects, they could prove to be more serious competitors for men's jobs after the war.

The Committee's findings were welcomed by women's organizations such as the Women's Industrial Council and the National Federation of Women, because the reports opposed excessive hours of employment for women, without implying that women were physically incapable of such work. It was stated that women's health had stood up to long hours in employment unexpectedly well (Cd 8185, 1916, p. 4), and this was attributed to their better pay and thus presumably an improved diet.[88]

The Committee's reports were also designed to influence employers, however. It was argued that excessive hours of employment were unproductive; that the last few hours of a 12-hour shift yielded little output, especially at the end of a night shift, when women who had been doing housework during the day were liable to fall asleep at their machines.[89] It was stated that women working seven days a week did only six days work,[90] and that long, crowded journeys to work added to the fatigue and loss of production (Cd 8186, 1916, p. 5). It was therefore recommended that eight-hour shifts and a weekly rest should be the norm (Cd 8186, 1916, p. 6).

Largely as a result of these reports, the government brought women's hours of paid employment largely back within the limits of the Factory Acts[91] and, in most cases, did not meet with obstructive resistance from employers. From June 1916, 60 hours per week again became the normal maximum for women and juveniles except for emergencies and 'reasonable amounts of overtime' (Andrews, 1918, p. 123). In November 1914 the avarage working week of women in munitions factories was given as 52 to 54 hours, plus 1–4 hours overtime (Cmd 8186, p. 4). Nonetheless, night work by women was regarded as inevitable while the labour shortage lasted[92] and was retained until the end of the war.

Women 'substitutes' were exposed to the same hazards as men in the work process. Poisonous substances such as TNT, aircraft dope and cordite caused fatalities among women, although this attracted less publicity than lead poisoning, which affected unborn children (Wrigley, 1982, p. 46). Fires and fatal accidents occurred in munitions factories[93] but women could not refuse to work in parts of factories known to be dangerous. If they attempted to do so they could be fined 10s–15s, more than half a week's wages, for breach of discipline. Since women could not leave without a Leaving Certificate without severe financial penalty they were, in practice, virtually conscript workers.[94] The similarity of their position to that of members of the armed forces was not entirely lost on the government. Eventually, women who had been munitions workers were given war-service badges for their services to the nation.[95]

In order to maintain women's energy levels and work incentives, facillities such as canteens and restrooms were provided, particularly in the newer factories, on the recommendation of the Health of Munitions Workers Committee.[96] In some cases, lighter work was given to pregnant women, and some crèches were provided with State grants.[97] Women welfare officers were appointed – particularly where there were large numbers of young women – whose duties were partly pastoral. However, there was a 'social control' element to welfare officers' work, since women workers, especially away from home, were often less docile than they were expected to be. 'Discipline problems', consisting of rowdiness, swearing and staying out late were widespread in munitions factories and government clerical work, among women in the auxilliary forces and in the land army (Marwick, 1977, pp. 101–4; Wrigley, 1982, p. 43). Some of the government's concern stemmed from the fact that many women had spending money of their own at their disposal and more freedom from the controls placed on them by husbands and families; there were fears of a rising illegitimacy rate and declining 'morality' among women who had been 'let out of the cage' (Braybon and Summerfield, 1987, pp. 107–16). A scheme for the cessation of separation allowances to women deemed 'unworthy' as a result of drunkenness, 'irregularity of conduct' or 'unseemly behaviour' was circulated by the Home Office to Chiefs of Police in October 1914, but it caused such an outcry that it was modified, although not completely abandoned (Braybon and Summerfield, 1987, pp. 107–10).

Much of the welfare policy was concerned with arranging travel and accommodation. Problems had arisen because rents became excessively high close to factories, but if workers lived further from work the travelling time and expense were considerable.[98] The government became concerned enough to take action in 1916 after the Health of Munitions Workers Committee had warned that mothers' long absences from home was threatening the destruction of home life.[99]

Policy reponses to travel and accommodation problems included the construction of huts close to factories by the Ministry of Munitions.[100] The standard of these varied greatly, and in Barrow they were said to be poor and overcrowded.[101] Nevertheless, huts remained in use until the end of the war. In 1917 it was also decided that women should be billeted, in the same way as soldiers, in areas where there was a severe shortage of housing.[102] Most of the work of organizing suitable accommodation and housing for women workers was given to the Women's Voluntary Committees which were formed by the government in 1914. These were said to be highly efficient[103] and by 1917 the Ministry of Labour was able to claim that no woman was sent for a job without suitable arrangements for travel and accommodation having been made.[104] Although concern was shown for working women's welfare at the stage of bringing a woman to the job and maintaining her working capacity, less was shown at holiday times when women wanted to return home to visit their families. Married men were gived cheap rail vouchers to go home, but women, whose low wages made it difficult for them to afford the full fare, only received these concessionary tickets if any were left over.[105]

Welfare policy was concerned, above all, with maintaining women's work incentives and labour discipline at a time of labour shortage. However, 'welfare' also had the effect of maintaining ideologies about women as a separate labour force with different (and expensive) needs, who were physically weaker and more vulnerable to moral danger. Despite this, few measures were taken to protect women in terms of their working hours and exposure to danger. Indeed, some employers seemed ready to take grave risks with women's lives and health in order to maintain production. Although the State intervened to a degree to protect women from excessive hours – and thereby undoubtedly reduced the incidence of industrial accidents – this was partly a response to the perceived threat to home life because women were out at work for long periods.

Policies towards Working Women at the End of the First World War

It is sometimes asserted that during the First World War there was a general assumption that women would cease to occupy men's jobs when the war ended (Lewis, 1984, pp. 182 and 202). However, it was not made completely clear to working women during the war whether or not they would continue to occupy men's jobs once the war ended. It is true that agreements had been made by unions, employers and the State for the 'restitution of prewar practices' and in particular the exclusion of women from many trades and processes at the end of the war. However, many women expected their access to skilled work and a living wage to have improved permanently as a result of their wartime efforts, and were encouraged by policy-makers to believe this.

Women on the whole did not disagree with the view that returning soldiers should have their old jobs back again (Strachey, 1978, p. 320; Hutchins, 1915, p. 217; Bosanquet, 1916, p. 217). Neither did women trade unionists support the notion of continued dilution after the war by employers who were simply interested in driving wages down and gaining more control over the labour force (Hutchins, 1917, pp. 191–3). However many women were opposed to being excluded from trades such as engineering purely on the grounds of sex, especially since losses in the armed forces meant that many men would not be returning to the jobs they had vacated (Braybon, 1981, p. 175). It was argued that since large numbers of women had also lost actual or potential male breadwinners in the war and needed to be able to earn a living wage, women should be allowed to remain in men's jobs where they would not be displacing returning soldiers (Drake, 1917, pp. 82–4). Some women also argued that since they had not been party to the Shells and Fuses Agreement, women should not feel bound by its conditions.[106] Barbara Drake stated clearly in 1917 that: 'Women cannot and will not accept a verdict of the men, excluding them from a trade for which they are and know themselves to be suited, for no other reason than sex' (Drake, 1917, p. 84).

While the war lasted, women were in fact encouraged by both employers and the government to believe that many of them would be retained in men's jobs after the war. Women war workers were eulogized for their efficiency and productivity and regarded as being in some ways superior workers. For example, it was pointed out that women did not engage in restrictive practices to reduce output,[107] whereas among male workers such practices had been rife.[108] Some employers hinted that they would retain women in men's jobs after the war,[109] whereas others openly declared their intention of doing so (Drake, 1917, p. 82). Eleanor Rathbone predicted that since employers had discovered women's capacity for doing men's work, they would be prepared to fight to retain women when the war ended.[110]

Leading politicians also hinted, when praising women workers, that they would be rewarded with 'wider avenues of employment';[111] that men would now have to 'look to their laurels';[112] and that gratitude to women would ensure that their improved industrial conditions were permanent.[113] However, most of these claims were extremely vague and the only firm statement made by the Prime Minister was that women would not be excluded from the new trades which had developed during the war.[114]

Women war workers were acutely aware of male trade unionists' hostility to the notion of the retention of women in men's jobs beyond the war. However, some feminists believed that blanket exclusionary policies would be recognized as 'naked self interest'[115] and that public opinion and the press, which had treated women as war heroines, would side with 'keeping the door open to women who had helped to win the war' (Drake, 1917, p. 83).

However, the sudden ending of the war in the autumn of 1918 was rapidly accompanied by a dramatic switch in public attitudes towards women war workers, who suddenly became portrayed as 'parasites, blacklegs and limpets' (Strachey, 1978, p. 371; Braybon, 1981, p. 185). Braybon provides convincing evidence that men thought that if women were allowed to remain in their wartime jobs for long after the war they would occupy these occupations permanently, so the objective was to remove women from men's jobs as rapidly as possible (Braybon, 1981, p. 174). Many women's last few weeks in their wartime jobs were made miserable by accusations that they were taking jobs that they had no right to or need for; and employers were put under pressure by a campaign in the press to sack women workers (Strachey, 1978, p. 371). Despite this, only half of the women who had made up the increase in the female labour force during the war chose to withdraw (Braybon, 1981, p. 179).

Contrary to many women's expectations, there were no attempts by employers and the State to shield women from being pushed out of their wartime employment. Instead, the government, employers and unions joined forces to put the exclusion of women on a more legal and institutionalized footing. The 1919 Restoration of Prewar Practices Act was presented simply as a way in which the government was fulfilling the terms of the agreements made with the trade unions in 1915.[116] However, under the terms of the Act, the practice of excluding women was extended to new industries and branches of industries which had not existed before the war,[117] despite opposition by the Women's Industrial League (Braybon, 1981, p. 201) and representations made to Parliament on their behalf.[118]

Employers had met to discuss the issue of women workers soon after the armistice.[119] Contrary to the expectations of some feminists at the time,[120] employers seemed to have become less keen to continue employing women. A survey by the Women's Industrial League showed that 439 employers, the majority of those interviewed, were not interested in keeping women on, apparently because of women's alleged unsuitability for heavy labour and the need for extra supervision. A fairly small minority, 97 employers, would have kept women on but for the opposition of trade unions; but a substantial minority of 228 would have preferred to have retained the women war workers. These were overruled by their fellow employers (cited in Braybon, 1981, p. 184). Employers who pressed for the restoration of prewar practices to be converted into legislation, not left as a voluntary agreement, did so because they were concerned that they might be undercut by employers who continued to use cheaper female labour.[121]

Although employers were aware of some of the problems involved in using male workers, such as restrictive practices, they seemed willing to work towards amicable solutions, such as profit-sharing schemes;[122] and employers spoke warmly of creating harmony between (male) labour and capital.[123] Working men in unions, not only in the Amalgamated Society of Engineers (ASE), but also in the General Workers' Union, pressed for the exclusion of women from many occupations.[124] The campaign to remove those women still occupying men's jobs was even actively supported by J. R. Clynes, who before the war had supported women's right to work.[125]

As a result of the Restoration of Prewar Practices Act, unions, particularly the ASE, were able to remove women still remaining in men's jobs in a range of trades (Braybon, 1981, p. 184). Thus, at the very time when a few mainly middle-class women were about to gain entry to the professions under the Sex Disqualification (Removal) Act, a far larger number of predominantly working-class women were being barred from earning a livelihood in men's trades, purely on the grounds of gender. This is in contrast to the viewpoint expressed at the time and by some historians since that women were well rewarded for their efforts in the First World War (Marwick, 1977, p. 163).

The government, as the largest wartime employer of labour, encouraged the dismissal of women workers in men's jobs by its own example. Even six months before the end of the war, in spring 1918, 8,000 women were dismissed from a government-controlled establishment at short notice,[126] demonstrating the State's adherence to a condition in the Shells and Fuses Agreement that women should be the first to be affected by redundancy during or after the war (Drake, 1917, p. 16). Similarly, the government made 'drastic reductions' in the numbers of women employed in the civil service in 1919 (Martindale, 1938, p. 87; Strachey 1978, p. 324). At the same time, pressure was being put on women to move back into low-paid, unpopular occupations, particularly domestic service (see Chapter 4) or into dependence on a husband. By 1921 there were fewer women in paid employment than in 1911 (Braybon, 1981, p. 179; Roberts, 1988, p. 68).

Conclusions

In general women war workers were not adequately rewarded for their part in the war effort. Despite receiving the vote and a formal right of entry to the professions, most working women were returned to menial work and economic dependency on men once the war ended.

For the duration of the war, policy had shifted away from the total exclusion of women from men's jobs, to the recruitment of women as substitutes for men. However, women were not interchangeable substitutes. The initial reluctance and delays of government and employers to recruit women, the way that women were purposely kept in subordinate positions to men in occupational hierarchies, the lack of consultation of women over matters affecting their long- and short-term interests and the much lower pay given to the women workers all reinforce the idea that women were seen as 'erzats' or inferior substitutes.

However, during the later stages of the war, partial gaps had opened in this ideology. Despite huge obstacles, including minimal training, obstructive attitudes from some male co-workers, lower pay and household responsibilities, combined with long hours in paid work, it became known that women had somehow managed to become much more productive workers than the men they had replaced. This raises the question of why, having discovered the worth of the women as workers, the government and employers did not choose to substitute women for men in paid employment more permanently at the end of the war.

Men in trade unions, despite having a vested interest in the exclusion of women from men's jobs, cannot be held fully responsible, because employers and the government were in a more powerful position and could have overridden the unions' wishes in many if not most cases. Indeed, during the war many male trade unionists feared that this was precisely what could happen. Only a small proportion of employers who were surveyed claimed to have given up employing women because of pressure from the unions.

Why, then, did the majority of employers give up these women workers without a fight, particularly given that nearly half of the employers who were surveyed would have preferred to keep women on? The unexpectedly sudden return of demobilized servicemen expecting a 'land fit for heroes', but finding a rapidly contracting job market, may explain the hurried manner in which many women were ejected from their wartime occupations, and the equally rapid reversal of public attitudes towards women war workers. In 1919, the collusion between capital and male organized labour at the level of the State, represented by the restoration of prewar practices, appears, as in the decade before the war, to illlustrate policy-makers' longer term desire to promote harmony between male labour and capital at the expense of working women.

Notes

1. Health of Munition Workers Committee, Memorandum No. 4, *Employment of Women*, Cmd 8185, 1916, p. 3.
2. Walter Long, President of the Local Government Board, House of Commons, *Hansard*, 5th series, Vol. 73, p. 439, 1915.
3. A. Marwick (1977) *Women at War 1914–1918*, p. 183; S. Pollard (1991) *The Development of the British Economy 1914–1990*, p. 30.
4. *Board of Trade and Labour Gazette*, March 1915, p. 78; Hutchins, 1915, p. 240.
5. G. Braybon (1981) *Women Workers in the First World War*, p. 44; Hutchins, 1915, p. 249.
6. *Hansard*, 5th series, Vol. 70, col. 434: Mr Whitehouse.
7. *Hansard*, Vol. 73, col. 439: Walter Long.
8. *Women's Industrial News*, April 1916, pp. 10 and 12: E. B. Ashford.
9. *Hansard*, Vol. 70, cols 406–32.
10. The *Labour Gazette* regularly published details of the extent to which Germany substituted female for male workers. See also *Hansard*, Vol. 72, col. 1495: Mr R. Maxwell.
11. *Hansard*, Vol. 71, col. 256: Mr J. M. Robertson.

12. *Hansard*, Vol. 71, col. 256: Mr J. M. Robertson.
13. Rosamund Smith, 'Women and munitions work', *Women's Industrial News*, April 1916, p. 14.
14. *Hansard*, Vol. 71, col. 563.
15. *Women's Industrial News*, January 1916, p. 116.
16. *Hansard*, Vol. 71, col. 563.
17. *Hansard*, Vol. 74, col. 300.
18. *Hansard*, Vol. 72, col. 1495: Mr R. McNeil.
19. Public General Acts and Measures 1916, pp. 115–20.
20. House of Commons, *Hansard*, Vol. 73, col. 439: Walter Long.
21. House of Commons, *Hansard*, Vol. 81, col. 1193.
22. House of Commons, *Hansard*, Vol. 81, col. 202: David Lloyd George.
23. *Board of Trade and Labour Gazette*, December 1915. However, many factories recruited women directly, so these figure do not show all the women who found work. Some of the men who found work must not have been registered as unemployed.
24. *Women's Industrial News*, April 1916, p. 10.
25. *Ibid.*, and Cd 8110, 1915: Report issued by the Clerical and Commercial Appointments Committee.
26. *Hansard*, Vol. 70, col. 439: Sir H. Verney.
27. *Women's Industrial News*, April 1916, p. 25.
28. *Women's Industrial News*, July 1916, p. 28; *Labour Gazette*, December 1916.
29. In November 1914 the Amalgamated Society of Engineers (ASE) secured an arrangement known as the Crayford Agreement with the Employers' Association whereby women were to be excluded from skilled employment and confined to purely repetitive work. See Barbara Drake (1917) *Women in the Engineering Trades*, p. 14.
30. *Ibid.*, p. 16; Braybon, 1981, p. 52.
31. *Labour Gazette*, March 1916, p. 83.
32. *Ibid.*, see also Andrews 1918, pp. 59–60.
33. *Women's Industrial News*, July 1916, p. 19.
34. *Labour Gazette*, October 1916: 'The extension of women's employment during the war'.
35. Sir William Beardsmore, *Manchester Guardian*, 16 May 1916; House of Commons, *Hansard*, Vol. 84, col. 203; Millicent Garrett Fawcett, *Economic Journal*, 1918, p. 3.
36. Jane Lewis, 1984, p. 181. However, the jobs were not exactly the same as before the war, because they had been rearranged in the process of dilution.
37. *Women's Industrial News*, July 1916, p. 65.
38. *Ibid.*
39. *Women's Industrial News*, July 1916, p. 13.
40. House of Commons, *Hansard*, Vol. 106, col. 325: Dr Macnamara, Parliamentary Secretary to the Admiralty.

41. *Labour Gazette*, October 1916: 'The extension of women's employment during the war'.
42. *Labour Gazette*, November 1916: 'Work of the Board of Trade Local Advisory Committees upon women's war employment'.
43. *Labour Gazette*, December 1916.
44. Eleanor Rathbone, Secretary of the Women's Industrial Council (Liverpool Branch), *Women's Industrial News*, July 1916, pp. 42–3; Eleanor Rathbone, 'The renumeration of women's services', *Economic Journal*, 1917, pp. 56–8.
45. Eleaor Rathbone, *Women's Industrial News*, July 1916, p. 66.
46. *Women's Industrial News*, July 1916, p. 66.
47. *Women's Dreadnought*, 1 January 1916, p. 396.
48. *Ibid.*, p. 398.
49. House of Commons, *Hansard*, Vol. 98, col. 2079: Mr Anderson; Vol. 96, col. 1250: Mr Kellaway, Parliamentary Secretary to the Ministry of Munitions.
50. Braybon, 1981, p. 68; *Labour Gazette*, 1918, p. 217.
51. *Women's Industrial News*, April 1916, p. 16.
52. *Ibid.*, pp. 11 and 19.
53. *Women's Industrial News*, April 1916, p. 16.
54. House of Commons, *Hansard*, Vol. 87, col. 228: Mr Anderson.
55. House of Commons, *Hansard*, Vol. 92, col. 896: Mr Anderson; Vol. 96, col. 2242; Vol. 101, col. 1001.
56. House of Commons, *Hansard*, Vol. 87, col. 228.
57. *Women's Dreadnought*, 1 January 1916, p. 395; Drake, 1917, p. 19.
58. Lewis, 1984, p. 203. In 1916 the government sent a circular to all government-controlled factories recommending that women on semi-skilled men's work receive equal piecework but not equal timework rates of pay.
59. House of Commons, *Hansard*, Vol. 72, col. 668: Mr Montagu, Secretary to the Treasury.
60. *Women's Industrial News*, July 1916, p. 66.
61. *Ibid.*
62. *Hansard*, Vol. 85, col. 2468: George Barnes.
63. House of Commons, *Hansard*, Vol. 83, col. 1204.
64. *Ibid.*, col. 1361.
65. House of Commons, *Hansard*, Vol. 92, col. 896.
66. House of Commons, *Hansard*, Vol. 101, col. 1001.
67. House of Commons, *Hansard*, Vol. 95, col. 581: Dr Addison.
68. Cmd 135, 1919, p. 5; Andrews, 1918, pp. 40 and 55. Other trades into which women were admitted into men's jobs in 1915 included printing, bleaching, dyeing, woodworking, biscuit and pastry baking, wholesale clothing and bootmaking, earthenware and china manufacturing. In 1916 they also included lace making, hosiery finishing, printing, silver plate, cutlery and brush making.

69. *Women's Industrial News*, 1917, p. 7. Women's unskilled factory work included occupations such as sweet making, pickle making and tea and tobacco packing. Orders were also made regulating the wages of women on women's work in government-controlled factories (Order 447 of 1916 and Orders 9 and 10 of 1917); girls on men's work (order 49 of 1917), women on general woodwork (order 313 of 1917) and women on aircraft work.
70. *Women's Industrial News*, 1917, p. 7.
71. *Labour Gazette*, 1918, p. 217.
72. House of Commons, *Hansard*, Vol. 82, col. 915.
73. *Women's Industrial News*, April 1916, p. 25.
74. *Labour Gazette*, December 1916: 'Women in agriculture'.
75. House of Commons, *Hansard*, Vol. 90, col. 2130.
76. House of Commons, *Hansard*, Vol. 91, col. 11; Public General Acts: 9 Edw. 7, col. 22.
77. House of Commons, *Hansard*, Vol. 95, col. 1730. This was done under the Corn Production Act of 1917.
78. *Labour Gazette*, March 1917: 'Migration of women's labour through employment exchanges'.
79. *Women's Industrial News*, 1917, p. 6.
80. Cmd 135, 1919; Lewis, 1984, p. 187.
81. House of Commons, *Hansard*, Vol. 105, col. 1148: Winston Churchill.
82. House of Commons, *Hansard*, Vol. 72, cols 1035–6.
83. House of Commons, *Hansard*, Vol. 78, cols 871–2.
84. Andrews, 1918, p. 123; *Hansard*, Vol. 81, col. 2064. A government survey in April 1916 showed that of employers who replied, over half employed no Sunday labour.
85. Cd 8186; *Women's Industrial News*, 1917, pp. 12–14.
86. Cd 8185, p. 4, Memorandum No. 4 'The employment of women'.
87. House of Commons, *Hansard*, Vol. 81, col. 1800: Mr Anderson.
88. Andrews, 1918, p. 8; Report of the War Cabinet Committee on Women in Industry, Cmd 135, 1919, p. 107, which stated: 'properly nourished women have certainly a greater reserve of energy than they have been credited with'.
89. Cd 8185, p. 4; *Labour Gazette*, 1916, p. 45; Helen Bosanquet, 'Women in industry', *Economic Journal*, 1916, p. 213.
90. Cd 8186, p. 4; Bosanquet, 1916, p. 212.
91. House of Commons, *Hansard*, Vol. 83, col. 1525.
92. Braybon, 1981, p. 114; House of Commons, *Hansard*, Vol. 82, col. 9243.
93. House of Commons, *Hansard*, Vol. 90, col. 1032. References to explosions in munitions factories were sometimes censored during the war. Marwick, 1977, p. 109, cites an instance of women receiving an OBE for fighting a fire at a munitions factory.
94. *Hansard*, Vol. 90, col. 1580: Mr Anderson.
95. *Hansard*, Vol. 97, col. 1711.

96. Cd 8185; *Labour Gazette*, 1916, p. 45.
97. Cmd 135, 1919, p. 106; *Hansard*, Vol. 71, cols 1899–1900.
98. *Women's Industrial News*, April 1916, p. 18; Bosanquet, 1916, p. 214. The government's attitude to women with some spending money and more freedom is worthy of a study in itself.
99. Cd 8185; *Labour Gazette*, 1916, p. 45.
100. House of Commons, *Hansard*, Vol. 81, col. 2065.
101. House of Commons, *Hansard*, Vol. 93, col. 1290.
102. Public General Acts and Measures 1917–18: Billeting of Civilians Act, May 1917.
103. *Labour Gazette*, March 1917.
104. *Ibid.*
105. House of Commons, *Hansard*, Vol. 96, col. 2243: Mr Kellaway.
106. *Ibid.*, p. 113. Mary McArthur, of the National Federation of Women Workers, and Susan Lawrence agreed with this view.
107. *Women's Industrial News*, April 1916, p. 15.
108. House of Commons, *Hansard*, Vol. 116, col. 1755.
109. *Women's Industrial News*, July 1916, p. 9.
110. Eleanor Rathbone, 'Equal pay for women's work', *Women's Industrial News*, July 1916, p. 9.
111. *Women's Industrial News*, July 1916, p. 35.
112. House of Commons, *Hansard*, Vol. 73, col. 439: Walter Long.
113. House of Commons, *Hansard*, Vol. 105, col. 1250: Mr Kellaway.
114. House of Commons, *Hansard*, Vol. 116, col. 1780.
115. Eleanor Rathbone, 'The renumeration of women's services', *Economic Journal*, 1917, p. 56.
116. Public General Acts and Measures, 1919, p. 144: Restoration of Prewar Practices Act, section 1(2).
117. *Ibid.*
118. House of Commons, *Hansard*, Vol. 118, col. 1779.
119. *Ibid.*, col. 1771.
120. Strachey, 1978, pp. 371–2, claims that employers wanted to keep women workers on.
121. *Hansard*, Vol. 118, col. 1754.
122. *Ibid.*, col. 1755.
123. *Ibid.*
124. Cmd 167 'Report of the Committee on Women in Industry', p. 41.
125. House of Commons, *Hansard*, Vol. 118, col. 1745.
126. *Hansard*, Vol. 103, col. 1251.

Chapter 4

Women and Unemployment Policy Between the Wars

After the First World War there was a dramatic fall in the number and range of employment opportunities available to women. Although the feminization of some occupations continued to take place, notably in clerical and shopwork, gender divisions in paid and unpaid work remained entrenched. Contemporary official sources denied that this was the result of State social policy, claiming that occupational segregation was the result of women's natural capacities and interests, employers' preferences and trade unions' exclusionary practices (Cmd 3508, 1920/30, pp. 10–14). However, closer inspection reveals that the State's employment policies towards women consisted of much more than a refusal to intervene to assist working women, although this played a significant part. This chapter therefore examines several aspects of the employment policies of British governments which affected the position of working women between the wars: the 'marriage bar', the policies of protecting women in some respects but not others, programmes for the unemployed and the manipulation of unemployment benefit regulations.

During the years following the war the government had a policy of continuing to remove women who still remained in the men's jobs they had occupied during the war. The Ministry of Labour was 'unremitting in its endeavours to secure the reinstatement of men in their prewar jobs',[1] and this policy continued until 1928, when the Southborough committee reported that there was 'no further field for the substitution of ex-servicemen for women'.[2] By this time women had been virtually eliminated from engineering jobs apart from monotonous, repetitive, unskilled positions in light industry, for which they were described as being 'naturally' suited (Cmd 3508, p. 14; Walby, 1984, p. 351). However, there were occupations such as clerical work and teaching which were open to both women and men, and to control the numbers of women in these occupations a 'marriage bar' was introduced.

The 'Marriage Bar'

A 'marriage bar' had existed before the First World War in some occupations but it was greatly intensified in Britain between the wars. Although it was never the subject of central government legislation as it was in Germany, where married women were prohibited from taking any paid work from 1933,[3] it was almost universally applied. Central government as an employer, for example in the Civil Service and in local authorities, took a lead in applying a marriage bar and some private employers followed suit. The 1919 Sex Disqualification (Removal) Act did not entitle women to the same treatment as men[4] and women were expected to resign on marriage. In the civil service, the Joint Substitution Board surveyed staff 'with a view to securing that married women whose husbands can maintain them are replaced by ex-servicemen'.[5] In 1921 the London County Council sacked its married women cleaners and in 1922 most local education authorities sacked married women teachers (Lewis, 1984, p. 199).

The marriage bar was almost but not quite universally applied. In Nelson, Lancashire, where married women were used to and expected economic independence, and were active in local politics, there was no marriage bar (Walby, 1984, p. 358). In other areas, married women were retained only if their husbands were unable to maintain them; but were subjected to humiliating questioning and sometimes criticized for depriving single women of jobs.[6] Opposition to the marriage bar, for example from the National Union of teachers, had little success. In 1923, 57 married women teachers from Rhondda unsucccessfully attempted to prevent their dismissal by invoking the Sex Disqualification (Removal) Act (Branson, 1976, p. 209). However, in 1925 one woman won her case against Poole corporation on the grounds that her employers had attempted to dismiss her 'to remove any possible inducements for married teachers to neglect their domestic concerns'. Since this woman had domestic help and no children, it was ruled that Poole were acting 'in pursuance of motives alien and irrelevant to the discharge of their duties as a Local Education Authority'.[7] For the vast majority of married women in the professions, however, and for many women in other forms of paid employment, the marriage bar remained firmly in place throughout the interwar period and was not formally removed until after the Second World War.

Policies of 'Protecting' Women

Many men in unions supported the marriage bar and, in redundancy situations, demanded the sacking of married women first; employers appear to have willingly agreed to these demands (Cmd 3508, p. 24). However, in contrast with the war years there was no government intervention to protect women's employment. For example, in the case of 90 women bakers dismissed in Glasgow as a result of union pressure, the government decided not to hold an enquiry;[8] and similarly no action was taken to prevent the sacking of women compositors as a result of trade-union exclusionary practices which resulted in the number of women printers falling from 1,000 in Edinburgh alone in 1911 to only 200 in the whole of Scotland by 1929 (Cmd 3508, p. 26).

The State imposed limits on the hours and types of work considered suitable for women by means of protective legislation, however (Lewis, 1984, p. 173). In 1920 the Women and Young Persons Act, which added to the provisions of the Factory and Workshops Acts of 1901–11, prohibited night work by boys under 18 and females of any age, although permitting 'double day shifts between 6 am and 10pm'.[9] Official sources denied that protective legislation adversely affected women's employment opportunities (Cmd 3508, p. 6), although some feminists disagreed and thought that all factory legislation should apply equally to men and women,[10] since in fact some employers at the end of the First World War had given protective legislation as a reason why they had not wished to retain women in their wartime employment (Braybon, 1981, p. 184). It is clear therefore that policies of 'protecting' working women consisted largely of protecting women from the harmful effects of too much paid work (although not of unpaid work) rather than protecting women from dismissal or discriminatory treatment in employment.

Programmes for the Unemployed

During the long period of high unemployment between the wars, governments remained reluctant to acknowledge the full extent of women's unemployment. Consequently, women were excluded from public works programmes, and only marginally included, under very different terms and conditions, in training programmes for the unemployed. In 1920 the Unemployment (Relief Works) Act was passed 'to make better provision for the employment of unemployed persons'.[11] Although jobs were created on a huge scale for unemployed men, it was clear that for the purposes of ths Act, women were not considered to be 'persons'. A very small scheme which had existed in London to assist unemployed women ended in 1920.[12] Thereafter, Ministers of Labour in all of the succeeding governments gave identical reasons why women should not be included in public works schemes. The work devised on schemes for the unemployed consisted almost entirely of 'pick and shovel' labouring work from which women were usually barred; so then it was argued that women were 'not suited' for the work provided.[13] Even Margaret Bondfield, the first woman Minister of Labour, expressed the official view that 'direct employment provided in relief of unemployment *necessarily* consists in the main of labouring work for which women cannot be engaged'[14] (emphasis added).

However, other, less senior women MPs of all parties, particularly Nancy Astor, Eleanor Rathbone and Jennie Lee, were outspoken in their criticism of the lack of provision for unemployed women. They strongly objected to the fact that in 1930, 160,000 places were provided for men at a cost of £60 million,[15] and 220,000 places in 1930,[16] while unemployed women were not catered for at all under these schemes. Policies of ejecting women from adequately paid work, combined with the lack of State provision for unemployed women, created desperation for work which paid a living wage (Strachey,

1978, p. 373). One advertisement for 40 women soda-fountain attendents in 1925 at a weekly wage of £2 10s produced 8,000 applicants, 6,000 of whom applied personally and rushed the gates, so that mounted police were called to disperse them.[17]

Women's unemployment was not considered important, since policy-makers assumed that the vast majority of women could be maintained within marriage. Whether young women, many of whom had enjoyed comparatively good pay and freedom during the war, would want to settle for a life of economic dependence and domestic servitude does not appear to have been considered important by the postwar government. In fact, however, the already larger number of women in the population and the losses of young men in the war meant that an estimated one-third of women still had to be completely self-supporting, whether or not they chose to be (Strachey, 1978, p. 371).

Nevertheless, many employers had taken advantage of high unemployment in 1921–2 by halving wages for both men and women;[18] and because women's wages continued to be fixed substantially below those of men by the Trade Boards, women's pay, which could be less than half the weekly minimum for men[19] often fell below subsistence level.[20] Women's desperation for a livelihood was such that by 1921 a delegation of unemployed women met by MPs agreed that women factory workers would accept domestic service if they were given training with grants,[21] and a group of unemployed women from Shoreditch actually paraded outside the House of Commons demanding training for domestic service.[22] This was despite the fact that resident domestic service was extremely unpopular. There was little personal freedom and a humilliating 'no followers' rule was observed in most houses (Graves and Hodge, 1941, p. 45). Until 1927, domestic servants were denied the vote (Branson, 1976, p. 203) and 'indoor servants' (cooks and housemaids) were excluded from national insurance cover longer than any other group of workers. Accommodation usually consisted of an attic or a cellar; uniforms (a hated badge of servility) had to be worn and there were long hours of physically demanding work for very low pay. These were thought to be among the main reasons why the numbers of domestic servants had fallen from around 1.4 million in 1911 to just over 1 million in 1921.[23] Nevertheless, resident domestic service, like the nineteenth-century workhouse, was a last resort which at least guaranteed food and shelter.

The government's domestic service training scheme which was provided was, with only very small exceptions, the only training provided for unemployed women between the wars. Even this was a relatively small scheme, training only 7,000 women per year at its height[24] although it was much larger than the prewar women's workrooms scheme. The chief aim of the scheme was to retrain 'redundant' industrial workers and make them more suitable domestic workers, either in meeting the demand that existed for servants in the homes of the better-off, or as good wives.

Training in domestic service had already existed before 1914, in the form of training schools for girls.[25] Female pupils of Poor Law schools and Dr Barnardo's homes were also sent into domestic service (Lewis, 1984, p. 186) having been prepared beforehand by years of routine domestic duties and the inculcation of 'good habits' which would make them 'good wives'[26] often to the neglect of their general education and mental development (Cmd 67, p. 10). In 1919 the Report of the Women's Advisory Committee on the Domestic Service Problem was commissioned and published, (Cmd 67, p. 10), following allegations that a fall in the numbers of domestic servants was caused by women remaining unemployed rather than accept such work, and the belief that munitions workers could not easily adapt to the discipline required of servants (Strachey, 1978, pp. 371–2). The Committee recommended that the leisure hours of domestic servants should be increased, that social clubs should be set up (Cmd 67, p. 4) and that more training should be provided, in order to raise the status of domestic work.[27]

The interwar domestic service training schemes were administered by the Central Committe for Women's Training and Employment (CCWTE). This body had already been in existence in 1914, when it had administered the Queen Charlotte Women's Workrooms in 1914–15; but a fall in women's unemployment in 1915 had left the Committee with a surplus of funds of £500,000,[28] which gave them a degree of financial autonomy. In 1920 the CCWTE ran a 'scholarship scheme' to give grants to women 'whose earning capacity had been injuriously affected as a result of conditions arising out of the war' to enable them to undertake training on existing courses in any vocational but non-industrial subject.[29] Women were trained in a variety of subjects, including horticulture, journalism and hairdressing (Lewis, 1984, p. 191). Equipment and uniforms were given to women who had obtained employment but could not afford to buy such items.[30] This scheme enabled 2,511 women to complete their training by the end of 1922. Between May 1921 and December 1922, the Committe also provided training with maintenance for over 10,000 women undertaking to enter residential domestic service. They also provided 2,538 uniforms and had a 'homemakers' scheme' designed 'to assist women with the domestic work in their own homes while they were awaiting the opportunity to return to their own trades'.[31] During 1922, however, the Committee's funds expired, and they became completely dependent on State assistance; thus their grant became exclusively tied to domestic service training.[32]

These new courses provided to train women in domestic duties were of three months' duration, although they were extended slightly for younger women. Trainees were paid allowances of 10s to £1 per week, according to age.[33] In 1929 there were 35 training centres. All the centres were non-residential (a residential centre opened in 1930) and used rented houses. Approximately 5,000 women per year were trained[34] in housework, needlework, cookery, laundry and personal hygene. Trainees also spent part of the course making their uniform, the cost of which was deducted from their allowance at the rate of 2s–3s per week.[35]

Despite superficial appearances to the contrary, there were few differences between the Labour and Conservative parties over domestic service policy. The Conservatives attempted to impose a condition on trainees that they would enter domestic service when their training was finished, whereas Labour made this optional. Labour opposed the direction of women into (low paid) domestic service, regarding it as a class rather than a gender issue. As one Labour MP expressed it:

> We object to the women of our class being made flunkeys for women
> who are far better able to look after their own families. If there is to
> be any home life, and domestic service is necessary, let the daughters
> of the workers stay at home and help their mothers.[36]

However, Labour were impressed by the argument that domestic service training created better (unpaid) working-class wives.[37] Margaret Bondfield claimed that Labour's less coercive approach to domestic service training was the reason why more women entered domestic service after their training while Labour was in power.[38] Further, more women were trained in the domestic arts under Labour than while the Conservatives were in office;[39] and even in opposition Labour, backed by women MPs of all parties, campaigned successfully in 1928 for increased funding for domestic service training.[40] At this time women's unemployment was particularly severe, and there were four times as many applicants as places on the courses;[41] and it was politically more feasible to obtain funds for domestic service training than for any other type of project to assist unemployed women.

By 1931, the number of female domestic servants had risen to 1.27 million. However, domestic service remained an unpopular occupation among women. Virtually no attempt had been made to improve the conditions in domestic work,[42] and policy-makers had instead relied on the desperation of unemployed women to fill the positions. Once unemployment began to diminish from 1937 onwards, relatively few women were willing to consider domestic work or training.[43] Politicians expressed much concern about this, with one describing it as a 'national disaster'.[44]

Other types of training for unemployed women were provided briefly by the second Labour government in 1929–30, but only on a tiny scale. Under the Individual Vocational Training Scheme candidates over 18 who were 'not suitable for domestic service' were taught shorthand and typing, nursery nursing, cookery, midwifery and institutional housekeeping on grants of £1 per week. Only 381 women were catered for between April 1930 and December 1931, and of these 90 had their grants cancelled because of inadequate funding.[45] Two small experimental workrooms were also set up at the same time 'to assist women who have been unemployed for so long that they have lost all hope and energy'.[46] Pressure was put on unemployed young women by the Ministry of Labour during the 1930s to take up hotel work, and the government gave grants to private bodies such as the Restaurant Public Houses

Promotion Company which trained young women (and some men) in hotel and bar work.[47]

It was also recommended that single unemployed women should receive State help in order to go to Canada and Australia and there become domestic servants.[48] The 1922 Empire Settlement Act granted financial assistance towards fares in 'suitable cases' (Public General Acts, 1922); and the CCWTE was given funding from the Colonial Office to provide training,[49] and a residential training centre established to train 'household workers' who would then qualify for a free passage to Australia.[50] Part of the cost was borne by the Overseas Settlement Committee, and part was met by the Australian government.[51] Four voluntary societies which assisted the emigration of women were also given grants by the Ministry of Labour.[52] Whereas employed spinsters were at best tolerated, unemployed spinsters were described as 'surplus' to the requirements of the nation; and the objective of the scheme was to channel them into the least desired jobs in another country.

Despite the lack of job creation for unemployed women, fewer places on training schemes were created for women than for men.[53] This was not through any lack of meeting the objectives of placing women in domestic service. The vast majority of the women trainees took up the work for which they had been prepared;[54] whereas the men's schemes were less successful in this respect.[55] Spending on training for women was also considerably less, mainly because the men's training centres were purpose-built, and had cost £880,000 just to equip;[56] whereas the women's training took place in rented houses, and the total cost was between £70,000 and £90,000 per annum.[57] Programmes for unemployed women between the wars were thus fairly minimal and cheaply run. Their overriding concern was to retrain women whose expectations had risen as a result of their war work and prepare them for domestic work either in their own working-class homes or those of the more affluent, in Britain or overseas.

Unemployment Benefit Regulations

Between the wars, unemployment benefit regulations were, like the training schemes, used as a means of transfering women from industrial employment to low-paid and unpaid domestic work, as well as economizing on public spending disproportionately at the expense of women. In the process it was often argued, as before 1914, that most out-of-work women were not genuinely unemployed because they were not really part of the labour force.

At the end of the First World War the government created an unprecedentedly generous unemployment benefit: the 'donation' benefit. Men were initially to be paid 24s per week and women 20s per week for thirteen weeks (although such was the level of alarm in policy-making circles that the actual amounts paid were raised higher still and women were receiving 25s) and thereafter men received 20s and women 15s.[58] This was an emergency

respose to the sudden return of servicemen with a low tolerance for unemployment and armed with rifles; but it was also paid to unemployed civilians. By
May 1919 488,486 civilian women and 1,012 ex-servicewomen were still claiming this benefit, compared with 209,486 civilian males and 305,621 ex-servicemen.[59] Although the total numbers of male and female claimants were similar,
and women had been ejected from employment in industry to make room for
men, it was the women who were the targets of attempts to cut spending on the
benefit. Women were said to be abusing the system by refusing to accept work
in laundries, dressmaking and domestic service at wages as low as 8s per week
for very long hours of work;[60] and to counteract this the Minister of Labour
proposed 'special tests' in areas where there was a demand for servants, to
appoint special investigators and to 'prosecute relentlessly'.[61] By November
1919 the number of women claiming the benefit had shrunk to 30,000. Already
in the short period up to April 1919, 66,000 women had been placed in
domestic service: an achievement described by the Minister of Labour as 'a
record we need not blush for'.[62]

Women had not initially been included in the 1911 National Insurance
scheme in any significant numbers,[63] but were brought in, ostensibly on the
same terms as men under the 1916 National Insurance Part II (Munition
Workers) Act. By 1920, women accounted for one million of the 3.75 million
insured workers.[64] By 1921, however, rising levels of unemployment had led to
the collapse of the contributory basis of the National Insurance fund (Deacon,
1977, pp. 15–17). Means of economizing were devised and, again, women were
the main target. The Not Genuinely Seeking Work Clause (NGSW), introduced as part of the 1921 National Insurance Act, was chiefly aimed at removing married women from the unemployment registers, as the Minister of
Labour made clear:

> It really would not be fair, I suggest, for a married woman who has
> definitely upon her marriage given up paid employment, to claim this
> emergency benefit on the basis of twenty weeks' employment during
> the last year if, in fact, she was not available for work and had no
> necessity or intention of returning to it. This Bill, in fact enables this
> claim to be tested.[65]

Although women were being *sacked* upon marriage as a result of the marriage
bar, their *intention* to work was thus denied, and they were to be regarded as
unavailable for paid employment.

However, unmarried women were also affected by the Not Genuinely
Seeking Work regulations. In an Umpire's decision in 1921 a group of young
female redundant glovemakers was refused benefit because there was a demand for domestic servants in their area.[66] The Minister of Labour also issued
an Order on Domestic Service to labour exchanges[67] and required them to
compile lists of all suitable female applicants.[68] Often young women under 18
were disqualified from receiving benefit for refusing domestic service up to 150

miles from home;[69] and seasonal and hotel workers were particularly vulnerable to being classed as 'suitable for domestic service'.[70]

The Not Genuinely Seeking Work clause was intensified from 1924. The first Labour government of that year introduced a clause that applicants for insurance benefit should 'normally be in insurable employment'. Women who had been temporarily pressed into accepting work in domestic service fell foul of this rule, since domestic service was not an insured trade. The Conservative Baldwin government from late-1924 used 'travelling committees' to ensure tight administration of the Clause.[71] One employment exchange which had appointed a special committee to interrogate women applicants for unemployment benefit was singled out for special praise.[72]

The effects of the Not Genuinely Seeking Work clause on women before 1925 are difficult to assess with precision since separate statistics for men and women were not introduced before that date. However, according to the *Woman Worker*, thousands of women were disqualified from receiving benefits under the NGSW clause by the Rota Committees.[73] The *Labour Gazette* admitted that the smaller number of women than men claimants was caused by the 'heavier incidence of disqualification of women'.[74] In 1926, one in three of women's claims was disallowed, compared with one in nine of men's; and by 1927 the proportion of male to female claimants had widened to 11 to two.[75]

It was made transparently clear that women were the target of the NGSW clause. For example, in the Not Genuinely Seeking Work regulations claimants were always referred to as 'she'.[76] There was little organized working-class opposition to the Clause during the early 1920s except by the Independent Labour Party. As long as it was seen as being aimed only at women it was mainly regarded as 'a legitimate defence of public funds' (Deacon, 1977, p. 21). However, in 1928 it became clear that in numerical terms, more men than women were falling foul of the Not Genuinely Seeking Work clause;[77] and from then on opposition increased.[78] By 1929 the Clause was a major election issue, and was discontinued by the second Labour government in 1930 (Deacon, 1977, p. 106). However, only unemployed men benefited, because single women continued to be disqualified if they refused domestic service, and married women benefited only briefly because from October 1931 they came up against the Anomolies Regulations.

The Anomalies Regulations

The Anomalies Regulations were presented as being simply an economy measure, passed during the financial crisis of the second Labour government. However, the total amount of money saved by the Anomalies Regulations was tiny – estimated at no more than £5.5 million per annum,[79] compared with a total National Insurance budget defecit of £115 million in 1931,[80] and minute compared with its major impact on married women. Morover, the Regulations remained in force until after the Second World War, even though the pressure on the National Insurance fund declined steadily after 1934.[81]

'Anomolies' meant the legal abuse of the benefits system. The Majority Report of the Royal Commission on Unemployment Insurance thought that employment after marriage was not the 'normal' situation for women. Since the number of married women claiments had risen briefly after the discontinuation of the Not Genuinely Seeking Work Clause, it was argued that married women were abusing the system (Cmd 3872, pp. 61 and 73). This view, although opposed by the Independent Labour Party, had much support from within the trade-union movement,[82] including from some single women who had made political careers within the trade union movement, such as Margaret Bondfield and Marion Phillips. Many unionists saw married women in the labour market as unfair competitors with single women and married men. They therefore opposed the payment of unemployment benefit to married women because this was seen as an acnowledgement that wives had a legitimate place in the paid workforce.

Under the Anomolies Regulations, a woman had to prove that she had not abandoned insurable employment *and* that she could reasonably expect to get work in the district where she lived (Cmd 3872, Majority Report, p. 457). A high proportion of married women claimants were affected by these provisions. Despite assurances to the contrary[83] the Anomolies Regulations also affected significant numbers of married women who were normally dependent on their own earnings, especially since the Regulations coincided with a recession in the cotton industry.[84] In 1932, the Regulations were also followed by an intensification of the marriage bar.

Women consistently paid more into the National Insurance fund than they received.[85] This was not only because of the higher rate of disallowance of women's claims compared with men's, but also because insured women were almost never able to obtain benefits for dependents, especially husbands. The assumption that the typical woman worker was single and without dependents, which was reflected in women's low pay, was strongly maintained; and the Royal Commission on National Insurance firmly resisted the notion that even an uninsured unemployed husband was the dependent of an insured wife.[86]

It is clear that the changing unemployment benefit regulations between the wars were far more than a means of containing the costs of the National Insurance scheme. They were also a policy statement of who was normally seen as a self-supporting employee in insurable employment, and who was a dependent and a low-paid, uninsured and/or unpaid domestic worker.

Effects of Government Policies on Women Workers

Several changes in the position of working women in the 1920s and 1930s are connected with the government policies described above. First, during the 1920s women's total full-time employment fell relative to the number of women in the population (Lewenhak, 1980, p. 215), at a time when a higher proportion of women than before was obliged to be self-supporting. In 1931, 90 per cent of married women and 30 per cent of single women were described as 'unoccupied' (Branson, 1976, p. 213). Although the accuracy of census data on economic activity is questionable, since large numbers of married women made money in the infomal economy by taking in lodgers, laundry and sewing and by making and selling a range of goods (Roberts, 1988, p. 49), this is nevertheless a higher proportion than in 1911. Women's unemployment appears to have been seriously and deliberately underestimated.

Second, there was a fall in the number of women engaged in skilled employment, which is said to have fallen by 34 per cent between 1911 and 1951 (Lewis, 1984, p. 182). It is true that some occupations were feminized during this period, particularly clerical and shopwork, and that women were recruited into new jobs in light engineering and electrical engineering. However, most of the new jobs were classed (and paid) as unskilled.

Third, government policy had a significant impact on the numbers of women dependent on low-paid and unpaid domestic labour for their livelihood (Branson, 1976, p. 212; Lewenhak, 1980, p. 203). By 1931, 1.6 million women were engaged in paid domestic service, either on a residential or daily basis; more than 10 million women were housewives (Beauchamp, 1937, p. 10); and an estimated two-thirds of adult women were primarily engaged in domestic work (Branson, 1976, p. 213).

Government policies towards working women were less overt in Britain than in some countries.[87] The impression was given that women chose the type of employment they entered. They were 'perfectly contented' with monotonous unskilled work, because of 'special aptitudes such as delicacy of touch' (Cmd 3508, p. 14) which made them ideal for assembly-line work. Young women's lack of training in skilled work was put down to a 'difference in attitude' which made them 'unwilling to spend much time on training', since they allegedly expected to 'retire' on marriage:

> Work in the factory is looked upon by most as a temporary career, which fills in the time, and enables them to earn a living between school and marriage, and for this reason they *tend to seek* the easily learned and repetitive work and are *apt to lack the enterprise and ambition* which would make such work seem irksome (Cmd 3508, p. 14). (emphasis added)

Finally, the impression was conveyed that the intensification of the sexual division of labour between the wars was natural, inevitable, and certainly not the result of government social policy. It was asserted that:

> The rapid and easy return to the prewar industrial condition indicates that the division of work *tends to settle itself naturally* on the basis of prewar tradition and experience[88] (emphasis added).

Conclusions

Government interwar unemployment policies were not solely responsible for the changes that affected women at work, but they reinforced gender divisions in paid work and the home. Women did not simply 'drop out' of better paid work between the wars as contemporary officials and and some historians have suggested;[89] nor were women appropriately recognized or rewarded for their work during the First World War. The 1919 Sex Disqualification (Removal) Act allowed more women to enter the professions, but only as long as they remained single, and even then not on the same terms as men. Feminist demands for family allowances sufficient to give wives and mothers economic independence, which could have been accompanied by equal pay for women in paid employment, were unsuccessful during this period.[90] Unemployed women received no public work, no significant amount of training except in domestic service, and in the majority of cases no unemployment benefit even when they had paid contributions. Women who either remained in jobs which would have appealed to men *or* claimed unemployment benefit were consistently seen as abusing the system. However, the fact that women's National Insurance contributions subsidized male workers was not commented upon.

Votes for women and the election of small numbers of women MPs to Parliament did not provide equality for working women (Beddoe, 1989, p. 7). Although backbench women MPs often united across party political lines to oppose gender discrimination, 'equal rights' feminists who wanted women to have the right to compete on equal terms with men in the paid workforce were less influential than the 'new' feminists and some women trade unionists who supported the family wage for men and 'protection' for women from having to work a double shift of paid and unpaid work (Beddoe, 1989; Braybon and Summerfield, 1987, p. 138). There were few differences in the dominant views expressed by the two major political parties where women's work issues were concerned and considerable continuity in policy during this period towards unemployed women, despite changes in government. However, perhaps because women by this time had the vote, the role of government policy in restricting women's access to adequately paid work while pressing women into domestic work was concealed. The impression was given that women's desires and aptitudes were being catered for – whereas in fact women simply 'chose' from the limited options made available to them.

Although one official reason given for dismissing married women was that single 'unsupported' women would be spared their competition, this does not apear to have arisen out of a concern for the economic wellbeing of unmarried women. Unemployed single women were pressed into very low-paid 'women's work', much of which did not pay an adequate living wage for a single person. Unemployed spinsters were regarded as 'superfluous' and encouraged to emigrate. A larger objective was to prevent women competing with men in the paid workforce. For example, the marriage bar was rigorously applied in teaching, in which women were in direct competition with men.

However, the marriage bar also made it easier to maintain a narrow range of occupations as 'women's jobs', which might have been more difficult had married women been competing for these jobs.

Women's economic position, as in the prewar years, was defined by policy-makers primarily in terms of their relationships within the family, not by their position *vis-à-vis* the paid workforce. Because it was assumed that married women would be supported by their husbands and would work at home for their keep, it was seen as 'anomolous' to regard a married woman as unemployed. It might be assumed that for middle-class wives, especially those who had well-paid, generous husbands and who were able to employ servants, this would not have incurred hardship; although the relatively late age of marriage during this period suggests that women with careers often hesitated before giving up their independent income.

Employment policies towards woman after the First World War treated even unmarried women and unemployed industrial workers as potential train-ees for marriage through domestic service. Some employed spinsters were able to benefit from the 1919 Sex Disqualification (Removal) Act and achieve economic independence through careers in the professions, despite receiving lower pay and status than their male co-workers. However, they were an increasingly stigmatized minority (Jeffreys, 1985). For most working women, the interwar period was one where the small gains achieved by hard work before and during during the First World War were systematically removed.

Notes

1. House of Commons, *Hansard*, 5th series, Vol. 135, col. 473; Deirdre Beddoe (1989) *Back to Home and Duty*, p. 53, shows how women who did not willingly relinquish their jobs to returning men were described as 'hussies'.
2. Southborough Committee; *Hansard*, Vol. 209, col. 387.
3. Sheila Lewenhak (1980) *Women and Work*, p. 215. Beddoe, 1989, p. 88 points out that France and Belgium also had measures to restrict married women's employment, although they were not as severe as Germany's.
4. Hilda Martindale (1938) *Women Servants of the State*, p. 99; Cmd 164; Jane Lewis (1984) *Women in England 1870–1950*, p. 196; Beddoe, 1989, p. 75.
5. House of Commons, *Hansard*, Vol, 135, col. 473.
6. *The Vote*, July 1925, p. 228.
7. *The Vote*, 7 August 1925, p. 252.
8. *Hansard*, Vol. 132, col. 1986.
9. *Labour Gazette*, 1920, pp. 669–70.
10. Letter to *The Times*, 9 August 1929.
11. Public General Acts and Measures, 1920. The Unemployed Grants Committee spent £69.5 million on assistance to local authorities with public works for men between December 1920 and January 1932, and 60,000 men

were provided with work in 1931, which Pollard, 1991, p. 129 describes as a 'grudging amount'.

12. *Hansard*, Vol. 129, cols. 1081, 1472 and 2061. These referred to the 'Joan of Arc' workrooms in Shepherds Bush, which employed 44 women in tailoring and dressmaking.

13. *Hansard*, Vol. 139, col. 1428: Dr Macnamara, Conservative Minister of Labour, 1921; Vol. 159, col. 1023: Sir Montagu Barlow; Vol. 244, col. 1410: Mr Hudson.

14. *Hansard*, Vol. 244, col. 1063: Margaret Bondfield.

15. *Hansard*, Vol. 244, col. 1321.

16. *Hansard*, Vol. 259, col. 992.

17. *The Vote*, 8 May 1925, p. 148.

18. *Ministry of Labour Gazette*, 1922, p. 398. For example, in bleaching, dyeing and printing, men's wages were reduced from an average of 49s 7d to 26s 2d, while women's were cut from 29s 6d to 15s 7d for a week's work.

19. *Ministry of Labour Gazette*, 1920, p. 577. For example, in hat and capmaking, women's hourly rates were fixed at between threepence halfpenny and sevenpence three farthings per hour, whereas the minimum hourly rate for a man was one shilling.

20. B. L. Hutchins, 'The present position of women industrial workers', *Economic Journal*, 1921, p. 246. She points out that in 1921 many women were already receiving as little as 4s–10s per week for full-time employment in catering.

21. *Woman Worker*, April 1921, p. 6.

22. *Ibid*, p. 13. Beddoe, 1989, p. 49, also describes other demonstrations by unemployed women, as well as a 'Right to Work' conference organized by the Women's Industrial League in 1919. The demonstration illustrates the extreme desperation of women for a livelihood at this time, since as Beddoe (p. 51) points out, in some labour exchanges only one woman in 3,000 stated that she was willing to accept domestic service. Beddoe provides graphic descriptions of the reasons for the unpopularity of domestic service.

23. Branson, 1976, p. 211. However, Elizabeth Roberts (1988) in *Women's Work 1840–1940*, p. 18, points out that there is a degree of unreliability in the census figures, since enumerators did not always distinguish between low-paid domestic servants and unpaid housewives.

24. *Labour Gazette*, September 1923, p. 317.

25. Cmd 67, 1919, p. 8. See also Beddoe, 1989, pp. 38–9, who points out that the prescriptions for training in domesticity for girls and young women was associated with policy-makers' concerns about the 'physical deterioration of the race'.

26. Pilgrim Trust 1968, *Men Without Work*, p. 233; *Ministry of Reconstruction Special Report*, No. 87, p. 29; Lewis, 1984, p. 186.

27. Cmd 67, p. 4. However, one of the Committee, Marion Phillips, put in a

memorandum (p. 6) that women should not be pressed to accept domestic service until definite hours, conditions and rates of pay had been agreed.

28. *Labour Gazette*, September 1923, p. 317; Lewis, 1984, p. 191.
29. *Woman Worker*, March 1921, p. 4.
30. *Labour Gazette*, September 1923, p. 318.
31. *Ibid.*
32. *Ibid.* and Lewis, 1984, p. 191.
33. *Labour Gazette*, 1929, p. 81.
34. *Hansard*, Vol. 223, col. 2039: Margaret Bondfield; *Labour Gazette*, 1931, p. 212. There was only one residential centre, at Leamington, which was opened by the CCWTE in January 1930.
35. *Labour Gazette*, 1929, p. 81.
36. House of Commons, *Hansard*, Vol. 121, col. 1035: Mr J. Jones.
37. Pilgrim Trust, 1968, p. 233; Lewis, 1984, p. 186.
38. *Hansard*, Vol. 223, col. 2039: Margaret Bondfield. During the six months ending 24 June 1924, 62,497 women were placed in domestic service by labour exchanges, compared with 56,993 during the corresponding period when the Conservatives were in office. House of Commons, *Hansard*, Vol. 175, col. 2484.
39. In 1923 the Conservatives allowed the number of training centres to fall from 61 to 38 through lack of government grant; whereas the 1924 Labour government started 40 new classes in 'hometraining and homemaking'. *Hansard*, Vol. 170, cols 2035 and 2081.
40. *Hansard*, Vol. 213, col. 1583. Pressure from Labour and women MPs was enough to persuade the Conservative administration to increase the funding for domestic service training.
41. *Hansard*, Vol. 205, col. 600.
42. One small exception to this was that the Ministry of Labour set up hostels for young women on their way to resident domestic service following complaints that very young women were being sent around the country for work and often were not even met at the station: House of Commons, *Hansard*, Vol. 319, col. 1800.
43. Of 30,000 unemployed women interviewed in 1937–8 about the possibility of training for domestic service, 20,000 refused to consider it, and eventually only 812 were admitted to the government's training centres (*Unemployment Assistance Board Annual Report* for 1938). The same year fewer than 44 per cent of domestic service vacancies notified to employment exchanges were filled (House of Commons, *Hansard*, Vol. 320, col. 210).
44. *Hansard*, Vol. 348, col. 143: Mr Brooke. A somewhat bizarre remedy proposed by one MP was 'the setting up of a Women's Service Board, somewhat like the Milk Marketing Board, in order to produce Grade A women': House of Commons, *Hansard*, Vol. 313, cols 465–6: Mr. Liddell.
45. *Royal Commission on Unemployment Insurance*, Cmd 4185, Final Report (Majority Report), para. 631.
46. *Hansard*, Vol. 175, col. 769: Dr Marion Phillips.

47. *Hansard*, Vol. 313, col. 1930.
48. *Labour Gazette*, 1923, p. 84. Two command papers, Cmd 403, 1919, *Openings in Canada for Women from the United Kingdom* and Cmd 745, 1920, *Openings in Australia for Women from the United Kingdom*, both stated that domestic service was the only suitable available work for women emigrants. The 1922 Overseas Settlement Committee Report on Emigration stated that 'the migration of women is especially to be encouraged, owing to the great excess of females over the male population and the urgent and unlimited demand for women in the Dominions, especially as household helpers'.
49. *Hansard*, Vol. 205, col. 634.
50. *Labour Gazette* 1929, p. 159.
51. *Ibid.*
52. *Ibid.*, p. 438.
53. The annual average output of training schemes was 8,500 men and 4,400 women (*Labour Gazette* 1931, p. 10).
54. In 1931, for example, 89 per cent of women who completed the domestic service training courses had found work (House of Commons, *Hansard*, Vol. 252, col. 38).
55. Also in 1931 some of the men's training centres were under threat of closure because too few of the men has found paid employment as a result of the schemes (House of Commons, *Hansard*, Vol. 257, col. 30).
56. *Hansard*, Vol. 332, col. 38.
57. *Royal Commission on Unemployment Insurance*, Cmd 4185, Majority Report, para. 630.
58. Braybon, 1981, p. 179. A dependents' benefit was also paid of 6s per week for the first child and 3s for each subsequent child: House of Commons, *Hansard*, Vol. 112, col. 225. See also Beddoe, 1989, p. 51.
59. Braybon, 1981, p. 181. The total cost of the donation benefit was £66 million, which 'seemed a small price to pay for social peace at a critical time': Pollard (1991) *The Development of the British Economy 1914–1990*, p. 126. See also Karl de Schweinitz, 1961, *England's Road to Social Security*, p. 218. At this time there were half a million women officially unemployed, and it was estimated that the total number was closer to a million (Beddoe, 1989, p. 49). Beddoe also points out that ex-munitions workers who turned down low-paid 'women's work' were described in the popular press as 'slackers in fur coats'.
60. *Hansard*, Vol. 114, col. 2013; Vol. 114, col. 387; Vol. 115, col. 48; Vol. 115, col. 49.
61. *Hansard*, Vol. 212, col. 993.
62. *Hansard*, Vol. 115, col. 48.
63. Only 9,000 women were included in the 1911 National Insurance Act (Part II) compared with over 2 million men.
64. Even then there was bitter criticism of this from some male politicians, one of whom complained that national insurance 'was not intended to assist

the woman worker at all: it was designed for the workman . . . that is a recognition of the economic difference between a woman and a man': House of Commons, *Hansard*, Vol. 90 col. 581: Mr Booth.

65. *Hansard*, Vol. 138, col. 2059: Dr Macnamara. Beveridge, in *Unemployment: A Problem of Industry* (1930 edition) p. 280 also argued that the main value of the NGSW clause lay 'not in keeping out the workshy and the unemployable but in the weapon of offensive defence it offered against the claims of married women who on marriage had practically retired from industry and were not wanted by employers'.

66. *Ministry of Labour Gazette*, 1921, p. 670 quoting selected Umpire's decisions: Case No. 1354 section 7(i) (iii).

67. *Hansard*, Vol. 146, col. 421: Dr Macnamara Minister of Labour.

68. *Hansard*, Vol. 179, col. 819: Dr Macnamara.

69. *Hansard*, Vol. 179, col. 819: Mr A. Maclean.

70. *Hansard*, Vol. 188, col. 1358; Vol. 192, col. 1709: George Lansbury.

71. *Hansard*, Vol. 192, col. 158: Sir Anthony Steel-Maitland, Minister of Labour.

72. *Hansard*, Vol. 182, cols 172–3: Steel-Maitland.

73. *Woman Worker*, July 1921, p. 13: D. M. Elliot.

74. *Labour Gazette* 1923, p. 395.

75. *Hansard*, Vol. 193, col. 1954; *Labour Gazette* 1927, p. 404.

76. *Hansard*, Vol. 146, col. 2155: Dr Macnamara: 'she has to make it clear that she wants work, that she is available for work . . . and that she is genuinely seeking whole time employment'.

77. *Labour Gazette*, 1928, p. 411: between September and October 1928, 13,355 men and 9,078 women were disqualified under the NGSW clause.

78. Deacon, 1977, p. 106. The opposition came not only from the Clydeside MPs and from the National Unemployed Workers' Movement, but also from Boards of Guardians, obliged to maintain the families of men denied National Insurance benefits.

79. *Hansard*, Vol. 133, col. 2103; Brockway (1931) *The Anomolies Bill: Why its Rejection was Moved*, p. 11.

80. Public General Acts, 1930–31.

81. *Reports of the Unemployment Insurance Statutory Committee 1935 and 1936*; House of Commons Papers, No. 63 1937/8 session, pp. 6–7; Tilyard and Ball (1949) *Unemployment Insurance in Great Britain 1922–8*, p. 154.

82. *Hansard*, Vol. 254, col. 2120.

83. *Hansard*, Vol. 254, col. 2108; Vol. 260, cols 43–4; Cmd 4346, *The Operation of the Anomolies Regulations*, p. 1.

84. *Hansard*, Vol. 240, col. 488; Vol. 241, col. 590.

85. *Royal Commission on Unemployment Insurance, Final Majority Report*, Cmd 4185, para. 216: Clara Rackham.

86. Initially under the Anomolies Bill it was possible for unemployed insured women to claim for dependent husbands. However, this was strongly criticized by the Royal Commission on Unemployment Insurance, who

argued that it was 'anomolous that a married woman should be presumed to have returned to the industrial field and be entitled to benefit purely on the grounds that her husband is incapacitated from work or is unemployed and not in receipt of benefit. Such a provision is in the nature of a grant of relief owing to the inadequacy of family means, rather than a proper exception to the Regulations' (Cmd 4185, Majority Report, para. 457). The Anomolies Regulations were amended so that a woman could not claim benefit for her husband (or herself) unless her husband had been incapacitated from work for more than six weeks (Unemployment Act 1934, Part 1, section II, sub section 3: Public General Acts, 1933–4).

87. Lewenhak (1980) p. 215 points out that in Germany, women could be compulsorily directed into domestic service and other unpopular occupations.

88. *Labour Gazette* March 1930, p. 85; Cmd 3508.

89. Constantine (1980) *Unemployment in Britain between the Wars*, p. 23.

90. Pedersen (1989) 'The failure of feminism in the making of the welfare state', *Radical History Review* traced feminists' demand for family allowances between the wars. These would have been set at a far higher level, and would have meant that the 'family wage' would have been dropped and women and men would have been paid the cost of maintaining an individual. The Labour movement and the civil service united against the idea of valuing women's unpaid work.

THE
NORTHERN COLLEGE
LIBRARY
BARNSLEY

Chapter 5

Women, Recruitment and Demobilization Policy during the Second World War

It has often been assumed that during the Second World War the government, recalling women's major contribution during the Great War, was quick to extend employment opportunities to women.[1] However, the wartime government's employment policies severely restricted women's access to paid work between 1939 and 1941, to the point where it was beginning to undermine the war effort. Moreover, the recruitment and demobilization policies during and after the war, which could have potentially extended 'a new social and economic freedom to women which could never entirely be lost' (Marwick, 1976, p. 142), were in fact designed to prevent such an occurrence. This chapter describes the series of ways in which wartime government policies maintained women's position as low-paid subordinates in the labour market and as unpaid domestic workers within marriage.

Recruitment of Women by the State before 1941

During the first two years of the Second World War the recruitment of women was not only extremely limited compared to that of men, but also effectively strengthened the hierarchical sexual division of labour before the very urgent demand for women workers which occurred in 1942–3 and which could potentially have altered long-term patterns of women's employment.

Delayed Recruitment of Women into Paid Work

In the early stages of the war, women flocked to register for employment. However, during the early months of the Second World War, as in the First World War, it appeared that the government wished to limit the recruitment of women, particularly into men's jobs. Men were conscripted into the forces immediately on the outbreak of war; but the legislation that allowed for the direction of both male and female labour into paid work, Regulation 58A, was in practice initially only applied to men. In the early stages of the war women were chiefly encouraged to enroll in voluntary work.[2] The Minister of Labour was said to have told women's organizations in the spring of 1940 that he anticipated a smaller demand for women in paid work than during the First World War because the machinery had become bigger and beyond women's capacities.[3]

One indication of policy-makers' reluctance to promote the widespread absorption of women into industry during the early stages of the war was the way in which government policy effectively removed many women from the labour force. During the first week of the war, for example, 1,230,000 women and children were evacuated from large cities to rural areas, and were accommodated with private householders. Many evacuated women had to give up their jobs. Soldiers and civil servants were also billeted on private householders, which created extra domestic responsibilities for the women in whose homes they stayed, making it more difficult for them to participate in paid work. In recognition of this the government announced in 1939 that women who took in evacuees would not be regarded as 'unavailable for work' and therefore could claim unemployment benefit.[4]

Older women were also removed from the labour force in 1940, following the passing of the Old Age and Widows' Pension Act, which reduced the retirement age from 65 to 60 for women, and meant that women over 60 could be sacked and would not obtain further employment. This also meant that some of the women who had worked during the First World War were denied the opportunity to use that experience. By contrast the employment of older men was encouraged.[5] The State in its role as a major employer, in the civil service and in local government, also delayed women's employment until after 1941, when all available men had been absorbed. Instead of recruiting additional women, services such as transport were reduced and existing staff worked longer hours.[6]

In 1939–41, women's unemployment was high, largely as a result of the government's deliberate policy of 'concentration' on private industry, which meant the deliberate contraction of 'inessential' industries, which in effect were those employing large numbers of women, such as textiles, pottery, boots and shoes, hosiery, lace and glovemaking. The aim was to create a 'pool' of available women workers, and it was assumed that when they were required the women affected would find work in munitions and related industries.[7] However, only about half of the women affected by 'concentration' policies found their way into war work; and in the meantime many women were obliged to live on unemployment benefit.

Wastage of Women's Skills and Potential

The slowness with which policy-makers began the call-up of women workers contrasts strongly with the official measures that were taken to prevent skilled men leaving their jobs or being sacked. Requests were made for the reporting of any wastage of skilled men in the services.[8] Policies of delaying the recruitment of women and of ensuring that skilled men were well established (and often promoted) before the widespread recruitment of women was allowed to occur had the effect of strengthening the gender divisions that already existed in the workforce.

During the early part of the war, government-funded training was aimed at men. As early as November 1939, 6,000 men were being trained in 'occupations of special importance'.[9] Women were generally given mainly 'on the job' training at this stage in the war: a policy encouraged by Ernest Bevin, the Minister of Labour.[10] In this way women were trained 'to order and not to stock', which reduced the chance that there would be significant numbers of women with recognized skills and qualifications who could be in a position to compete with men at the end of the war.

As a direct result of this policy, women were largely confined to unskilled repetitive work when they entered wartime industry (Lewis, 1984, p. 18). In aircraft production some women were said to receive no more than half-an-hour's training (Riley, 1981, p. 67). Women thus continued to earn lower wages, to be less assertive and to be more vulnerable to dismissal than men.

Treating Women as Temporary Reserves

State-recruitment policies also facilitated the temporary employment of women. There was a careful avoidance of recruiting in ways that could have given the majority of women long-term ease of access to the range of jobs normally open mainly to men. This was done partly by discriminating in recruitment policy between single women, who were still treated as normally only short-term members of the paid workforce, and married women. The marriage bar was officially kept in place during the war and, although married women were recruited, they continued to be classed as temporary members of the workforce during the war.[11]

Throughout the war, only single women (who were presumed to have no domestic responsibilities) were officially classed as 'mobile' and thus could be transferred to 'men's jobs' in other areas, while married women were expected to fill the (often lower paid) jobs that the single women had vacated. Before the introduction of conscription these policies were put into place by the labour exchanges and enforced by umpires' decisions; women who did not comply with these rulings were disqualified from unemployment benefit.[12] Women workers did not necessarily approve of these classifications. Young women often felt unhappy about leaving home to go to work, while older women, especially skilled workers, found it galling to take on young women's jobs and rates of pay. A group of married women in Glasgow with experience of war work demanded to be allowed to take up munitions work instead of their daughters.[13]

The temporary nature of women's work in men's jobs was also reinforced by the 'Extended Employment of Women' agreement between the Engineering and Allied Employers' National Federation and the Amalgamated

Engineering Union. The first clause of the document stated that 'Women drafted into the provision of this Agreement shall be regarded as temporarily employed.'[14]

Recruitment of Women from 1941

The main difference between the recruitment policies of 1939–41 and those that followed after 1941 was that in the later stages of the war, when there were no more men available, drives to recruit women were stronger and greater efforts were made to persuade employers to recruit women into jobs usually performed by men. Even so, there was still considerable reluctance on the part of the government to use coercion on either employers or potential women recruits into industry.

Although efforts were made by the government to persuade employers to employ more women workers, propaganda rather than compulsion was used.[15] As in the First World War, employers were slow to substitute women for men on a large scale, even where trade unions were relatively weak, despite the fact that women were considerably cheaper to employ.[16] When recruiting women, there was an obvious unwillingness on the part of the government to use the provisions of the national service legislation,[17] and as late as November 1941 it was proposed in Cabinet that there should be a continuation of the policy of diverting women from 'less essential industries'.[18] This was hardly an example of the State seizing the chance to bring women to men's jobs on a large scale. It appears more as if the government was taking the opportunity to remove women from the skilled women's jobs they still retained at the end of the interwar years.

Initially more women were exempt from conscription than were called up. It continued to be the case that only single women were regarded as 'mobile'. Married women, even if childless, were seen as 'immobile' and were not conscripted in 1941 and 1942. It was believed in policy-making circles that the conscription of married women would antagonize working men, and that the fighting spirit of servicemen would be dampened if their wives were not at home waiting for them.[19] Women with children under 14 at home continued to be exempt from conscription throughout the war, and it was claimed that mothers were already performing 'national service': 'Nothing is more important to the future of the race, and clearly there is no higher focus of national service than the guidance of a home and the upbringing of young children'.[20]

Also exempt were women with billetees or evacuees, those caring for sick or elderly dependents, pregnant women and those with 'special domestic responsibilities' such as a very large home. By 1943 10 million women were still engaged solely in unpaid household duties and looking after only nine million children.[21] Even the registration of young, mainly single women was progressing very slowly in 1941, and it was alleged that Ministry of Labour interviewers encouraged young women to make excuses to avoid direction into employment (Summerfield, 1984, p. 50).

Many women did not feel inclined to volunteer for war work, often because the available work was monotonous, dirty and sometimes dangerous. Others felt angry about the 'concentration' policies and snubbed at having been refused work during the earlier part of the war (Summerfield, 1984, pp. 32 and 37). In October 1941, 32 per cent of a sample of 1,000 women declared that they were unwilling to accept war work of any sort, and the War Works Weeks recruitment campaigns fell below target (Summerfield, 1984, pp. 37 and 42). Nevertheless, despite their relative ineffectiveness, voluntary methods of recruitment continued to be used as far as possible; and although the pressure on women to volunteer increased as the war progressed, the conscription of women played a relatively small part in their recruitment throughout the war (Marwick, 1976, p. 338).

During 1941, however, the worsening labour shortage highlighted a growing concern that, as Sir Ralph Assheton admitted on behalf of the Ministry of Labour: 'we have somehow failed to approach [women] in the right way'.[22] In an attempt to compensate, the Ministry of Labour appointed a Women's Consultative Committee, over which Sir Ralph presided. The committee had narrow terms of reference, and it could only advise on matters of recruitment and not on wider issues affecting women's employment such as childcare and shopping; it had no decision-making power and meetings were only held fortnightly;[23] but it represented an attempt to appease women. A day was also devoted to a discussion on woman power in the House of Commons which allowed women MPs to air their grievances.[24]

It was also coming to be recognized as inevitable that many older and married women would have to be drawn into war work.[25] A memorandum from the Ministry of Supply in November 1941 complained to the Cabinet that:

> The unsatisfied demand for labour is the most crippling influence on munitons production in this country . . . there are dangerous shortages . . . week after week the total shortage mounts . . . Female labour is available. It awaits direction from the Ministry of Labour.[26]

The Minister of Labour, Ernest Bevin, agreed that 'we shall have to call into service many women who in normal circumstances would not take employment'.[27]

From late 1941, the recruitment of women was vastly intensified and involved a greater measure of compulsion and direction. Under the 1942 Employment of Women (Control of Engagement) Order (Summerfield, 1984, p. 35) women could only obtain paid work through employment exchanges: this was to ensure that women only went into work which was regarded as essential. In Northern Ireland, where conscription was not introduced, women were directed into war work through the unemployment benefit administrative machinery, just as women on the mainland had been during 1939–41.[28]

After September 1941 single women had to prove that they had 'domestic responsibilities' if they wished to avoid conscription.[29] It became far more difficult for unmarried women to avoid direction into war work, and objectors had to present their case to 'hardship committees' similar to those that had disallowed women's claims to unemployment benefit between the wars, and in some cases had the same chairmen.[30] Usually the committees were all male and if a woman objected to this a woman member would be added to the committee. Bevin regarded one woman and three men as a 'fair proportion'.[31] 'Women's panels' were also appointed to advise the committees, but again these were given no decision-making power.[32]

Initially, conscripted women could choose between the women's services, the Land Army and the munitions factories. Later in the war, however, the choice was narrowed to between munitions factories and aircraft works, although choice was always constrained by demand.[32] The conscription of young Scotswomen to munitions works in towns such as Coventry, which were prime targets of bombing raids, drew great criticism from male Scots MPs, who objected to the transfer of 'their' women away from home.[34] Although women themselves did not complain about the danger, the pressure from the men was such that the policy was reversed, and aircraft factories were established in Scotland.[35] By 1945 the government was inviting Scotswomen in England to apply to be transferred home.[36]

In 1942–43 women aged up to 45 and then 45–51 were registered and conscripted. Experienced nurses could be called into employment up to the age of 55, and midwives could be directed into work up to the age of 60. Attempts were made not to alienate older women, and the Ministry of Labour made a point of employing interviewers aged over 30,[37] and paid the expenses of several thousand women to enable them to attend a meeting held by the Ministry. Bevin promised that the 'utmost consideration' would be given to the domestic responsibilities of these women.[38] Women in the older age ranges were still not regarded as 'mobile', and new aircraft factories were located close to where 'immobile' women lived.[39]

Objections to the conscription of older women do not appear to have come from the women themselves. Criticism came largely from men, including some employers, who argued that older women's health and strength would not be able to stand the strain of working in men's jobs. One doctor warned of the 'attacks of vertigo, to which women of this age are so prone'.[40] However, once employers had been persuaded to accept older women workers they found, according to the Minister of Labour, that middle-aged women were more efficient and less prone to absenteeism than younger workers and had a steadying influence on other employees: in short, their employment was a great success (Summerfield, 1943, p. 249). Married women (without children under 14 at home) were not conscripted until 1943.[41] Even then, they could only be directed into part-time employment, which was a creation of the wartime government designed to allow women to do war work without abandoning their household duties. However, there was increasing pressure on wives and mothers to 'volunteer' for full-time employment.

By 1943, when the wartime employment of women had reached its height, the combined results of the Ministry of Labour's conscription and voluntary recruitment policies was that women now formed 38.8 per cent of the total 'occupied' population, compared with 29.8 per cent in 1931.[42] An additional two million women had been brought into the paid workforce, so that there were now 7,750,000 women in full-time employment or the services, 700,000 women working part-time and one million women unpaid volunteer workers (Boston, 1980, p. 205). Contrary to the initial expectations of the Minister of Labour, women had been brought into industry and the services to a greater extent than during the First World War and older and married women, whom the government had been most reluctant to recruit, became the largest group to enter paid work in 1943 (Boston, 1980, p. 185).

Nevertheless, in 1943 the mobilization of women was said to have reached its limit,[43] even though by 1944 the labour shortage was 'more stringent than ever before',[44] which suggests that there was still a strong resistance to recruiting wives and mothers. Moreover, although many women had gained access to a wide range of occupations from which they had formerly been excluded, an hierarchical gender division of labour still existed. Women tended to have male supervisors and were seldom in authority over men (Summerfield, 1984). Thus despite the tremendous drive to bring more women into wartime production there were definite signs of continuity in employment policies towards women.

Policies to Assist the Retention of Women War Workers

During the Second World War, far more than during the First World War, a number of temporary policies were put into place to enable wives and mothers to manage the combination of paid and unpaid work, although politicians had no intention of removing unpaid work responsibilities from women either in the short term or after the war. There were also once again policies to promote the 'welfare' of all women workers and so maintain productivity and reduce absenteeism.

It was recognized early in the war that the State would have to provide some help, especially with childcare, to enable women to do war work. Ernest Bevin, the Minister of Labour, argued that if women came forward for war work the State would have to take a bigger responsibility for caring for their children;[45] but he encountered a certain amount of resistance from officials within his own Ministry who believed that women looking after children at home were already doing 'national service'.[46]

Effective opposition to the expansion of childcare also came from the

Ministry of Health, which was the provider of day nurseries. Its usual policy was to regard pre-school children as their mothers' responsibility,[47] and to provide day care chiefly in cases where the mother was too ill to cope or was forced into paid employment by the lack of a male breadwinner. Day nurseries were designed to be mainly for the benefit of the children rather than the convenience of working mothers, some of whom were obliged to work shifts and be away from home for very long hours (Summerfield, 1983, pp. 254 and 262). There was particular opposition from the Ministry of Health to the provision of 24-hour nurseries for night-shift workers' children, on the grounds that mothers might cease to take responsibility for their children (Summerfield, 1984, p. 81).

As a result, nursery provision increased slowly by wartime standards. In February 1940 there was a total of 30 wartime day nurseries open in Britain,[48] and almost a year later in January 1941 the number had only increased to 223, although 313 were due to open and a further 267 were in preparation.[49] Even when the provision of wartime nurseries reached its peak in 1944, providing 71,806 places, as well as substantial numbers of places for children in nursery schools and elementary schools, only 6.4 per cent of the child population aged 0 to 4 was catered for by the State (Summerfield, 1983, p. 250). Instead, the policy from 1941 was to leave most childcare to 'private arrangements made by the mother' which in practice usually meant childminders (Boston, 1980, p. 196; Summerfield, 1984, p. 81). These mainly informal arrangements were often unreliable, enabled fewer women to take better paid work outside the home, and tended to be seen by mothers as the least satisfactory arrangement. This policy drew criticism from the Standing Joint Committee of Working Women's Organizations and the Women's Trade Union Congress in 1941 (Boston, 1980, p. 196), and in Parliament Edith Summerskill claimed that the men did not want mothers to be freed from the burden of childcare responsibility.[50]

Women's responsibility for providing food for families was recognized by policy-makers as another obstacle to the mobilization of married women. Summerfield (1984) describes the disagreement between the Ministry of Labour, which planned to make arrangements with retailers so that working women did not have to waste time queuing for basic foods, such as bread, in the shops, and the Ministry of Food, which refused to countenance any scheme that could complicate shopkeepers' businesses. Eventually the Ministry of Labour simply recommended to employers that women workers be given unpaid time out from work in order to queue in the shops.[51] Thus the 'sexual contract' was upheld whereby women were to be available to provide services such as shopping even to the detriment of their wartime employment in a national emergency.

The provision of school dinners increased during the war, although meals were not made available to all school children until after 1944.[52] Nevertheless, these, together with the popular and inexpensive wartime British Restaurants which catered for adults, freed many wives and mothers from the obligation to shop and cook for a family midday meal (Summerfield, 1984, pp. 99–122). Nevertheless, working women usually still had to provide the evening meal (Summerfield, 1983, p. 251). Thus women were relieved of shopping and food preparation enough to enable them to undertake war work, but not enough to allow them to slip out of the responsibility for feeding the family (Lewis, 1984, p. 153). Nonetheless there were signs that policy-makers were relying on women's contribution to the war effort, particularly after 1941. Once the shortage of skilled labour became sufficiently severe, many women volunteers and conscripts were given considerably more formal training than had been provided in the early part of the war. Women were admitted to government training centres,[53] and were provided with training allowances. The Technical Services Register was established so that women could be trained as skilled electrical technicians, draughtspeople and engine testers (Boston, 1980, p. 198).

During the war, especially in the later years, women workers were also provided with somewhat better conditions of employment than in peacetime. The Select Committee on National Expenditure in 1942–43 suggested that women's health and productivity would be improved by the provision of better facilities such as canteens, washrooms, cloakrooms and restrooms.[54] The unions also helped to negotiate a better working environment for women, although sometimes at the expense of better pay.[55] The State-sanctioned focus on conditions of employment had the unfortunate effect of encouraging employers to continue to see women as a 'different' workforce with differing and sometimes expensive needs, such as 'welfare workers'; although in fact male workers also benefited from much of the investment in better facilities in the workplace and the productivity of the workforce as a whole tended to increase (Lewenhak, 1980, p. 239; Boston, 1980, p. 214).

Recruitment Policy and Women's Hours of Employment

There was an acknowledged relationship between government recruitment policy and permissible hours of paid employment. Policy-makers had a choice between recruiting more women, but for fewer hours per week, or being slow and cautious in the recruitment of women, but allowing the hours of the employment of recruits to rise to meet any shortfall in production. Early in the war official sources claimed that the government had learned from the experience of the First World War not to unduly expand the working hours of women in employment. A Command Paper stated in 1940 that:

> It is the policy of the government, while authorising hours where necessary not permissible in peace time, not to authorise hours which in the light of experience and scientific investigation would be detrimental to health or efficient production.[56]

However, in practice, once again the wartime government compensated for its hesitation to recruit women who were not normally in employment by expanding the hours of the existing workforce. The 1937 Factories Act which allowed a maximum of 48 hours per week for adult women (and 44 hours for girls) and which prohibited night work (Public General Acts, 1937) was suspended once war began. In August 1940 an Emergency Order covering munitions workers allowed women to be employed for up to 60 hours per week, on nights, on Sundays and for continuous seven-day weeks (Summerfield, 1984, p. 132). In State-owned industries, such as the Ministry of Aircraft Production factories, women often worked for 11-and-a-half hours without a proper break (Lewenhak, 1980, p. 236); and in 1942 28 out of the 42 Royal Ordinance Factories (ROFs) required women to work a basic week of at least 55 hours and sometimes more (Summerfield, 1984, p. 133). This was despite the fact that the remoteness of many of the ROFs, combined with wartime travelling difficulties, often added two or three hours to both ends of the working day (Lewenhak, 1980, p. 236). It was reported that at Euxton ROF near Chorley many women workers had to leave home in Blackpool at 4.30 am and did not arrive home until 10.00 pm, having had only one hour's break for lunch, much of which was spent travelling to and from the canteen.[57]

This policy of expanding the workforce through the extension of hours of employment only became acknowledged as 'official' once it was practised on so large a scale that it could no longer be denied. The number of premises granted modifications of the factory legislation rose steadily from 6,500 in 1940, to 11,000 at the end of 1941 and 19,000 at the end of 1942.[58] By 1943 the policy was to grant authority for employing women for more than 55 hours per week 'wherever circumstances appear to justify it'.[59] Mass Observations commented that the lessons of the First World War had been neglected to an extraordinary extent (Summerfield, 1984, p. 133).

Women war workers, although not described as being in bad health, were seen as 'lacking their full vitality'[60] and were often anaemic (Summerfield, 1984, p. 125). Married women workers were particularly prone to 'nerves and fatigue',[61] which was attributed to the strain of doing two jobs.[62] Women's rate of absence from paid employment was twice that of men (Summerfield, 1984, p. 125), and about half of women's absences were said to be caused by sickness and accidents. Women's health was thought to deteriorate as a result of combining long hours of employment with queueing in the shops at lunchtime for the family's evening meal instead of sitting down for a midday meal (Summerfield, 1984, p. 126). Women working night shifts got insufficient sleep during the day because of the pressures of shopping, childcare and housework; and in one sample of 1,000 women working nights, 40 per cent were getting less than 6 hours' sleep (Lewis, 1984, p. 187). The accident rate rose sharply, mainly affecting adult women on dangerous processes.[63] In 1940 there were 1,372 fatal and 230,607 non-fatal recorded industrial accidents, far higher than the peacetime rates; and in 1942 there were 1,642 fatal and 269,652 non-fatal accidents.[64] Although women's inexperience may have been partly responsible for the increase, fatigue also undoubtedly played a part.

Absenteeism and lateness among both women and men became common enough to affect production and to be seen as requiring State action. Married women were particularly prone to absence for domestic reasons: 62 per cent of married women, compared with 1 per cent of men, took time off work to care for children or dependent relatives or to catch up with the housework (Summerfield, 1984, p. 130). At weekends, when the schools and nurseries were closed, the rate of absence for women was four times that of men (Summerfield, 1984, p. 135). Married women took more time off for family reasons than single women (Lewis, 1984, p. 187) but even single women took significant amounts of time off work for reasons associated with domestic responsibilities (Summerfield, 1984, p. 130).

In April 1942 it became an imprisonable offence to be absent from work or persistently late.[65] However, the Ministry of Labour recognized that it was not feasible to prosecute wives and mothers, since they were 'volunteers' rather than conscripts, who would simply leave if the pressures of paid work made it impossible for them to take adequate care of their dependents. The Ministry's response was therefore to look leniently on married women's absenteeism and to recognize that if a wife and mother was able to perform two jobs by having a mere half day off from her paid work each week, she was 'achieving something marvellous'.[66]

The Ministry of Labour also recommended to employers that wives of servicemen be given unpaid leave not only to do the shopping, but also to spend time (up to a fortnight) with their husbands when they were home on leave.[67] However accommodating this appears, married women continued to pay a high price in terms of having two major sets of responsibilities, of losing wages for the time taken away from paid work and, perhaps of the most lasting significance, of gaining a reputation as employees whose domestic responsibilities affected their reliability and commitment to paid employment. At the same time, male workers were being forced by law to be regular and reliable employees, and denied the option of sharing more equally in family responsibilities.

The introduction of part-time employment was another means by which the government attempted to recruit and retain women war workers, while reaffirming women's responsibility for unpaid domestic and caring work.[68] As early as 1941 Winston Churchill proposed to Cabinet that employers might be persuaded to take on married women on a part-time basis, to enable the women to shoulder the 'dual burden'.[69] At this stage there was no clear idea about how many hours might constitute part time (Summerfield, 1984, p. 141), but the Lord President of the Council, in a Cabinet memorandum, recommended that 'part time' be understood as half time (*ibid.*), and this formula was generally accepted during the war years. The government began to promote the idea of employing women part time from 1942. A Command Paper recommended that women part-time workers be used to replace men in banking;[70] and the Ministry of Labour produced a booklet called *Mobilization of woman power; Planning for part-time work*.[71] This aimed to appeal to employers by suggesting that part-timers could be given the heaviest and most monotonous jobs, and that two part-timers would be more productive than one full-timer (Boston, 1980, p. 199). Although employers were initially reluctant to recruit part-time women workers (Summerfield, 1984, p. 143), some employers came to appreciate the avantages it had for industry. Nonetheless, part-time working remained on a relatively small scale during the war years, accounting for less than one-tenth of women employees; and the government continued to recruit women into full-time paid work except where their family commitments made this impossible (Summerfield, 1984, p. 141).

From 1942 to 1943, a more general reduction in working hours was forced upon employers (including the State) by the prevalence of absenteeism and turnover among women in the 'volunteer' classes (Summerfield, 1984, p. 138). The average hours of women in paid employment was 45.9 in 1943[72] and 45.2 in 1944, excluding time lost.[73] Nevertheless, these were still long hours by peacetime standards, especially for women who had been given only the minimum assistance by the State to carry this double burden.

Recruitment Policy and Women's Wages

It is often thought that women's pay in wartime rose significantly in relation to men's (Fraser, 1973, p. 193; Lewis, 1984, p. 183), because of the strong drives by the Ministry of Labour to recruit women into men's jobs after 1941; especially since the unions were assumed to be pressing for equal pay so that women could not be used to undercut men's wage rates. However, during the war women's average weekly pay remained well below that of men, moving only from a little under 44 per cent to just over 50 per cent of men. In 1940 women earned an average of 43s lld per week and men 103s 3d;[74] whereas by January 1944 women's average wage was 63s 9d and men's 123s 8d.[75]

Although Bevin, the Minister of Labour, was also a prominent trade unionist and Labour were highly influential in the wartime coalition government's work and welfare policies (Pollard, 1991, p. 183), State policies actually played a key role in holding down women's wages relative to men's. The State as an employer paid lower wages to women, often even when women substituted for men on a one-for-one basis. In the civil service, armed forces and local authority employment, women were paid between two-thirds and three-quarters of the men's rate for particular jobs (Boston, 1980, p. 192), but were also concentrated in the lower paid positions. In ROFs the policy was to pay the women's rate if women predominated, even on men's work, although their male workmates were still paid the men's rate (Summerfield, 1984, pp. 170–1).

Women on the government-training schemes were also paid lower allowances than men. Soon after the admission of women, the allowances, which had paid 60s to men and 58s to women with dependents was altered so that all men were paid 60s 6d and all women 38s, regardless of commitments;[76] al-though women had to pay equally high lodging costs, which were often around 30s per week (Boston, 1980, p. 200). Lower State training allowances reduced women's expectations about the wages they could comand when they qualified and moved into men's jobs in industry.

The government also facilitated a number of agreements between trade unions and private employers such as the 1940 Extended Employment of Women Agreement. This stated that women could not be paid at the men's rate until they had served a probationary period of 32 weeks, and then only if they could carry out the work without supervision (Lewenhak, 1980, p. 227; Summerfield, 1984, pp. 153 and 193). Employers were enabled to keep wages low simply by imposing unnecessary supervision on women workers (Lewenhak, 1980, p. 227; Summerfield, 1984, p. 159). Three-quarters of women employees in wartime were classed as being on women's work (Summerfield, 1984, p. 169) and paid accordingly. The State tended not to inhibit the reclassification on jobs in this way (Boston, 1980, p. 199; Lewenhak, 1980, p. 227; Summerfield, 1984, p. 163), and employers were largely left free to organize their workers in whatever way they wished – although this was opposed by unskilled workers' unions who feared the permanent displacement of men in this process (Summerfield, 1984, pp. 163 and 168).

During the early part of the war there was strong support from the Trades Union Congress (TUC) for equal pay for women on men's jobs (Boston, 1980, p. 207), although in practice many unions continued to negotiate separate and lower pay rises for women (Summerfield, 1984, p. 170). In 1942, however, the government passed the Restoration of Prewar Practices Act (Boston, 1980, p. 192), and this made male unionists more confident about the removal of women from men's jobs at the end of the war, whether or not the women had equal pay. At the 1942 TUC conference there was no mention of equal pay (Summerfield, 1984, p. 173). By giving male trade unionists virtually guaran-teed control over access to the best-paid jobs at the end of the war, the government had deflected a major source of support for equal pay for women, albeit one based on self-interest.

Campaigns in favour of equal pay by women's organizations met with only limited success (Summerfield, 1984, p. 173). In 1942 pressure by women was successful in altering the system of compensation for war injuries, which had been earnings-related, and so had paid lower rates to injured women employees and even less to housewives. Women MPs condemned this as putting a lower value on women's lives;[77] and following this a Select Commit-tee proposed the adoption of flat-rate compensation for all injured civilians regardless of sex,[78] which was subsequently implemented. However, when women MPs argued that the equal valuing of women also meant giving equal pay for the same work, they were informed that since the link between wages and compensation had been broken, equal compensation could not be used as a vehicle for claims for equal pay.[79]

In 1944 the International Labour Organization conference in

Philadelphia advocated equal pay for equal work regardless of gender;[80] and the British delegates, representing government, trade unions and employers all voted in favour.[81] However, when asked by women MPs whether this was a signal that Britain was to implement equal pay, Bevin replied that the delegates had only voted for equal pay: they did not advocate it.[82] When an amendment to the 1944 Education Act, which would have given equal pay to women teachers, was passed and then reversed following a vote of confidence in the government (Summerfield, 1984, p. 174), the uproar that followed was contained by means of appointing a Royal Commission on Equal Pay. However, it was not empowered to make recommendations, but only to examine the issues.

The government frequently ran the risk of alienating large groups of women because of its discriminatory wages policy, so the extent of the government's role in maintaining the wages gap between women and men was generally not made explicit. Although the head of the Treasury said openly towards the end of the war that the government's pay policy was based on differentiation of the sexes,[83] this admission was unusual. State wages policy was sometimes disguised as 'non-intervention'. For example, Bevin argued in 1941 that it would not be appropriate for him to 'intervene' in wage negotiations between employers and trade unions to provide women with minimum rates of pay.[84] It is true that employers' leaders, such as Sir Alexander Ramsay, vehemently opposed equal pay for women and argued that no employer would keep women on if they were paid men's wages.[85] Yet the Second World War was the period when the Ministry of Labour exercised greater powers in the labour market than at any other time in the twentieth century and could have used these to equalize pay rates between women and men to a far greater extent.

Demobilization Policy, Reconstruction and Women Workers

The Second World War ended less unpredictably but also in a more complex manner than the first. The demobilization of troops and war workers after the war in Europe ended in 1945 took place at the same time as conscription for the war against Japan. Despite the apparent scope for chaos, however, the government worked effectively to retain unequal gender divisions in the labour market, to reaffirm the distinction between married and single women workers and to reinstate distinctions between men's work and women's work during the process of demobilization and postwar reconstruction.

Within days of the end of the war in Europe, following calls from men for the release of older and married women from industry[86] the call-up of women over 40 ceased, although young women reaching the age of 18 continued to be called-up for industrial work.[87] A government White Paper also proposed that all women with domestic responsibilities (whom they referred to as 'Class K') be released on compassionate grounds and allowed to retire as a matter of overriding priority.[88] Married women in the auxiliary services who wished to join their husbands were also given priority of demobilization.[89] By December 1945, although men up to the age of 31 could still be called into service, there was no further registration of women of any age;[90] and although workers in establishments covered by Essential Work Orders still could not leave or be dismissed, this did not apply to Class K (Cmd 6568, 1945, p. 4).

However, the apparent compassion for women in Class K hid an element of compulsion. It was recommended that even in factories covered by Essential Work Orders, 'arrangements should be made for the release *or discharge as appropriate* for persons in Class K' (*ibid.*) (emphasis added). It was also recommended by the government that decisions concerning who should first be made redundant should be made 'in accordance with current practice, as determined by industrial agreements' (Cmd 6568, 1945, p. 5). This was done in full knowledge that unions such as the AEU would certainly ensure that married women were the first to be dismissed from men's jobs if the government provided them with no protection (Summerfield, 1984, p. 193).

In planning for reconstruction the government strongly reaffirmed traditional gender divisions between occupations. Under the 1944 Reinstatement in Civil Employment Act, the ex-servicemen, and the smaller number of ex-service women, were given rights of access to their prewar jobs,[91] although there were few cases brought by women,[92] presumably partly because the jobs they had vacated to join the forces would have normally been lower paid women's jobs and less worth fighting for. Both men and women were given priority of release from the forces if they would accept essential reconstruction work (Cmd 6548, 1943–4, p. 2), but the work available was divided according to gender. For men there was a long and varied list of alternatives which included the building trades, teaching and coal mining, whereas for women there was a much shorter list that included laundry, clothing, textiles and boot and shoe making.[93]

The training of women in all men's trades apart from draughtmanship, motor mechanics and instrument making had already ceased at the end of 1944;[94] and it was made clear that women who had been trained in men's jobs during the war would not normally be encouraged to use their skills for reconstruction, even where there were severe labour shortages. One example of this was the housing shortage at the end of the war which was serious enough for the Minister of Labour to register all men up to the age of 60 who had any experience of building work and to aquire the power to direct them into it.[95] However, despite the fact that many women had more recent experience of all branches of building work, including the skilled trades such as electrical wiring, the Minister of Labour refused to recruit women.[96]

The Minister of Labour put considerable energy into the recruitment of women into domestic service, however. During the war a high proportion of domestic servants had either been called-up or had volunteered for better paid work. By 1944 the shortage of domestic workers was seen as a 'grave question' (Lewis, 1984, p. 191) and it was made possible to direct women compulsorily into domestic work in schools, hospitals and sanitoria, although not as politically feasible to direct women into private domestic service.[97] Bevin differed somewhat from his prewar predecessors by attempting to improve the status, wages and conditions in domestic service, and he argued that the most needy households, not the wealthiest should receive domestic help.[98] Nevertheless, he took the traditional view that domestic labour was women's work; and the Ministry of Labour put considerable pressure on women to enter private domestic service in 1945, reinforced by the threat of withdrawal of unemployment benefit, as a result of which 25,000 women were placed in 'hardship households'.[99]

Although some women appear to have been glad to have had the opportunity at the end of the war to leave employment, especially if they had been working long hours in tedious and sometimes dangerous jobs or were ready to start a family (Boston, 1980, p. 205), three-quarters of women working in professional jobs wished to remain in their career after the war (Boston, 1980; Lewis, 1984, p. 153). However, large numbers of women who had done men's jobs during the war were only given a choice between lower paid women's jobs and unpaid domestic work at home when the war ended. It became much more difficult for mothers to remain in the paid workforce, however, when the number of State-funded nurseries contracted. In 1945 the Ministry of Health stopped funding the wartime nurseries and passed the responsibility to local authorities, which were obliged to meet the cost by charging higher fees. This put the cost beyond the means of many women who had moved back into lower paid jobs and many nurseries closed because of 'lack of demand'. The Minister of Health nevertheless made it clear that:

> Wartime nurseries have been provided at the cost of the exchequer and to aid war production. Their purpose has been to enable women with young children to help in the war effort, and when these facilities are no longer required, their continuation ... cannot be justified.[100]

Nevertheless, the negative effects of discriminatory policies were somewhat softened and delayed by the shortage of labour which continued after the war. The 1942 Restoration of Prewar Practices Act was not implemented until the end of 1951, for example,[101] and because of this there were still three times as many women in engineering in 1950 than in 1939 (Summerfield, 1984, p. 199), although by 1960 only about one in 500 engineers were women.[102] Some positive changes were also brought about at the end of the war. One important change was the removal of the marriage bar in 1945, although it continued to be informally applied in many cases. However, the justification for its removal was that it would allow 'career women', who were still regarded as exceptional, to continue paid employment after marriage; whereas there was an assumption that most married women would prioritize home-making.[103] The Anomolies Regulations were initially only temporarily suspended for one year for married women who had been doing 'work of national importance' in the war, but they were later abolished.[104] There was also a sizable rise in married women's labour force participation rates by 1951 compared with 1931 (Summerfield, 1984, p. 196). This may have been partly attributable to changes in women's expectations and somewhat increased bargaining power.[105] However, it seems unlikely that married women would have been allowed to remain in paid work to as great an extent if the Second World War had been followed by another recession.

Conclusions

During the Second World War the government used its substantial powers to intervene directly in the labour market and recruit women on an unprecedentedly large scale, but chose not to break down sexual divisions at work. Although wartime politicians were undoubtedly forearmed with the realization of the crucial part that women had played during the First World War, they appear to have used this knowledge to *limit* women's long- and short-term access to better paid occupations. Throughout the war, the sexual division of labour was maintained, sometimes even at the expense of production, and these divisions were simply raised higher as women moved on to the lower rungs of men's jobs (Milkman, 1987, p. 335). This was achieved in several ways.

First, hierarchical (vertical) gender divisions in the workplace were maintained throughout the war by delaying the recruitment of women into men's jobs, especially of older women with experience of war work, until all available men had been absorbed. Young, inexperienced women were then recruited into the lowest positions in men's jobs even before single older women. This ensured that women would almost always be subordinate to men in the paid workforce. It also meant that women would be the last hired, and therefore the first to be fired when redundancies occurred.

Second, divisions between men's jobs and women's jobs (which are often referred to as 'horizontal' divisions, although men's jobs have tended to be considerably better paid) were partially broken down, in the sense that for the most part jobs remained gendered, but far more women gained access to men's jobs for the duration of the war only. The temporary nature of women's access to this wide variety of jobs was made clear during the war. As soon as the war ended, many married women were asked to leave and men were invited under the Reinstatement in Civil Employment legislation to claim their old jobs back from the women (married or single) who had performed them (Public General Acts, 1944).

Third, care was taken that women's responsibility for domestic work and caring was never removed.[106] Indeed some policies, such as the billeting of evacuees, soldiers and civil servants on private households, served to increase women's unpaid work in the home. Women's responsibilities for housework and caring for families were known to have a major effect on recruitment, retention and productivity. However, the assistance that was given in order to enable wives and mothers to take up war work in industry, such as additional nursery places, was both minimal and temporary.

Finally, distinctions continued to be made throughout the war between married and single women; and at no point could even childless wives be conscripted into full-time employment. The government was prepared for the possibility of another slump after the war and clearly wished to avoid treating married women as a permanent part of the workforce. The policy of prioritizing the placement of young single woman (who, it was assumed, would marry and leave before long) rather than older married women into men's jobs helped to maintain the position of all women as a temporary workforce.

The main shift that occurred in policy toward working women at the end of the Second World War was in the way married women came to be regarded by politicians as having a 'dual role' in the postwar world. Wives became the largest marginal secondary labour force, who still had primary responsibility for unpaid work and did not have permanent access to enough adequately paid work to provide them with economic power within the household. As a result of these policies, women found that despite having done the full range of men's jobs, worked long hours in paid employment, coped with long arduous journeys to and from work, often while maintaining responsibility for the physical and emotional wellbeing of a family, at the end of the war they were in a subordinate position in both the paid workforce and the home.

Such policies may be seen as unremarkable, given the earlier history of employment policies towards women, coupled with the fact that the wartime Minister of Labour was a male trade unionist. What remains surprising, however, is that once again at the end of the war employers seemed willing to give away the opportunity to retain women who had more recent experience in the full range of men's jobs at half of men's pay. It would appear that employers' interest in maintaining profitability at the end of the war was overtaken not only by a wish to keep the peace with working men but also by their wish to maintain a gendered workforce. This theme is explored in more detail in Chapter 9.

Notes

1. For example, Marwick, 1976, p. 132 writes that although there had been extreme reluctance to recruit women during the First World War, in the Second World War: 'conscription was introduced from the very beginning and the government was forearmed with the knowledge of the very crucial role women had played in the previous war'. See also Pollard, 1991.
2. Summerfield, 1984, p. 34; House of Commons, *Hansard*, Vol. 388, col. 1340 and Vol. 342, col. 48. A similar situation appears to have existed in

the United States, where the War Department took the view that defence employers 'should not be encouraged to utilise women on a large scale until all available male labour has first been employed', US Manpower Commission *Survey of Employment Prospects for Women in War Industries*, Jan–Jun 1942, pp. 1–2, in S. M. Hartmann, 1981, p. 54.

3. House of Commons, *Hansard*, Vol. 370, col. 383: Mrs Tate. Appeals to women to come forward for wartime employment were made by Bevin in the summer on 1940, but the recruitment process ensured that gender divisions at work were mantained.

4. *Ministry of Labour Gazette*, 1939.

5. Cmd 6301, (iv 181), 1941, p. 1.

6. *Ibid.*, p. 2; *Hansard*, Vol. 355 col. 219; Marwick, 1976, p. 138; Summerfield, 1984, pp. 32–3.

7. *Ministry of Labour Gazette*, 1939, p. 369; Summerfield, 1984, p. 32.

8. Sarah Boston, 1980, p. 187; Cmd 6307, 1941: iv 473: Interim Report of the Beveridge Committee. The second report of the Committee reported that there was still a search for skilled men.

9. *Ministry of Labour Gazette*, 1940, p. 76. Such was the sense of urgency that the men were being trained in shifts by March 1940 because of a shortage of instructors.

10. House of Commons, *Hansard*, Vol. 362, col. 574–5: Ernest Bevin.

11. Cmd 6886 (1945/6) Civil Service National Whitley Council Committee on the Marriage Bar, p. 4. During the war married women were recruited into the civil service and local government, but only as temporary workers. However, there were cases of nurses and teachers being sacked on marriage even at their height of the labour shortage in 1943–44 (House of Commons, *Hansard*, Vol. 399, col. 2066).

12. *Ministry of Labour Gazette*, 1940, pp. 208 and 296. Three Umpire's decisions were published which were taken as test cases. Two related to young women aged 18 and 19 who were disqualified from benefit for refusing to move away from home to take up factory work, when the cost of their lodgings would have been more than half their wages. The other was of an experienced saleswoman who was disqualified from benefit for refusing 'work of national importance' as a grocery assistant at 35s per week, when she normally earned 50s.

13. House of Commons, *Hansard*, Vol. 367, cols 1322–4.

14. *Ministry of Labour Gazette*, 1940, p. 159.

15. One example of such propaganda was the Ministry of Labour's brochure: 'Women in shipbuilding' which made comparisons between welding and knitting in order to present welding to employers as a trade suitable to the 'feminine' woman. See also Riley, 1981, p. 67.

16. Lewis, 1984, p. 184; Boston, 1980, p. 199; Braybon and Summerfield, 1987, p. 157. Employers in the USA were similarly reluctant to employ women and also had to be prompted by the State when the labour shortage became severe. See Milkman, 1976, p. 338; S. M. Hartmann, 1981, p. 54.

17. Preparations for the conscription of women had been made in the form of the 1941 National Service (No. 2) Act which put all persons of either sex between the ages of 16 and 51 under an obligation to perform National Service (Cmd 6324, 1941/2: 4).

18. PRO Cab 65/20:2: 7 November 1941, Memorandum by the Lord President of the Council.

19. Summerfield, 1984, p. 35; House of Commons, *Hansard*, Vol. 368, cols 1070–7; Vol. 376, col. 1481.

20. *Hansard*, Vol. 370, col. 321: Sir Ralph Assheton, Parliamentry Secretary to the Minister of Labour.

21. *Hansard*, Vol. 392, col. 460: Ernest Bevin.

22. *Hansard*, Vol. 370, col. 318.

23. House of Commons, *Hansard*, Vol. 378, col. 824; Summerfield, 1984, p. 36. The Committee included two women MPs, Irene Ward and Edith Summerskill, and a number of feminists. A similar Committee was established in the USA in September 1942, with similarly limited powers. See S. M. Hartmann, 1981, p. 55.

24. *Hansard*, Vol. 370, cols 396 and 400.

25. PRO Cab 65/29 p. 2: 'a large balance will have to be found by a more intensive recruitment of women outside industry . . . (including) the very large and hitherto untapped reserve of unoccupied married women'.

26. PRO Cab 65/220, Memorandum by the Ministry of Supply, 20 November 1941.

27. *Hansard*, Vol. 368, col. 95: Ernest Bevin, Minister of Labour.

28. *Hansard*, Vol. 392, col. 47.

29. Ministry of Labour Gazette, 1941, p. 174.

30. *Hansard*, Vol. 382, col. 1293.

31. *Hansard*, Vol. 376, col. 1421: Ernest Bevin.

32. *Hansard*, Vol. 383, col. 50.

33. *Hansard*, Vol. 392, cols 54–5 and 226.

34. *Hansard*, Vol. 382, col. 1300: Mr Kirkwood.

35. *Hansard*, Vol. 382, col. 1300: Mrs Hardie.

36. *Ministry of Labour Gazette*, 1945, p. 47.

37. *Hansard*, Vol. 386, col. 314; Vol. 392, col. 466: Ernest Bevin.

38. *Hansard*, Vol. 391, col. 2148: Mr McQuorquodale, Joint Parliamentary Secretary to the Minister of Labour.

39. *Hansard*, Vol. 392, col. 466: Ernest Bevin.

40. *Hansard*, Vol. 392, col. 47.

41. *Ministry of Labour Gazette*, 1945, p. 61. This was done under the Control of Employment (Directed Persons) Order of 1943.

42. *Hansard*, Vol. 392, col. 460: Ernest Bevin.

43. *Hansard*, Vol. 392, col. 460: Ernest Bevin. September 1943.

44. *Hansard*, Vol. 399, col. 143: Mr McQuorquodale.

45. *Hansard*, Vol. 368, col. 95: Ernest Bevin.

46. *Hansard*, Vol. 370, col. 321: Sir Ralph Assheton. For a fascinating account of the disagreements between the Ministry of Health and the

Ministry of Labour over the issue of nursery provision, see Summerfield, 1983, p. 68.

47. In the USA official policy also discouraged the mothers of small children from taking paid employment, and it was argued that a woman's primary responsibility was to her home and children. See S. M. Hartmann, 1981, p. 58.
48. *Hansard*, Vol. 368, col. 813: Ernest Bevin.
49. House of Commons, *Hansard*, Vol. 377, col. 411.
50. House of Commons, *Hansard*, Vol. 378, col. 851: Dr Edith Summerskill.
51. In the United States there was also conflict between government departments which wanted to recruit women and others which took the view that this would be harmful to the children; S. M. Hartmann, 1981, p. 58.
52. School meals were only made available to all children following the 1944 Education Act.
53. Summerfield, 1984, p. 168. Some employers objected to having trained women in their establishments and gave them work that was beneath their capabilities.
54. HC 19 1942/3 *Health and Welfare of Women in War Factories*; *Ministry of Labour Gazette*, 1943, p. 8.
55. Boston, 1980, p. 214. Again this was also the case in the USA. See S. M. Hartmann, 1981, p. 57.
56. Cmd 6182 (iv 225) 1940, *Hours of Employment of Women and Young Persons during the First Five Months of the War*, p. 15.
57. *Hansard*, Vol. 356, col. 798.
58. *Hansard*, Vol. 389, col. 945. These modifications mainly affected women over the age of 18.
59. *Hansard*, Vol. 388, col. 936: Ernest Bevin.
60. Report of the Chief Inspector of Factories, 1941: reported in *Ministry of Labour Gazette*, 1942, p. 174.
61. *Ministry of Labour Gazette*, 1945, p. 62. This quotes a report of the Industrial Health Research Board called 'A study of certified sickness amongst women in industry'.
62. Royal Commission on Equal Pay, 1946; Lewis, 1984, p. 147.
63. Report of the Chief Inspector of Factories, 1941; *Ministry of Labour Gazette*, 1942, p. 174.
64. *Hansard*, Vol. 328, col. 120.
65. *Ministry of Labour Gazette*, 1942, p. 82.
66. PRO Cab. 2631, *The Problem of Absenteeism* September 1942.
67. *Ministry of Labour Gazette*, 1945, p. 79. The MOL in 1942 had asked employers to give wives 'reasonable leave of absence' (about 14 days, normally unpaid) when husbands were home on leave from the services.
68. Part-time working came to be one of the primary ways in which gender divisions were maintained in paid and unpaid work during the postwar years. See Briar, 1992b.
69. PRO Cab. 65/20, Memorandum by the Prime Minister.

70. Cmd 6402, 1942, *Manpower in Banking and Allied Businesses, in Ordinary Insurance and Industrial Insurance.*
71. PRO Cab 65/20, Memorandum by the Lord President of the Council.
72. *Ministry of Labour Gazette*, 1944, p. 26.
73. *Ibid.*, p. 126.
74. *Ministry of Labour Gazette*, 1940, p. 159.
75. *Ministry of Labour Gazette*, 1944, p. 126. Pollard, 1991, p. 185 argues that women's rates rose more than men's, which they did but not to a large extent.
76. *Ministry of Labour Gazette*, 1941 (March), p. 53.
77. *Hansard*, Vol. 368, cols 254–6: Dr Edith Summerskill.
78. *Report of the Select Committee on Equal Compensation*, 1942, p. xvi. The TUC gave evidence to the Select Committee in favour of equal compensation for women on the grounds that war injuries could reduce a women's chances of economic support through marriage.
79. *Hansard*, Vol. 391, col. 2216: Mrs Cazalet Kier.
80. *Hansard*, Vol. 403, col. 397.
81. *Ibid.*, col. 1109.
82. *Ibid.*
83. *Hansard*, Vol. 391, col. 2182.
84. *Hansard*, Vol. 373, col. 1373: Ernest Bevin.
85. Royal Commission on Equal Pay, Minutes of Evidence, 20 July 1945, paras 2858–9.
86. *Hansard*, Vol. 403, cols 386, 1105, 1912 and 2546.
87. *Hansard*, Vol. 410, col. 2604.
88. Cmd 6568 *Reallocation of Manpower between Civilian Employment during the Interim Period between the Defeat of Germany and the Defeat of Japan*, 1945.
89. Cmd 6548, *Reallocation of Manpower between the Armed Forces and Civilian Employment during any Interim Period between the Defeat of Germany and the Defeat of Japan*, p. 4.
90. *Ministry of Labour Gazette*, 1945, p. 217.
91. *Hansard*, Vol. 481, col. 350. The Restoration of Prewar Practices Act was prepared for implementation late in 1950: Public General Acts, 1950.
92. House of Commons, *Hansard*, Vol. 481, col. 350: George Isaacs, Minister of Labour.
93. *Hansard*, Vol. 413, col. 795.
94. *Hansard*, Vol. 406, col. 701.
95. *Hansard*, Vol. 410, col. 1749.
96. *Hansard*, Vol. 407, col. 2201.
97. *Hansard*, Vol. 403, col. 2404. Compulsory direction resulted in the placement of 34, 211 women in institutional domestic work during the first eight months of 1944. Domestic service was described by Bevin as 'the band that holds the national family together'.

98. *Hansard*, Vol. 391, col. 363. This was one of the wartime practices which carried over into peacetime as the 'Home Help' service for the elderly, the sick and mothers of new babies.
99. *Hansard*, Vol. 413, col. 795.
100. *Hansard*, Vol. 406, col. 1967.
101. *Hansard*, Vol. 480, col. 1262. The Restoration of Prewar Practices Act was presented as 'non-controversial' (*Hansard*, Vol. 480, col. 1264: George Isaacs).
102. *Hansard*, Vol. 782, col. 632.
103. Cmd 6886, 1945/6, X 871, p. 9.
104. *Ministry of Labour Gazette*, 1945, p. 147.
105. At the TUC Women's Advisory conference in 1942 a proposal to give married women refunds of their National Insurance contributions as an incentive to 'retire' from paid work was turned down by delegates, and the National Advisory Women's Council had to issue a circular stressing that they had no intention of attempting to restrict married women's right to work (see Lewenhak, 1977, p. 245 and Lewenhak, 1980, p. 228). Women's membership of trade unions had risen from 500,000 in 1939 to 1.3 million in 1945 (Boston, 1980, p. 209), and women's organizations during and after the war generally supported the right of married women to paid employment. However, some attempts were made by the government to convince women's organizations of the fairness of the system, such as the 1944 Reinstatement in Civil Employment Act which gave ex-servicewomen the same rights of access to their old jobs as men. However, unlike men, few women had been in employment that merited a struggle for reinstatement.
106. *Hansard*, Vol. 782, col. 632.

Chapter 6

Women's 'Dual Role' and the Postwar Boom 1945–1970

For a long time to come there will be an acute labour shortage, and we will need the services of every man and woman who can stay at work.[1]

what we are asking is that all women who can will come and serve. We do not want women with young children to desert them, and to upset their home life, because that upsets the menfolk and the factories. There must be many many thousands of women who can help.[2]

Did women finally gain the 'right to work' after 1945? During the long postwar boom, which continued until the early 1970s, employment policies certainly shifted to the extent that the Ministry of Labour and National Service actively recruited married women into certain branches of paid employment. In these circumstances the rate of labour force participation by women rose markedly. Between 1951 and 1968 the total number of women in paid employment increased by 1.6 million,[3] and the number of married women in paid work rose from 2.25 million in 1947 to 3.75 million.[4] However, it has been an overstatement to suggest that there were radically changed attitudes among policymakers towards working women,[5] or that wives finally gained the 'right to work' (Wilson, 1980, p. 208) or emancipation and equality of opportunity (Robertson, 1979, p. 35). In fact, in many ways, despite superficial changes, employment policies during the postwar labour shortage continued to reinforce gender inequality in paid and unpaid work. Governments and the 'free market' continued to discriminate in employment and related policies on the grounds of gender. Policies nevertheless did diverge from those of the interwar period, which had been typified by the marriage bar. Instead, wives from the end of the Second World War were seen as having a dual role. This chapter looks in more detail at what the dual role entailed.

Recruitment Policy and Sexual Divisions at Work

Between the peak of women's wartime mobilization in 1943 and 1948, women's employment fell by almost a million, despite remaining at a million higher than in 1939.[6] By 1947 the competing demands of national service, reconstruction work and the export industries meant that there was a severe labour shortage and no unemployment. The government was unwilling to recruit young people and delay the raising of the school-leaving age, since this would have been seen as sacrifcing the long-term interests of the nation.[7] Therefore women were seen as 'the only large reserve of labour left' and it was to women that the government again made a 'special appeal'.[8]

As during the Second World War the government acquired strong powers to direct people into employment.[9] On 6 October 1947 an Order came into force giving power to control engagement in industry of men aged 18 to 50 and women aged 19 to 40.[10] Once again, however, the majority of women were exempt from these controls, and the Minister of Labour instead appealed to them to come forward voluntarily to 'actively help in the national effort'[11] and 'serve the country'.[12]

During these postwar labour shortages, several government recruitment programmes were aimed specifically at attracting married women back into paid work. In 1947–49 and again in 1966–67 campaigns were launched to recruit experienced women workers into a number of occupations, including textiles, nursing and domestic service. Attempts were made in 1948–49 to bring more women into teaching,[13] and throughout the 1960s there was a drive to bring married women teachers back to work.[14] A 'women in industry' recruitment drive was launched in 1947 through the radio, film trailers and the press, concentrating on 69 districts where the need for women workers was particularly acute.[15]

Nevertheless, these appeals to women implied that the demand for their labour would be temporary, and the Minister of Labour stated that this would be the case.[16] The assumption that married women were temporary and marginal in relation to the paid workforce was still in evidence in 1968, when after a long series of recruitment drives married women were still described as 'the only major reserve of potential recruits into the labour force'.[17]

By contrast, women's responsibility for domestic work and childcare was still regarded as central and permanent. Mothers of young children were exempt from direction into paid work;[18] and women with 'great domestic responsibilities' were not asked to volunteer.[19] It was seen as important not to upset husbands' domestic comforts in the process of recruiting wives.[20] Only women whose household responsibilities were manageable enough to allow time for paid employment were encouraged to re-enter the paid labour force. The dual role was thus one in which housework and caregiving were intended to be central and constant, and paid work was peripheral and sporadic.

To enable more wives and mothers take up this dual role, the Ministry of Labour and National Service persuaded employers to expand the employment of part-time women employees.[21] In 1950 the government instigated 'house-wife shifts' in the evenings via the Factories (Evening Employment) Order (Lewis, 1984, p. 153). In 1955 it was proposed that part-time working be expanded in occupations which already employed part-timers, such as clerical work, distribution, teaching and nursing, and extended into branches of employment which had barely begun to do so.[22] The Minister of Labour was obliged to overcome the resistance of employers. Except in the occupations where women were already employed part time, it was reported that 'most employers seem to regard part-time schemes of any sort as both complicated and uneconomic'.[23] Nevertheless the government met with some success, since there was an increase of 37 per cent in the numbers of women working part time between October 1948 and April 1958, bringinging the proportion of women workers who were part-timers to 16 per cent.[24]

Part-time employment was presented by the government as granting wives' and mothers' wishes to retain their position in the home and have some additional opportunites for paid work.[25] However, this was an option given only to women, and it was made clear that the place of men of working age was to be in full-time paid employment. Cmd 9628 (1955/6) *The Employment of Older Men and Women*, argued that older men should only be offered part-time employment as an alternative to retirement, not instead of full-time paid work. The paper also saw all married women as 'older workers' but only put men who were close to the official retirement age in this category.[26] The encouragement of part-time employment meant than gender divisions in unpaid work were maintained because women but not men were still available for unpaid caregiving responsibilities.

The government also continued to reinforce gender divisions in paid work through its recruitment policies. During the 'women in industry' campaign, the Minister of Labour made it clear that women were not expected to fill men's jobs in industry. Instead, women were recruited into traditional women's jobs in which there were severe shortages, particularly in textiles, hospital domestic service, hosiery and boots and shoes.[27]

Finding that there were too few women in Britain willing or able to fill these positions, the government recruited overseas workers from 1946. Women from displaced persons camps in Europe were brought to Britain to work in textiles and 'public sector domestic service' (mainly cleaning jobs in hospitals), on schemes with titles such as 'Westward Ho!' and 'Blue Danube'.[28] These migrant 'European Volunteer Workers' were, like their British counterparts, regarded as helping to meet a temporary labour shortage; but it was envisaged that they would return to their country of origin once their services were no longer required. They were recruited on two- and three-year contracts, and could be repatriated before that time elapsed if they became ill or were unsuitable.[29] Migrant workers were originally expected to leave any dependents behind,[30] although once the scheme was established a limited number of family members for whom accommodation could be found were allowed to follow.[31]

The direct recruitment by the government of women workers from Europe into public sector domestic service reached a peak in 1949 and dwindled to only 2,613 by 1951.[32] However, in 1947 the government lifted all restrictions on the recruitment of European women as employees in private households.[33]

Within a short time, commercial agencies were recruiting women from Europe for private domestic service, and in 1951 such organizations brought 36,570 workers, mainly women, to work in private homes in Britain.[34] There were allegations that these women were often obliged to work excessive hours and were underpaid.[35] The government claimed to have no control over the agencies[36] and refused to 'intervene' in the work arrangements in private households, although in fact it was responsible for issuing work permits for immigrant workers.[37]

From the early 1960s overseas domestic servants began to be replaced by *au pairs*.[38] These were in a potentially even more vulnerable position because they were not classed as employees and did not require work permits.[39] In 1964 an estimated 20,000 women were brought to Britain by private agencies to work as *au pairs*, some of them as young as 15.[40] It was claimed that some *au pairs* in Britain were subject to 'the most blatant exploitation'.[41] The government issued booklets to *au pairs* and their hosts, containing guidance to avoid 'misunderstandings and abuse'[42] but provided no legal backing. The fact that *au pairs* did not require work permits and were not classed as employees served to blur any distinction between paid domestic servants and unwaged housewives.

This outcome was contrary to what had been envisaged at the end of the Second World War when, following the recommendations of the 1947 Markham Committee,[43] the National Institute of Houseworkers was established (Lewenhak, 1977, p. 246). Its aim had been to improve the pay, status and conditions in domestic work by introducing training and qualifications in the same way as industry (Cmd 6650, 1944/5, p. 21). However, its attempts to do so were thwarted by the small size of its government grant,[44] but even more so by the State-led recruitment of European women into domestic work who were in a vulnerable bargaining position. By the time the Institute's grant was stopped in 1971 it was already seen as ineffective.[45]

Private domestic service did not disappear after the Second World War as is often supposed. However, there was a loss of distinction between domestic service as a trade and unpaid housewifery. *Au pairs* lived as part of the family and were seen as 'helping' the woman of the house, who was increasingly likely to be doing two jobs. Domestic labour, though no less time-consuming, was becoming de-skilled and less heavy and increasingly seen as something that could be done (still by women) in addition to full- or part-time paid employment.

The role of the State became much less obvious once the immediate postwar reconstruction period ended. Moving away from the situation in the 1940s when the government had the power to compulsorily direct women into 'women's jobs' such as domestic service, the Conservative governments of 1951–64 had a more libertarian and market-based approach to employment policy; yet domestic work and other low-paid and low-status jobs continued to be performed by women. Terms and conditions not only failed to improve but in some cases actually declined.

Women and Training Policy in the Postwar Boom

The distribution of funded places in government-sponsored education and training schemes is an important indicator of gendered employment policies. After the Second World War, and especially later in the postwar period, sex discrimination education and training policy was partly obscured by rhetoric claiming equality of access,[46] and by the argument that it was 'lack of demand' for appropriate training from young women themselves that barred them from the best-paid jobs in science and engineering.[47] Nonetheless, there were clear patterns of inequality in training provision after the war. Only 'exceptional women' had effective access to the same education and training as men;[48] whereas most women received training that was of shorter duration and prepared them for traditional women's occupations. Domestic subjects continued to be viewed as excellent training for girls.[49]

At times discrimination was particularly overt. In 1946, for example, the Minister of Labour, George Isaacs, persuaded the vice-chancellors of British universities not to accept female school-leavers unless they were of 'exceptional' ability, in order to give priority to ex-servicemen.[50] He stated without apology that:

> With regard to girls leaving school, I asked that if their admission would result in excluding men of the priority classes, they should not be admitted except where they are of exceptional promise. I feel this to be an equitable arrangement.[51]

These arrangements were continued until 1949, which resulted in the exclusion of most girls for three years. However, this exclusion was not confined to university education. Throughout the 1940s, when the postwar labour force was receiving training or retraining for their position in the postwar world, women also received less access to vocational education than men. The Vocational and Disabled Training Scheme trained 93,777 men and 10,572 women between 1945 and 1952.[52] The Further Education and Training schemes catered for a total of 203,401 men and 15,346 women between 1943 and 1952.[53] This scheme was modified in 1947 to exclude all women (but not men) who had not done at least one year's 'work of national importance', beginning not later than August 1945.[54] This mainly affected the same cohort of young women school-leavers who were barred from the universities.

The vocational training given to young women at the end of the war was typically shorter and provided access to a different and narrower range of lower paid occupations. While young men were apprenticed in the various building trades and skilled occupations such as clock and watch making (Mackie and Patullo, 1977, p. 97), young women were taught canteen cookery, cotton textiles, dressmaking, hairdressing, shorthand typing and tailoring, although a few women also continued to learn engineering and draughtsmanship.[55] This situation had scarcely altered by the 1970s. In 1974 only 15,500 girl school-leavers went into apprenticeships (mainly hairdressing), compared with 118,200 boys (Mackie and Patullo, 1977, p. 97). While a high proportion of young women went directly into clerical work after leaving school, fewer girls than boys went into jobs with opportunities for further training, and young men on day release schemes consistently outnumbered young women by about four to one during the 1960s.[56]

For older women returning to paid employment after a 'career break' spent rearing children there were virtually no training programmes (Titmuss, 1976, p. 102). Relatively little use was made of the skills, experience and qualifications that women already had. A survey commissioned by the Ministry of Labour in 1965 found that more than half of women who already had professional qualifications were employed at lower levels after a career break (Hunt, 1966, p. 168). In 1975 the Department of Employment predicted that up to 25 per cent of women graduates might have to accept non-graduate employment, compared with only 5–10 per cent of male graduates (Mackie and Patullo, 1977, p. 99).

The relative lack of education and training for women and girls and the underuse of women's existing skills and qualifications took place against a background of increasing concerns about a shortage of skilled workers which was threatening the competitiveness of British industry. In 1957 a government White Paper called *Technical Education* pointed out that only one-fifth of girls took any form of further education, and that of those who did the majority took nursing, homecraft and secretarial subjects and that only one-sixth of students on degree level courses were women.[57] While implicitly blaming girls themselves for having made the wrong choices, the White Paper gave cautious support to the idea of encouraging girls to train for jobs in science and technology.[58]

Domestic subjects formed a significant part of the curriculum for girls in schools during the 1950s and 1960s.[59] However, the Minister of Education made it clear that he did not envisage any change in the school curriculum for girls which might encourage them to go on to training in science and technology:

> I am, of course, very much aware of the need to encourage science teaching, but . . . I have admiration for the domestic science teaching which is being given . . . I believe that modern mothers will want their daughters to have . . . up to date information about nutrition and the use of modern domestic appliances.[60]

Despite the considerable anxiety expressed about the severe shortages of skilled 'manpower' in a long series of government papers throughout the 1960s,[61] the number of girls taking science subjects at A-level actually fell between 1960 and 1964.[62] The number of skilled women in engineering had fallen to a low level by 1967, having been declining since the war.[63] Although there was a shortage of skilled workers, this was clearly not severe enough to prompt the government to take decisive action to train and recruit women into men's jobs.

By contrast, expansion took place in the training of young men in skilled craft work and science to meet the shortages. More boys leaving school were recruited into work offering planned training such as apprenticeships (Mackie and Patullo, 1977, p. 99), additional government training centres were opened and the Industrial Training Board created on the grounds that:

> the economic well being of the country depends on an early increase in the numbers of skilled men, particularly in the engineering and construction industries, to meet persistent shortages in the engineering and construction industries.[64]

The Minister of Labour commented: 'I hope we do not forget the girls: we are rather apt to forget the girls.[65] Nonetheless, the proportion of women workers in jobs classed as skilled was continuing to decline during this period, having fallen from 15.5 per cent in 1951 to 13.9 per cent in 1961 (Mackie and Patullo, 1977, p. 99). In 1968 it was somewhat belatedly proposed that there should be a 'revolution in attitudes' towards where the training of women was concerned, after the Donovan Report warned that:

> Lack of skilled labour has consistently provided a brake to our economic expansion since the war, and yet the capacity of women to do skilled work has been neglected . . . the failure to train sufficient girl school leavers now will have ill effects for a long time ahead . . . women provide the only substantial new source from which extra labour, and especially skilled labour, can be drawn during this period (Cmnd 3623, 1967/8 (Donovan Report), p. 92).

There were some modifications of education and training policy towards women in the early 1970s. In 1973, HM Inspectors of Schools studied school curricula to see how these contributed to unequal opportunities in paid employment (Cmnd 5536, 1972/3, p. 13); and it was announced that women were to receive equal training allowances when undertaking further education and training (Cmnd 5536, 1972/3, p. 15). However, these changes had been delayed until the end of the long period of high demand for labour. Training policy during the postwar years served to create women as a secondary and subordinate workforce and to reinforce the dual role.

Women and Wages in the Postwar Boom and Beyond

During the 1940s and 1950s there was strong public pressure for equal pay for women in Britain. The International Labour Organization passed a resolution in favour of equal pay in 1951[66] and some countries such as France had equal pay policies early in the postwar period. In this political climate it was no longer feasible for governments to argue against the concept of equal pay. Instead successive governments claimed to favour equal pay for women in principle but found reasons to delay its implementation for as long as possible.

In 1950 and 1951 it was claimed that the cost of rearmament took precedence over equal pay for women.[67] In 1953 the Chancellor of the Exchequer claimed that he was bound by the decisions of the previous (Labour) government in relation to equal pay.[68] However, unions in the public sector such as NALGO and the Civil Service Clerical Association were particularly active in support of equal pay (Lewenhak, 1977, p. 254); and so were the TUC and some strong private sector unions such as the engineers' unions. In 1952 a motion in favour of equal pay was passed in the House of Commons without a division, having been proposed by Charles Pannel, an engineer.[69] Pannel believed that women's place was at home and, like many men in unions, hoped that equal pay would protect working men from women's competition.[70] Equal pay for women public servants was finally approved in 1954, following the ending of the Korean War and the revelation that the cost of equal pay – a little over £17 million – was merely equivalent to the amount underspent on the defence budget in that year.[71]

Equal pay in the public service was implemented in fixed installments, beginning in 1955 and ending in 1961.[72] It was a limited application of equal pay and was only applied in grades where there was common recruitment of women and men. Because of occupational segregation, large numbers of women's jobs such as typing were outside the scope of the public service equal pay regulations (Lewenhak, 1977, p. 281). Private industry did not voluntarily follow suit by introducing equal pay in the private sector; in fact the wages gap between women's and men's pay widened in the early 1960s.[73] Both the Labour and Conservative parties were opposed to introducing equal pay legislation to cover the private sector,[74] strengthening the wages councils[75] or introducing a national minimum wage.[76]

Governments delayed legislating for equal pay in the private sector thoughout most of the 1960s. Equal pay was presented as an exceedingly complex issue, and became the subject of apparently interminable investigations.[77] Although it was calculated that it would only have added a maximum of 1 per cent to the national wages and salaries bill if spread over seven years,[78] it was seen as a low priority, for example:

> Mr Hattersley reaffirmed the government's commitment to the principle of equal pay, but said that in the present economic circumstances it was not possible to give full implementation to the principle. But the government was anxious to be ready to take action when circumstances were more favourable.[79]

The final implementation of equal pay legislation covering the private sector was partly precipitated by a women's strike for equal pay at Ford's in Dagenham in 1968. A firm promise of equal pay legislation covering the private sector followed in December 1969, with Britain's admission to the European Economic Community, since Article 119 of the Treaty of Rome was binding on all Member States.[80] The Equal Pay Act was passed in May 1970.

Although the Equal Pay Act was described by some politicians as a 'progressive measure'[81] as indeed it was, potentially, it was again limited in scope. It was never intended to apply more than the relatively small numbers of women working alongside men on the same job.[82] Equal pay was phased in over five years, but this time not in fixed installments. This gave employers ample opportunities to find ways of avoiding equal pay completely. Their usual strategy was to separate male and female workers and reclassify their jobs; so there was a marked increase in occupational segregation during this period.[83] The Act was also poorly enforced. Under the 1970 Act the government was empowered to compel employers to have made substantial moves towards equal pay within three years,[84] but declined to do so because of the 'overriding consideration of the counter inflation policy'.[85]

Once the Act became enforceable, in 1975, its shortcomings became more apparent. It had two methods of enforcement. The first was through collective wage agreements, wages councils and employers' pay structures. Cases could be brought by trade unions (but not by individuals) to the Central Arbitration Committee if they were thought to be discriminatory. Second, there was provision for individual women to take cases before an industrial tribunal. However, there were problems with both systems.

Collective agreements had the greatest scope for raising women's wages and the impact of the Equal Pay Act upon them was significant. For the first time many women with skills and qualifications began to earn more than male unskilled labourers.[86] However, women still did not earn wages that matched their ability and effort. This was partly because of employers' practices of regrading jobs and putting women in the lowest grades, and partly because trade unions were often loath to take up cases because male members wanted to preserve differentials. Employers often gave men bonuses to avoid hostility from male workers (Snell, 1979, pp. 43 and 46).

The tribunal system had considerably less impact on the 'gender gap' in wages. The proceedings were formal and court-like – and most had male chairmen and prodominantly male tribunal members (1,769 men and 494 women) (Coussins, 1977, p. 43). Moreover, there was no legal aid, and the onus was on the individual woman to prove that her unequal pay was on the grounds of sex.[87] If she successfully did so, her employer was invited to prove that the discrimination was due to a 'genuine material difference' between her work and that of a male counterpart. Often, material differences were assessed in a prejudiced manner. For example, a woman cleaner lost her claim for equal pay with a male warehouse cleaner on the grounds that 'office cleaners work in the comfortable surroundings of carpeted offices, very similar to the environment of one's own home'.[88] Not surprisingly, therefore, between 1979 and 1982 only between 15 per cent and 22 per cent of women won their cases, and in 1983 a total of seven successful cases were brought before tribunals.[89]

There were other problems with the British equal pay legislation. There was an awkward split between the Equal Pay Act and the Sex Discrimination Act. The Equal Pay Act dealt with pay but not with indirect discrimination, while the Sex Discrimination Act dealt with indirect discrimination but not with pay, so there was no cover for cases of indirect discrimination that affected pay.[90]

On 6 July 1982 the European Court of Justice gave judgment that the deficiencies in the 1970 Equal Pay Act were such that Britian had failed its Treaty obligations.[91] The British legislation contravened the EEC's 1975 Directive on Equal Pay on several counts, particularly in its lack of equal pay for work of equal value, and Britain was obliged to amend its 1970 equal pay legislation.[92] The government made a few changes to comply with the EEC regulations. Under the Equal Pay Amendment Act, which came into force in January 1984, the principle of equal pay for work of equal value was introduced. However, there was no increased scope for disputes over equal pay to be referred to the Central Arbitration Committee, which dealt with collective agreements. In tribunal cases, a woman was still obliged to compare her work with that of an actual man rather than a hypothetical man.[93] An extra stage was introduced into tribunal hearings: a 'pre-hearing pre-hearing', allegedly to eliminate 'frivolous cases'[94] and to encourage out-of-court settlements.[95] The definition of a 'genuine material difference' as a justification of unequal pay was widened, making it legal to pay a man more if his job had a higher market value.[96] Even if a woman survived these obstacles and won her case, the decisions of tribunals still did not set legal precedents, so that other women in the same jobs were obliged to go through the tribunal process. The legislation did nothing to address the undervaluing of entire 'women's occupations' such as nursing and clerical work. Nonetheless, the government claimed to be satisfied with the Equal Pay Act as amended and made it clear that no further alterations were envisaged.[97]

Throughout the long period of high demand for labour, when women were in a comparatively good bargaining position, the government had been able to delay implementing equal pay. When they could delay no further, the legislation helped to reduce the hourly 'wages gap' for full-time workers to four-fifths by the end of the 1970s, but thereafter no significant improvements occurred. The legislation did not deal adequately with women's low and unequal pay. In 1983, of seven million workers earning less than £2 20p per hour, three-quarters were women.[98] Outworkers, not included in these figures, averaged only 40p per hour (Lowe, 1980). The dramatic growth in low-paid insecure part-time employment and the reduction in the number of regular full-time jobs, especially in the staple women's jobs in manufacturing during the 1970s, counteracted any tendency towards equalization in the weekly and annual incomes of women and men.

Childcare Policy and the 'Dual Role'

The 'dual role' during the postwar boom was mainly a response to pronatalist concerns about the birth rate, which had considerably declined between the wars, and concerns about standards of childcare. After the war, it was taken for granted that 'normal' hours of employment were incompatible not only with mothers' responsibility for preschool children but also with caring for school age children. Gone were the days when schools would extend their hours to help working mothers. As one Command Paper expressed it in 1967:

> There are some obvious practical reasons why opportunities for women are restricted . . . Married women with family responsibilites cannot work the full normal hours of a factory or office. (Cmnd 3623, 1967/8, p. 91)

During the postwar boom, motherhood was seen as women's most important role and to a great extent, therefore, replaced marriage as women's main barrier to full-time paid employment. At the same time there was a labour shortage, although not as urgent as in wartime. The solution to this dilemma could have been to expand State day nursery provision. Governments did not generally make it easier for mothers of young children to take full-time paid work, however. Childminders, the childcare solution least preferred by working mothers, were most preferred by the government (Hunt, 1966, pp. 94–5). One compromise position adopted was that day nurseries and nursery classes in schools with the specific aim of assisting working mothers were provided, but only at times and in places where there was exceptional demand for women's labour.

In 1946 there was a shortage of women workers in the cotton textile industry in Lancashire, which was seen as a vital export industry.[99] The government estimated that about 6,000 women would be prepared to return to this work if nursery places were available.[100] Early in 1948, a special Parliamentary Secretaries' committee, under the charmanship of the Minister of Labour, Ness Edwards, was established and given authority to 'drive right ahead' with day nursery provision.[101] Huts and other equipment were provided by the Ministry of Works, and by 1950 places had been provided for 863 children in cotton areas by local authorities; and, following appeals from the Minister of Labour, 1,612 further places were provided by employers in cotton areas and 267 in wool textile districts.[102] A further twelve special day nurseries were established in the Potteries around Stoke-on-Trent where there was also a great demand for women workers.[103]

Similarly, during the 1950s and 1960s there was a shortage of school teachers. In 1963 the Minister of Education expressed willingness to provide nursery classes in schools where suitable premises already existed, if this would 'release' married women teachers to work in primary schools.[104] Priority was also given to teachers' children in nursery schools; and by 1969 236 nursery classes had been set up to enable mothers to return to teaching.[105] This policy continued into the 1970s.

Childcare provision by local government to help working mothers was very much the exception, however. Subsidized places in local authority day nurseries were provided for the children in families which were seen as 'unsatisfactory' in some way: where the mother was 'obliged' to work because she was unmarried, widowed or separated, or if she was seen as incapable of taking proper care of the children; or where the home conditions were unsuitable from a health point of view.[106] The Ministry of Health played a large part in maintaining this policy. In 1965 the Ministry of Labour commissioned Audrey Hunt to undertake a survey of women's employment. One of her findings was that there were many women who would take paid employment if they could obtain day nursery places for their children (Hunt, 1966, pp. 94–5). However, the Ministry of Health inserted a comment into the report that:

> as far as day nurseries are concerned, they have been provided since 1945 primarily to meet the needs of certain children for day care on health and welfare grounds. Their service is not intended to meet a demand from working women for subsidised day care facilities. The number of places provided is therefore considerably less than the demand shown in the survey. (Mackie and Patullo, 1977, pp. 94–5)

Whereas the Minister of Labour would have preferred the creation of additional (although temporary) preschool care and education, in order to allow more mothers into the paid workforce, he was successfully opposed by policymakers in the Ministries of Health and Education, who expounded their view about the dangers of separating a young child from its mother and the need for women to create a 'proper' home.

Children from 'normal' two-parent families were not formally barred from local authority day nursery places, however. A minority of mothers and wives were seen by government as 'exceptional' because they were able to pursue a full-time, well-paid career. Childcare places were made available to their children in local authority day nurseries – but at a price that would deter other woman. When unsubsidized daycare fees were being calculated, the incomes of both parents were aggregated in the assessment, even though it was the common practice for wives to pay the childcare fees out of their own lower earnings. This put day nursery places out of reach of any but the most highly paid wives and mothers.

The Ministry of Health also refused to give assistance to private employers who wished to set up crèches, although it would help voluntary organizations 'where the day nursey in question is mainly for children on health and welfare grounds'.[107] The number of local authority day nurseries actually declined during the labour shortages of the 1950s: there were 785 in 1952, dropping to only 500 in 1956;[108] and by 1975 there were 453 (Lewenhak, 1977, p. 292).

After the war, nursery schools continued to be provided with the educational needs of the child as their priority, with hours similar to a school day. During the 1950s and 1960s they were thus of as much help to working mothers as were schools (although this was not their intention): a woman could take part-time employment, or she could work full time and pay for childcare outside of school or nursery school hours. There was a similar lack of expansion in nursery education; and in 1948 restrictions were placed on the building of new nursery schools.[109] In 1960 a circular (8/60) to local authorities forbade any expansion in nursery education except for the children of women teachers.[110] By 1967 only 0.9 per cent of the child population aged between one and five attended nursery schools in England (and 1.4 per cent in Wales).[111]

There was an expansion in the provision of State preschool childcare in 1973–74 following the recommendations of the 1968 Plowden Report. However, it was recommended that 85 per cent of nursery school places should be part time,[112] which meant for only half of a school day,[113] which further reduced their usefulness to employed mothers. The Plowden Report recommended that nursery education:

> should be part time rather than full time, because young children should not be separated for long from their mothers. Attendence need not be for a whole half day session, and in the earlier stages, only one, two or three days a week will often be desirable.[114]

Further, the programme of expansion in nursery education soon came to concentrate on areas of 'deprivation'. It was recommended that full-time nursery school places should go to helping children from 'poor or unstable home conditions, or whose mother is the sole parent and has to go out to work' (Mackie and Patullo, 1977, p. 117). In the recession of 1974–5 the expansion in nursery schools was cut back and more limited resources went to 'deprived' children. This had the effect of stigmatizing single parents and working mothers and idealizing two-parent families with dependent wives as the best place in which to raise children. Children were also being removed from the influence of homes considered unsuitable for more of the time, whereas for children in 'normal' families it was argued that: 'the nursery school is not a substitute for a good home: its prime function . . . is to supplement the normal services which the home renders to its children'.[115]

Childcare policy helped the institutionalization of women's dual role during the postwar boom, because there was paid work available for wives and mothers, but the shortage and cost of childcare meant that low-paid women's employment tended to be sporadic and increasingly part time. The policy thus made use of women's labour, but acted as an effective barrier to any tendency towards economic independence for most women.

Welfare and Women's 'Dual Role'

Women's 'dual role' was closely associated with the notion of companionate marriage which was popularized at the end of the war and widely discussed by policy-makers. It was generally understood that wives would have greater entry to public life, including paid work, but were still expected to know how to cook. Companiate marriages were not intended to be equal partnerships: men were still intended to be the main breadwinners and women the main carers, using their equal-but-different talents to promote the common good of family members (Finch and Summerfield, 1991). In the postwar period of the expansion of the Welfare State, women's economic welfare was still regarded as being primarily derived from marriage.

The Beveridge proposals put forward in 1942 in *Social Security and Allied Services* involved extending the insurance principle to all employees, but treating housewives as a separate class to be covered by their husbands' National Insurance. This meant that housewives continued to be denied a reliable source of income when not in full-time employment. Wives were allowed and encouraged to pay a 'married woman's stamp' which did not entitle them to either unemployment pay or sickness benefit. Married women could opt to pay the full National Insurance contributions, but even then if they claimed a benefit they were paid at a lower rate than men. Insurance benefits were in any case of less help to working women than men because of the sporadic nature of women's paid employment and the fact that National Insurance had been devised with the 'regular workman' in mind. This meant that any contributor who had taken time out of paid work within the three years before claiming would usually find that they received reduced rates of benefits or none at all. After 1975 the 'married woman's rate' was phased out, but it was estimated that it would be well into the twenty-first century before the majority of married women were fully covered by National Insurance.[116] The Beveridge scheme also provided a social security safety net to those deprived of their 'normal source of income', which meant wages or salaries for men and single women, and husbands' earnings for wives. Dependents' benefits in respect of non-employed wives were paid to husbands under this scheme.

An alternative proposal, for a universal basic income or 'social contract' in Britain was published in 1943 by Lady Juliet Rhys Williams[117] but it did not receive the vast amounts of publicity given to Beveridge's scheme, and was not accepted. Rhys Williams's 'social contract' would have paid an unconditional universal basic living allowance to all citizens, irrespective of marital or employment status. The basic income would have been tax free, although additional income from paid employment would have been taxed. Astonishingly, it would have cost £10 million per year *less* to implement than the Beveridge plan and would have required taxes on earned income of only 8s in the £ (40 per cent). Although proposing to pay women slightly less than men – 19s for women compared with 21s for men (it was also proposed that 10s should also be paid for each child) – her scheme would have dispensed with wives' economic dependence. Arguably if this proposal had been adopted, women's lives in postwar Britain might have changed more than they actually did. Family allowances were the only universal benefit paid directly to women in Britain after the Second World War, and were a welcome development, although they were paid at a level that did not reflect the cost of maintaining a child or pay anything towards the living costs of the carer.

The welfare policies associated with the dual role which came to be adopted were not without their inconsistencies and contradictions, however. Benefit abatement levels encouraged lone mothers who, traditionally, far more than wives, had been seen as part of the paid work force (see Chapter 2) to stay at home with their children;[118] while women in two-parent families, who until the end of the war had been marriage barred from many areas of work, were drawn more and more into paid employment. Since wives did not receive State benefits, they had less to lose financially by taking on paid work. To an extent in the postwar years, the notion of the dual role was aimed at wives more than at lone mothers. Governments encouraging evening 'housewife shifts' assumed the presence of another adult – normally the father – in the home when the mother was out at work. Yet local authority day nurseries charged considerably lower fees to single mothers than wives and continued to pursue their traditional policy of giving priority to the children in one-parent families.

Similarly, conventional marriage was still regarded by policy-makers as the best type of family arrangement, but at least lone mothers were able to obtain a reliable income via a State benefit, which wives were not. The rising divorce and illegitimacy rates during this period prompted governments to take the place of the absent father – as long as a woman abstained from entering a regular heterosexual relationship! Married women were still treated as the responsibility of their husbands whether or not their men were willing or able to provide properly for a family and they received nothing from the State for their essential work of raising children (other than their family allowance). Single mothers remained visibly poor; but State benefits nonetheless offered an opportunity for some wives to escape from very unhappy or abusive relationships and in the process opened up a degree of choice not generally available to women in earlier parts of the century.

Conclusions

Unlike the period of economic slump after the First World War, the post-Second World War years were characterized by a labour shortage that was perceived by government as being serious enough to require the greater recruitment of women in the paid labour force, although not sufficiently major as to require women to be trained for and recruited into men's jobs. The rising rates of participation in waged labour by married women may have given the superficial impression that all women had finally gained the 'right to work'.

However, the notion of the dual role allowed British governments to recruit most married women into poorly paid and relatively unskilled work. Further, most wives and mothers were expected to continue keeping their home and family as their central responsibility and it was made clear to wives and mothers that they should not engage in paid employment if this meant neglecting their unpaid work. Generally no State assistance was given to help married mothers into paid employment except in occupations such as teaching and textiles where there were labour shortages.

This does not mean that the State was acting in a monolithic manner. There was disagreement at times within government circles, for example, when the Minister of Labour attempted unsuccessfully to press for the expansion of childcare places against the opposition of the Ministries of Health and Education.[119] Much State policy took the form of 'non-intervention': for example, in failing to attempt to overcome employers' reluctance to recruit or train women in men's jobs (Cmnd 3623, 1967/8, para. 57) or to act to prevent the numbers of women in occupations such as engineering from continuing to fall. Governments continued to accept the excuse that an expensive training would be poorly invested in women who would take time out to have children, despite a series of official document reporting that large numbers of expensively trained men were joining the 'brain drain' overseas.

The dual role was just one mechanism by which most women could be treated as marginal reserves in the paid workforce. It was assumed that if the labour shortage ended, housewives would still have their main work and livelihood within the home and family. Not all women were treated in precisely this way, however. The 'exceptional' clever girl entering university or training for men's jobs, the 'career woman' and the older spinster in the professions were more likely to be treated as permanent, but aberrant. The 'normal' British woman was expected to marry and have children. Women migrant workers, by contrast, were treated as temporary reserves, but not as family members, so were parted from their families and sent overseas, not back to the home, when they were no longer needed.

Nevertheless, during this period the trend was for the vast majority of women to marry, to do so at a younger age than before the war, and for more women to have children, even though families were smaller. Therefore the dual role affected the huge numbers of working women, although not always in precisely the same ways. Despite diversities, women's overall levels of participation in paid work increased markedly during the postwar years. However, this did not give most women economic equality with men. Much of the expansion in women's employment was in the traditional and newer women's jobs, which were typified by lower pay, short career ladders or none at all. Part-time employment, designed for married women, was low-grade, low-paid and often insecure. The British equal-pay legislation was delayed until the boom was ending and most women still did not obtain economic independence through paid work.

The dual role during the postwar period meant that most women of childbearing age were increasingly doing two jobs, but most were still not receiving a regular independent income from either. Many adult women's financial dependence on male partners was changing its form somewhat: it was now more likely to be partial than complete and unmarried mothers during this time became able to obtain a regular income, albeit a low one, from the State (Joshi, 1989; Lewis, 1992). Nevertheless, throughout this long period of economic expansion, despite now officially doing two jobs, most working women continued to be defined in policy terms as dependents and thus denied full citizenship.

The dual role as a solution to the labour shortage was not without its costs. This was a period when acute shortages of skilled workers were seen as undermining Britain's position as a major industrial nation. Women's existing skills, many of which were acquired during the war, were scarcely utilized and there was a systematic avoidance of providing education and training for more than a tiny minority of women which would qualify them for men's jobs. Despite a certain amount of rhetoric during the 1960s about the equality of access to training and employment, the reality was that in Britain employment policies continued to create hierarchical divisions in the workforce by gender and policy-makers appeared to prefer to watch British industry become un-competitive, if the alternative was to allow women to compete on equal terms with men. In short, preserving the existing 'sexual contract' remained paramount.

Notes

1. *Hansard*, Vol. 417, col. 618: George Isaacs, Minister of Labour and National Service, December 1947.
2. *Hansard*, Vol. 440, col. 593: George Isaacs, Minister of Labour and National Service.
3. *Employment and Productivity Gazette*, 1968, p. 360.
4. R. M. Titmuss, 1976, p. 102. It seems likely that married women's increasing participation rates varied by social class initially; and in fact the recruitment by government of married women in the 1940s was mainly into working-class occupations. Married middle-class women's labour-force participation appears to have grown more slowly until the late 1960s and 1970s, and even then much of it was part time. In addition there continued to be considerable regional differences in women's labour-force participation rates, with areas like Wales still having the traditional lower rates. Thanks to Dulcie Groves for alerting me to these variations. Further, anecdotal evidence (including personal experience) suggests that in some middle-class occupations, including the civil service, an informal marriage bar still operated as late as the 1970s.
5. *Employment and Productivity Gazette*, 1968, p. 362.
6. *Ministry of Labour Gazette*, 1958, p. 97.

7. Cmd 7046, 1946/7, *Economic Survey for 1947*, p. 27.
8. *Ministry of Labour Gazette*, 1947, p. 183.
9. *Ibid.*, p. 286.
10. *Hansard*, Vol. 446, col. 1611.
11. Cmd 7046, 1946/7, p. 27.
12. *Hansard*, Vol. 440, col. 593: George Isaacs.
13. There was an attempt to attract an additional 6,000 women into teaching which only brought in 4,000 (Lewis, 1984, p. 152).
14. There are numerous references to this campaign in *Hansard* throughout the period 1961–69. The policy changed in 1969 in favour of giving priority to attracting men teachers, especially in maths and science. *Hansard*, Vol. 779, col. 661: Alice Bacon.
15. *Ministry of Labour Gazette*, 1947, p. 183.
16. *Ibid.*
17. *Employment and Productivity Gazette*, 1968, p. 360.
18. *Ministry of Labour Gazette*, 1947, p. 286.
19. *Ibid.*, p. 183.
20. *Hansard*, Vol. 440, col. 583.
21. Cmd 7046, 1946/7, p. 28 reported that 'industries will have to adjust their conditions of employment to suit, so far as possible, the convenience of women with household responsibilities and to accept, as they did in the war, the services of women on a part time basis.'
22. Cmd 9628, 1955/6, *The Employment of Older Men and Women*, para. 54 reported that: 'we understand that the Minister of Labour is endeavouring to stimulate the production of part time jobs to meet the needs of industry.'
23. *Ibid.*, para. 57.
24. *Ministry of Labour Gazette*, 1958, p. 453.
25. Cmd 9628, 1955/6, para. 54. As Lewis, 1984, p. 193 points out, women took their responsibilities in the home very seriously and many were not prepared to take paid work which conflicted with their domestic work. At the same time, however, the government was not providing women with any supports which would have given mothers a realistic choice between caregiving and employment.
26. *Ibid.*, para. 55. The 1951 census showed 750,000 women and 45,000 men in part-time employment. See also Klein, 1965.
27. *Ministry of Labour Gazette*, 1947, p. 183; Lewenhak, 1977, p. 245.
28. *Hansard*, Vol. 433, col. 2278; *Ministry of Labour Gazette*, 1950, p. 192, and 1951, p. 9. In 1947 the Minister of Labour was hoping to recruit 500 European women per week into textiles and domestic service in the public sector. Men were also recruited from Europe during this period and were sent into agriculture, coal mining and ironfounding.
29. *Ministry of Labour Gazette*, 1948, p. 264; 1950, p. 192.
30. *Ibid.*, 1947, p. 148.
31. *Hansard*, Vol. 443, col. 60.

32. *Hansard*, Vol. 497, col. 1246; *Ministry of Labour Gazette*, 1948, p. 130.
33. *Hansard*, Vol. 434, col. 1398.
34. *Hansard*, Vol. 497, col. 1246.
35. *Hansard*, Vol. 534, col. 2570.
36. *Hansard*, Vol. 447, col. 93.
37. *Hansard*, Vol. 462, col. 964. The government refused to issue work permits for women over 55, on the grounds that 'the period of full and useful service such foreigners will be able to give is limited'.
38. *Hansard*, Vol. 855, col. 135. In 1968–69 there were still more than 10,000 people coming to the UK on work permits each year to work as servants, but by 1972, to number had fallen to below 8,000.
39. *Hansard*, Vol. 691, col. 976.
40. *Hansard*, Vol. 693, col. 800.
41. *Hansard*, Vol. 654, col. 135.
42. *Hansard*, Vol. 691, col. 976.
43. Cmd 6650, 1944/5, VI *Report on the Post War Organization of Domestic Employment*.
44. *Hansard*, Vol. 487, col. 803. In 1949, for example, the government awarded the Institute a grant of £77,637 for the year, plus a loan of £77,000 on which to carry out training and the setting of employers' standards. Training for domestic service ceased in 1957, after a series of cuts to the budget of the Institute (*Hansard*, Vol. 467, col. 2082; Vol. 574, col. 199).
45. *Hansard*, Vol. 827, col. 1494; Vol. 509, cols 1305–6.
46. *Employment and Productivity Gazette*, 1968, p. 363.
47. Cmd 9703, 1955/6, *Technical Education*, p. 35.
48. Cmd 6886, 1945/6, p. 4, *Civil Service National Whitley Council Committee on the Marriage Bar*; John Newsom (1948) *The Education of Girls*, who thought that only 'clever' girls should be educated to their full potential; Mackie and Patullo, 1977, p. 38.
49. *Hansard*, Vol. 584, col. 324.
50. *Hansard*, Vol. 423, cols 107 and 1348.
51. *Hansard*, Vol. 423, col. 534: George Isaacs. After these three years women could be offered university places, but most did not receive student grants to enable them to take them up because Local Education Authorities had quotas for the numbers of young women to be given financial assistance to attend university. Instead women were offered financial assistance to take two-year teacher-training courses. Universal grants for students obtaining university places only became available in the early 1960s. Until 1973, women's training grants were lower than men's.
52. *Ministry of Labour Gazette*, 1953, p. 32.
53. *Ibid.*
54. *Ministry of Labour Gazette*, 1947, p. 33.
55. *Hansard*, Vol. 463, cols 1–2 and 182.

56. *Hansard*, Vol. 625, col. 88. In 1956–7 148,700 boys and 36,000 girls were on day release schemes. By 1961–2 there were 199,600 boys and 50,000 girls on such schemes.

57. Cmd 9703, 1955/6, *Technical Education*, p. 35.

58. *Ibid.* The Report argued that 'much needs to be done to stimulate among girls a greater demand among girls for further education *if only to bring the numbers up to what they should be in subjects traditionally regarded as suitable for girls.* But an even greater problem confronts us in tapping the resources of talent and labour available among girls in the strictly technical occupations' (emphasis added).

59. Lewenhak, 1977, p. 246; *Hansard*, Vol. 497, col. 2082; Vol. 584, col. 324; Vol. 585, col. 1360.

60. *Hansard*, Vol. 594, col. 324.

61. Cmnd 902, 1959/60, xx 795, *Scientific and Engineering Manpower in Great Britain*; Cmnd 1490, xx 1003 1960/61, *Long Term Demand for Scientific Manpower*; Cmnd 1892, 1962/3, xxxi, *Industrial Training: Government Proposals*; Cmnd 3102, 1966/7, xxxix, *Interim Report of the Working Party on Manpower: Parameters for Scientific Growth*; Cmnd 3103, 1966/7, xxxix, *Report on the Triennial Manpower Survey of Engineers, Scientists and Technologist and Technical Supporting Staff*; Cmnd 3417, 1966/7, xxxix, *The Brain Drain*; Cmnd 3760, 1967/8, xxv, *The Flow into Employment of Scientists, Engineers and Technologists*.

62. Cmnd 2800, 1964/5, Committee on Manpower Resources for Science and Technology, *A Review of the Problems of Scientific and Technical Manpower Policy*, Appendix A, p. 8.

63. Cmnd 3623, 1967/8, xxxii, *Report of the Royal Commission on Trade Unions and Employers' Associations* (The Donovan Report), p. 91. By 1967 there were only 13,200 women doing skilled work in engineering, compared with 580,000 men.

64. *Ministry of Labour Gazette*, 1964, p. 196.

65. *Ministry of Labour Gazette*, 1963, p. 435.

66. *Hansard*, Vol. 494, col. 299.

67. *Hansard*, Vol. 524, cols 1910–11; Cmd 7895, 1950, xvii, 1061, *Statement on Defence, 1950*; Cmd 8146, 1950/51, xxxvii, 65, *Defence Programme 1951*.

68. *Hansard*, Vol. 514, col. 1375.

69. *Hansard*, Vol. 500, col. 1857: Charles Pannel.

70. *Hansard*, Vol. 794, col. 495. Charles Pannel argued on another occasion that 'we know the terrible price we pay in juvenile crime when married women go into the factories. I have great admiration for the woman who can realise herself through her growing family and looking after her husband. I am always greatful that my wife realised herself through me.'

71. *Hansard*, Vol. 524, col. 1916: Emmanuel Shinwell.

72. *Hansard*, Vol. 536, col. 31; *Ministry of Labour Gazette*, 1955, pp. 426 and 221; 1956, p. 46; 1957, pp. 51 and 360.

73. *Hansard*, Vol. 650, col. 160; Vol. 736, col. 896.

74. *Hansard*, Vol. 533, col. 543; Vol. 833, col. 261.
75. *Hansard*, Vol. 761, col. 829.
76. *Hansard*, Vol. 578, col. 1129; *Ministry of Labour Gazette*, 1954, p. 154. Wages councils continued to fix women's wages below men's, and women working as outworkers, and in catering and domestic work were particularly badly paid.
77. *Hansard*, Vol. 750, cols 3–4 and 63–4; Vol. 756, col. 894; Vol. 764, col. 23.
78. *Hansard*, Vol. 714, cols 3–4; Vol. 750, cols 63–4; Vol. 755, col. 894; Vol. 790, col. 159.
79. *Hansard*, Vol. 755, col. 894 (1967).
80. *Hansard*, Vol. 756, col. 894; Vol. 767, cols 152–3; Vol. 790, col. 1166; David, 1990, p. 119; Lewis, 1992, p. 117.
81. House of Lords, *Hansard*, Vol. 445, col. 884: Lord Gowrie.
82. Jean Coussins, 1977, p. 7. As Bruegel, 1983, points out, women's work, when they were not working alongside men in the same jobs, was not regarded as having equal worth.
83. *Hansard*, Vol. 814, col. 850; *Sunday Times*, 4 February 1973. It was alleged that employers were given guidelines on how to avoid giving equal pay, and that the government took no action against this.
84. *Hansard*, Vol. 842, col. 75.
85. Cmnd 5205, 1972/3, *Counter Inflation Policy*; *Hansard*, Vol. 855, col. 254.
86. Coussins, 1977, p. 14; Snell, 1979, p. 40.
87. *Ibid.*, p. 20. Once the Equal Opportunities Commission was established it could bring selected test cases.
88. *Ibid.*, p. 49.
89. *Hansard*, 6th series, Vol. 48, col. 138.
90. Equal Opportunities Commission (1982) *Proposed Amendments to the Sex Discrimination Act and the Equal Pay Act (as amended)*, p. 26.
91. *Hansard*, 6th series, Vol. 46, col. 479.
92. *Hansard*, 6th series, Vol. 32, col. 427.
93. *Hansard*, 6th series, Vol. 46, col. 485.
94. House of Lords, *Hansard*, Vol. 445, col. 887.
95. *Hansard*, 6th series, Vol. 46, col. 486.
96. *Ibid.*
97. *Hansard*, 6th series, Vol. 82, col. 419.
98. *Hansard*, 6th series, Vol. 39, col. 448. The existence of Wages Councils was important during this period in preventing women's low wage from falling even lower.
99. Cmnd 7046, 1946/7, *Economic Survey for 1947*, p. 27.
100. *Hansard*, Vol. 448, col. 1860.
101. *Ibid.*, col. 1861.
102. *Ministry of Labour Gazette*, 1950, p. 192.
103. *Hansard*, Vol. 560, col. 783.
104. *Hansard*, Vol. 745, col. 783; Mackie and Patullo, 1977, p. 116.
105. *Hansard*, Vol. 745, col. 783; Vol. 796, col. 351.

106. Cmnd 495 (1957): *Report of the Ministry of Health for 1957*, Part 1, p. 97.
107. *Hansard*, Vol. 751, col. 1362.
108. *Hansard*, Vol. 560, col. 700.
109. *Hansard*, Vol. 526, col. 136: Mr Pickthorne, Parliamentary Secretary to the Minister of Education. This was said to be in order to give priority to the provision of new school buildings for children of compulsory school age. Despite this the number of nursery schools increased slightly during the early 1950s from 454 in January 1951 to 477 in January 1954.
110. *Hansard*, Vol. 664, col. 72; Vol. 672, col. 1422.
111. *Hansard*, Vol. 736, col. 475; Mackie and Patullo, 1977, p. 117.
112. *Report of the Central Advisory Committee for Education (The Plowden Report) Children and their Primary Schools*, Vol. 1, 1967.
113. Cmnd 5536, 1972/3, Department of Employment, *6th Report of the Expenditure Committee*, p. 16.
114. *Report of the Central Advisory Committee for Education*, 1967, (Plowden), p. 121. These ideas were already familiar and well-rehearsed, having been expounded in John Bowlby's (1951) highly publicised work, *Maternal Care and Maternal Health*.
115. *Report of the Central Advisory Committee for Education*, 1967, (Plowden), p. 102, quoting Susan Isaacs.
116. This took place under the 1975 Social Security Pensions Act.
117. Rhys Williams, 1943. The concept of universal basic income had also been widely discussed between the wars in Britain, and was familiar to writers such as Cole and John Maynard Keynes.
118. Lewis, 1992, p. 97 quotes Marsden, 1969, as finding that *unmarried* mothers were still put under pressure to find paid work, whereas widowed and divorced women were not.
119. Summerfield, 1984 points out that a similar scenario – with a similar outcome – took place during the Second World War.

Chapter 7

Equal Employment Opportunities, or Women as a Flexible Reserve Labour Force?

> To say that the [Sex Discrimination] Act is revolutionary is not just a platitude. If it is effective . . . it will indeed accomplish a revolution in the British way of life.[1]

The introduction of the Sex Discrimination Act in 1975 was hailed by both the government and contemporary commentators[2] as a sign of British policy-makers' increasing willingness to reform away gender inequalities at work. However, equal opportunities legislation was introduced reluctantly and was severely restricted in scope, while at the same time other government employment and family policies made it *more* difficult for women to compete with men in the paid workforce. This was partly obscured by fluctuations in the implementation of equal opportunities during the first twenty years after 1975. Equal opportunities legislation initially came to Britain at a time when economic recession, coupled with policies of reduced government intervention and the pursuit of 'flexibility' in the labour market, created a cold climate for any initiative to improve women's position in paid employment. From the late 1980s there was increased demand for women workers and the concept of equal opportunities was more vigorously pursued by the government. Even then, however, women continued to be treated as 'atypical' workers, particularly in equal opportunities policies, with male working patterns still seen as the norm. In this way, arguably, policy-makers continued the long tradition of treating the majority of working women – and this time especially mothers – as a marginal reserve labour force.

Background to the 1975 Sex Discrimination Act

Before 1975, although women in principle were not usually legally barred from occupations or training, discrimination on the grounds of sex was not illegal and it certainly must have appeared revolutionary to give women permanent equality of access to and opportunities within the full range of men's jobs in peace time.[3] Between 1967 and 1973, leading politicians of both major political parties were strongly resistant to pressure for equal employment opportunities for women.[4] The Labour government opposed equal opportunities policies for women, arguing that work and training opportunities were already open to them. There was particularly strong denial that the State itself might have been guilty of discrimination against women in its employment policies.[5] Harold Wilson claimed that the under-representation of women on government-appointed committees was because of the women's unsuitability:

> The real way, of course, to establish and honour the principle of equality is to appoint the best person for the job, regardless of whether the person is a man or a woman. If one starts arguing that we have to appoint women just because they are women, that is a denial of equality in itself.[6]

A spokesman for the Department of Employment similarly denied that there was any discrimination against women in the employment policies of his Department.[7] In fact, however, the Fulton Report on the Civil Service pointed out that women were seriously under-represented in the administrative grades of the civil service.[8] In 1972 Marcia Williams commented that women who did get in 'remained spinsters or left'. (Williams, 1972, p. 352). The Conservative Party which took office in 1970 claimed to be in favour of equal opportunities for women in principle, but was opposed to legislation.[9]

Why then was the Sex Discrimination Act implemented at all? The adoption and especially the timing of equal employment opportunities for women was partly the result of 'second wave' feminists' demands on the State for equality in paid work and some means of achieving it: equal pay, equal treatment in paid work and equal opportunities in education.[10] International agreements on equal opportunities initially had limited influence in Britain. In November 1967 a declaration against discrimination against women was adopted unanimously by the General Assembly of the United Nations, which Britain signed only with the longest list of exceptions ever submitted to the United Nations. In any case, there was no requirement to conform to such agreements unless the signatory country had ratified them. In March 1969 it emerged that Britain was unable to ratify International Labour Organization Convention 111 of 1958 against sex discrimination in employment because British law and practice did not confirm to its requirements. In fact, even if Britain had ratified the agreement and then fallen short of meeting its recommendations, no legal action could have been taken. However, the European Economic Community's anti-discrimination measures put much stronger pressure on Britain to conform. In 1972–73 a recommendation was made by the Council of Europe Ministers' Deputies about the equitable treatment of working women[11] and it was then that the British government made a commitment to introducing its own equal opportunities legislation.[12]

Continued pressure for equal opportunities from within the House of Commons and the House of Lords only gradually made an impression. Four private members Bills against sex discrimination and a proposal for an equal oportunities commission, all introduced by Joyce Butler between 1968 and

1972, and two by Willie Hamilton, were defeated. Parliamentary Question Time was used extensively by one Mr Bishop, who aimed to find out about the lack of adequate representation of women in key government positions. He was given an assortment of weak excuses.[13] In 1972 Baroness Seear succeeded in bringing a Bill on anti-discrimination as far as a second reading in the House of Lords, where it was defeated (Mackie and Patullo, 1977, p. 131) but made the subject of a Lords Select Committee report.[14] This document conclusively showed that women were discriminated against in employment, training and education. In the same year, Willie Hamilton brought his second anti-discrimination private members Bill to the House of Commons (Mackie and Patullo, 1977, p. 131; Byrne and Lowenduski, 1978, p. 134) and this, too, was referred to a Select Committee.[15] Because its timing coincided with pressure from Europe for Britain to adopt anti-discrimination legislation, the Committee's fairly conservative recommendations were largely accepted.

By 1974 both the outgoing Conservative Party and the incoming Labour Party had committed themselves to some form of anti-discrimination legislation. On gaining office the Labour government issued a White Paper called 'Equality for women' (Cmnd 5724, 1974). The Conservatives issued a remarkably similar document called 'Equal opportunities for men and women'. The Sex Discrimination Act became law only months later.

Provisions and Adequacy of the 1975 Sex Discrimination Act

The 1975 Sex Discrimination Act appeared to be an ambitious and comprehensive measure (Schmidt, 1978, p. 158) which covered direct or indirect discrimination on the grounds of sex or marriage (Coussins, 1977, p. 51) although not parenthood and covered the fields of employment, training, education, housing and the provision of goods, facilities and services.[16] The Equal Opportunities Commission was set up to monitor and evaluate the progress of the Acts implementation, and also had some limited powers to take up test cases.[17] A system of Employment Appeals Tribunals was also set up (Gregory, 1987). Although the Act applied to both men and women it was understood that the Act applied mainly to women, who generally worked under less favourable circumstances than men.

The Act placed employers covered by the legislation, including the State, under an obligation to recruit, train and promote employees on the basis of their 'individual qualities and qualifications' irrespective of sex or marriage. Limited provisions were made for positive discrimination in training, to allow more woman into areas of employment which had previously been heavily male-dominated. As with the Equal Pay Act the onus was on the individual woman to prove that discrimination had taken place (Robarts, Coote and Ball, 1981, p. 12). The government made it clear they hoped that most of the changes would come about through voluntary initiatives by employers and that legal proceedings were intended only as a last resort (Cmnd 5724, 1974, p.

18). As with the Equal Pay Act, enforcement was to be through tribunals (*ibid.*, p. 19). There was provision for compensation to be awarded in successful cases. However, up to November 1975 only 55 cases were brought, and of these only 10 were successful (Coussins, 1977, pp. 52 and 54). The Equal Opportunities Commission, which was set up along with the Act, initially appeared reluctant to take test cases to court (Cockburn, 1991). Not surprisingly, in these circumstances the measurable results of the equal opportunities were limited. As late as 1991 it was reported by the National Economic Development Office that only 1 per cent of top managers and 4 per cent of middle managers were women (NEDO, 1991).

The potential effectiveness of the Sex Discrimination Act was further reduced by its numerous exceptions. These included childbirth, retirement, pensions (including occupational pensions) and death; taxation, social security payments and employment in private households; firms with fewer than ten employees (later reduced to five); 'personal and intimate relationships'; the clergy and religious orders and charities, as well as occupations where being of one sex rather than the other was a 'genuine occupational qualification': for example acting, or teaching in a single-sex school.[18] The majority of the provisions of the Sex Discrimination Act could also be waived if this was necessary to comply with earlier legislation, such as the Factories Acts.

By 1982 concern was being expressed at the ineffectiveness of the legislation. There was opposition to some of the exceptions to the Sex Discrimination Act from the Equal Opportunities Commission, particularly to the sections excluding small firms, partnerships and pension schemes.[19] However, the Prime Minister, Mrs Thatcher, claimed to be 'satisfied' with the existing anti-discrimination laws.[20] Once again, however, the European Court took a different view: in November 1983 it ruled that Britain's anti-discrimination legislation did not comply with the Community's Equal Treatment Directive of 1978[21] or with EEC rulings on social security. Accordingly, the British government passed new Sex Discrimination legislation in 1986.[22]

Changes to the legislation were largely superficial. The new Act included private households and small firms in line with other EEC Member States but 'maintained the principle of respect for private life'.[23] There was little affirmative action in the new legislation, except that it was made easier to set up single-sex training courses for occupations in which one sex was seriously under-represented. One change, however, was that women were to be treated more like men in the workforce, and Clauses 3–8 removed much of the protective legislation thought to restrict women's employment opportunities.[24] The work of removing protective legislation continued with the 1988 Employment Act which lifted obstacles preventing women working nights, on oil rigs, underground in mines or cleaning machinery in factories.[25] These changes were 'warmly welcomed' by the Confederation of British Industry and given a cautious welcome by the Equal Opportunities Commission. It was perhaps not surprisingly strongly criticized by the Trades Union Congress and also by the National Council for Civil Liberties, who feared that women lacking proper childcare facilities would be pressured into working nights when they were unable to get proper sleep during the day, to the detriment of their health (Coussins, 1977, pp. 81–4). The National Council for Civil Liberties thought it would be better to extend protective legislation to men than to remove it from women (*ibid.*).

Underlying Problems with the Sex Discrimination Act

Was equal employment opportunities for women a revolutionary idea? Some of the reasons for the lack of success of improving working women's employment opportunities can be traced to deficiencies in the use of the concept of equality by policy-makers. In Britain the 1975 Sex Discrimination Act and its subsequent amendment were based principally on the notion of creating equal opportunities to become unequal. It was thus concerned with equality of *access* not of *outcomes* and firmly embodied the 'merit' principle, which assumes that if women and other target groups still fail to secure the most attractive jobs it is because of the disadvantaged groups' unsuitability and not because of discrimination.[26] Further, little attention was given to the cumulative effects of past discrimination which had prevented women from gaining the qualifications and the experience regarded as necessary for many jobs.[27]

Greater emphasis on the principle of equality of outcomes may have proved a partial solution. However, although the 1975 British legislation contained some provision for 'positive action', this was limited to allowing employers to provide single-sex training courses for non-traditional areas and encouraging women to apply for jobs in occupations where women were under-represented.[28] It remained illegal under British legislation for women to be given priority at the point of selection for jobs.[29] In the USA, where the principle of equality of outcomes was more accepted, organizations top heavy with able-bodied white males were liable to be assumed to have discriminated and could be forced by law to change their recruitment, training and promotion policies and redress the balance (Robarts, Coote and Ball, 1981, p. 35). Affirmative action, including the use of quotas, seemed an effective short-term strategy for transforming embedded patterns of prejudice and discrimination. It was hoped that in the longer term employers would come to recognize the value of the target group members, and that the legislation would then become unnecessary. However, as the labour markets of the English-speaking countries of the 1970s became increasingly characterized by unemployment, inequality and fierce competition for the better jobs, an outraged white male backlash in the United States made the spread of American-style affirmative action to Britain politically impracticable. In the British situation some men were able to oppose equal opportunities intitiative on the grounds that they constituted discrimination against men.[30]

Throughout the period after the Second World War women have been perceived by leading British policy-makers as equal-but-different. Sex equality legislation was seen as perfectly compatible with women continuing to have the main responsibility for childcare (Cockburn, 1991, pp. 33–4). The drawback has been that women's equal-but-different work has been largely unpaid or low-paid and in reality has had lower status. After 1975 women's 'difference' was used as a rationale for creating low-paid, dead-end jobs for women. Since the late 1980s mothers have been increasingly expected to compete on equal terms with men in the public sphere, while the effects of women's 'difference' on their ability to compete with men who have the domestic support of wives have been largely overlooked. The 1975 Sex Discrimination Act was an outcome of a struggle for 'equal rights' and so has liberal and liberal feminist roots. It stated an important principle, but was not enough to alter long-established patterns of gender inequality in paid and unpaid work.

During the first three-quarters of the twentieth century, policy-makers and employers claimed that it was 'natural' to categorize most positions in the paid workforce and the home as 'men's jobs' or 'women's jobs'. However, since 1975 there has been an assumption that there should be no 'unnatural' barriers in the labour market and that in their own interests enlightened employers will recruit and promote good female employees. 'We are unreservedly against sex discrimination,' said the Employment Minister, Ian Lang, in 1986. 'Not only is it unfair, but it is in the interests of the economy for jobs to go to the best people irrespective of sex'.[31] British governments have used this argument as a rationale for preferring voluntary equal opportunities rather than strong legislation. They have therefore used *reactive* policies, where discrimination must be proved to have already occurred before a case may be brought. *Proactive* legislation, where employers can be legally obliged to begin by producing a plan to overcome structural inequality in their workplace, was found to be more effective in the United States.

Research sponsored by the Equal Opportunities Commission in Britain to investigate sex discrimination by employers 10 years after the Sex Discrimination Act found that employers were still seeking women to fill jobs with low pay and poor prospects (even though 86 per cent of jobs attracted applicants of both sexes); that employers believed they had every right to ask about and take account of women's (but not men's) domestic situations, and that these circumstances were central in making selection decisions (Curran, 1986). In short, employers were continuing to recruit and promote 'in their own image' while the legislation, which contained no analysis of patriarchal prejudices and practices, was not designed to cope.

Patriarchal attitudes and actions were not confined to employers. Equal opportunities legislation has been ineffective partly because working men have opposed it, in attempts to safeguard their pay and status in paid work, as well as their domestic comforts at home (Cockburn, 1991, p. 18). Unfortunately, the Sex Discrimination Acts operated in a period of a shrinking economy, in which men in unions often regarded equality of opportunity for women with suspicion, as a potential management device for weakening the position of skilled men by introducing competition from lower paid women and were consequently less than wholeheartedly supportive (Snell, 1979; Cockburn, 1991).

Women were in fact put in the position of having to compete for jobs which had been male preserves. Breaking down gender segregation at work was presented as the major objective of equality legislation. Although the 1970 Equal Pay Act was amended to allow for equal value, its effectiveness was limited and there were few benefits to women in women's jobs (see Chapter 6). Women were thus given the message that in order to receive equal pay they would have to conform to a male norm by performing the same jobs and following similar pattern of employment. The cost to women of the congeniality of working with other women was poorer pay and prospects. The legislation also did nothing to revalue, resource or encourage a more equal sharing of the valuable work that women were already doing.

The legislation even as amended in 1986 was too narrow, weak and poorly enforced to make a significant difference to gender inequality at work. Although sex discrimination in employment was unlawful and a civil offence, discrimination in recruitment was not a criminal offence and so prosecutions could not be brought.[32] Further, if a woman was to win her case, tribunals could not enforce reinstatement or prevent further abuse (Cockburn, 1991, pp. 33–4). Finally, the spirit and intent of the 1975 Sex Discrimination Act and its 1986 amendment were weakened by exemptions and by other pieces of legislation which could override the equal opportunities laws. Moreover, during this period the government was also strongly promoting other labour market policies, which undermined equality of opportunity.

Equal Opportunities, 'Flexibility' and Part-time Employment

Labour market 'flexibility', which was pursued vigorously as a policy goal from the early 1980s onwards, affected women to a greater extent than men. Wives and mothers had been perceived as a flexible reserve labour force throughout the century but there was an intensification of the process during this period. Further, 'flexibility' acquired different forms for women and men. Men were mainly given full-time fixed-term contracts (typically lasting a year or more), were increasingly expected to work overtime and were expected to be geographically mobile. By contrast, more women were recruited into part-time jobs, which before this period, as we saw in Chapters 5 and 6, had generally been regular, although usually dead-end and too low-paid to provide women with economic independence. From the mid-1970s, part-time employment also became increasingly 'flexible' and insecure.

The British government played a major part in this. Employers were given incentives to employ more low-paid part-timers by being given exemption from the employer contribution of National Insurance contributions (Walby, 1983, pp. 159–60), estimated at 13 per cent of the wages bill (Clark, 1982, p. 285; Hakim, 1995), provided that their income was kept below the

National Insurance threshold, which even by 1995 was only £58 per week. This also affected entitlement to unemployment benefits and the level of retirement pensions. A further incentive given to employers to employ women part-time was the exclusion of workers employed for less than 16 hours per week from protection from unfair dismissal, maternity benefits and statutory redundancy payments (Walby, 1983, p. 159). In 1986 the government attempted to raise the threshold to qualify for employment protection to 20 hours per week (even then a woman had to have been in two years' continuous employment with the same employer) or 12 hours per week for women with five years' continuous service.[33]

These policies appear to have been highly effective: part-time employment continued to expand rapidly after 1975, despite the economic recession. Whereas the 1951 census had shown only 750,000 women in part-time employment, by 1984, 4,117,000 women were employed part-time: 46.4 per cent of all women employees. In 1981 women were described as being 41 per cent of the paid workforce. The continued expansion of part-time employment led some writers to conclude that low-paid women were being used to displace men (Gardiner, 1976; Dex and Parry, 1984, p. 151). However women were only 29 per cent of the *full-time* paid workforce; and women's participation in full-time employment was declining steadily during this period,[34] especially in the traditional women's areas of manufacturing such as textiles, clothing and footwear (Clark, 1982, pp. 284–5). Part-time jobs, mainly in the service sector, which were generally regarded as unacceptable by men because of the low status and wages (Milkman, 1976), became available, and women were spared men's competition for such jobs partly because many of these jobs were irregular and discontinuous (Bruegel, 1979, p. 16).

Even regular part-time employment tended to be more insecure than full-time jobs. Although nearly a million new part-time jobs were created during the 1970s – almost the total number of new jobs – part-timers' positions were also more vulnerable than that of full-timers. As Bruegel pointed out in 1979, in every industry where contraction took place during the 1970s, part-timers were more severely affected than full-timers (*ibid.*). In fact employers usually tended to make women redundant more than men generally.[35] In 1982 the Employment Appeals Tribunal ruled this practice illegal (Robinson and Wallace, 1984, p. 396), but it continued under the guise of 'last in, first out' which also caught the same cohort of wives and mothers who had taken 'career breaks' (Walby, 1983, p. 164). Statistics on women's *underemployment* (the number of women in part-time jobs who would have preferred full-time employment) were not available in Britain.[36] Women's unemployment also rose during the period after the passage of the Sex Discrimination Act, although the full extent of this was disguised by the fact that most women were discouraged by the benefit regulations from registering as unemployed. Nevertheless, even using these figures, between 1979 and 1985 the number of women officially registered as unemployed tripled from 366,000 to more than a million.[37]

The expansion in part-time employment and the contraction in full-time work undermined the 1970 Equal Pay Act, since part-timers, who were predominantly women, seldom earned a living wage and normally earned appreciably less than men, even on an hourly basis. The policy of encouraging increasingly casual and insecure part-time employment also undermined the 1975 Sex Discrimination Act, since career paths were largely absent from part-time work. The promotion of flexible part-time employment was nevertheless presented by the government of the 1980s as equal opportunities and even as positive action for women.[38]

The government's claim that part-time employment was what women wanted[39] contained some truth but it overlooked women's reasons, which lay in the difficulty of combining paid and unpaid work.[40] One reason why part-time employment did not represent a move towards equal opportunities was that it reinforced women's 'housewife' role which has in turn constrained women in terms of time and energy available for paid work, and reinforced employers' prejudices about women's attachment to the paid workforce. Research has shown that although a higher proportion of women in full-time employment have managed to share domestic responsibilities with male partners, women part-time employees were as almost as likely as non-employed women to be carrying the main responsibility for caregiving and unpaid domestic labour.[41]

It was also claimed that lack of employment protection was in women's interests because it increased the number of opportunities to work part-time: 'flexible part-time work is *especially welcome* to women, and therefore regulations which tend to reduce its availability place women workers at a disadvantage[42] (emphasis added). Nonetheless, Britain's trading partners in Europe were unconvinced, and pressure was put on the British government to improve the conditions of part-time workers. In 1981 the European Commission published a draft directive on part-time work.[43] At the same time, calls for improved conditions for part-timers were made in a House of Lords document that highlighted the discriminatory treatment of part-timers in Britain.[44] However, there was no indication that the government intended to voluntarily eradicate discrimination against part-timers. Leading policy-makers' response was to defend part-time employment, to present it as the working pattern of the future and to try to blur the distinction between flexible part-time employment and other, less discriminatory forms of shorter time working such as job-sharing (in which job-sharers had equal access to promotion, fringe benefits and employment protection) and early retirement.[45] The government's attempt to raise the threshold number of hours for employment protection to 20 per week was a disincentive to the continued growth in job-sharing, which in the early 1980s had become available in 41 local authorities.[46] Central government instead introduced a 'job splitting' scheme in which participants worked an average of 15 hours per week: one hour less than those needed to qualify for employment rights.[47]

The 'needs of the economy' were also allowed to take precedence over the prevention of sex discrimination. A 1991 High Court ruling found that although depriving part-timers of equal employment rights was a form of indirect discrimination, it was not illegal if it could be justified on 'economic grounds' (Millar and Glendinning, 1992, p. 1). It was only in 1995, after the House of Lords invited a judgment by the European Commission, that part-time employees gained the same statutory rights at work as full-timers.[48] Even then, employment rights were restricted to regular workers.

The promotion of part-time employment and the disguising of much of women's unemployment were just some of the ways in which women's subordinate and marginal position in the paid workforce has been maintained, and the centrality of wives' and mothers' domestic role reaffirmed. The rhetoric has enabled traditional discriminatory policies to be continued behind a façade of equal opportunities.

Equal Opportunities and the 'Demographic Time Bomb'

The fall in job opportunities between 1975 and the late 1980s had created an inhospitable environment for anti-discrimination measures. From the late 1980s, by contrast, grave concerns were expressed about a fall in the number of school-leavers entering the workforce and policy-makers recommended that this should be made up mainly by mothers of young children returning to paid employment. It was thought that by 1995, 80 per cent of the increase in the workforce would be made up by mother 'returners'[49] and that in the period up to the year 2000 women would take 90 per cent of the new jobs and become 50 per cent of the workforce in the UK.[50] Other groups, such as older workers, were also to be drawn on and by 1992 firms were being urged by the government not to make older workers redundant.[51] However, as in previous labour shortages, women were the main group of 'reserves' to be called upon. This time, however, it was mainly mothers who had left the paid workforce who were targeted as the main recruits.

The government therefore began a recruitment programme aimed primarily at mothers. The Advisory Committee on Women's Employment, originally set up in the Second World War, was reassembled to advise on barriers to women returing to paid work after having children.[52] The Employment Department mounted a series of conferences aimed at women returning to work in conjunction with BBC 'Women's Hour', dealing with issues faced by returners and offering advice.[53] The Department of Employment also produced a leaflet telling women returners what opportunities were open to them.[54] A number of relatively expensive information packages were advertised in the *Employment Gazette*.[55]

The recruitment of mothers to compensate for a temporary shortfall in the numbers of younger workers was presented by leading politicians as a series of equal opportunities initiatives. The government, the Confederation of British Industry and the Equal Opportunities Commission all aimed to appeal to employers' self-interest and encouraged them to voluntarily invest in a diverse workforce which reflected the balance of the local population, arguing that this was good business. Employment Secretary Michael Howard put forward a ten-point plan, announced in 1991, to advise firms on how to avoid discrimination.[56] A Department of Employment-sponsored national intiative, Opportunity 2,000, urged employers to 'drop outdated and unfair practices' and persuaded a significant number of employers to offer flexible arrangements to staff, in the form of childcare or a career-break option.[57] The government, as in wartime, did not force employers to take on more wives and mothers, but it did set an example by producing frameworks and guidelines on equal opportunities for managers in the Civil Service,[58] and boasted proudly of the results.[59]

There was, however, still the entrenched view that family responsibilities were women's domain and that this would prevent mothers working 'normal' hours. Women were still perceived as 'atypical' workers. The Prime Minister, John Major, asked: 'Why should women be forced to conform to traditional working patterns?'.[60] In their attempt to 'harness the female resource', rather than providing direct help in the form of additional local authority day nursery places, the government encouraged employers to 'adapt traditional working practices to accommodate the needs of women'. By this they meant 'more flexibility in hours of work and in holidays, job sharing, career breaks, part-time working and where possible help with childcare costs'.[61] 'Family friendly' firms such as ESSO, BP, IBM and ICI were held up as good examples,[62] with awards given to firms which provided employment and training opportunities to women returners and other target groups.[63] Within government departments, such as the Department of Employment, equal opportunities policy also took the form of providing more flexible hours or part-time jobs and special leave for domestic purposes.[64] This encouraged women to continue spending less time in paid work and more time in unpaid work than men. However, this was still not presented by leading British politicians as discriminatory, but rather as normal and natural and the result of the exercise of free choice.

By contrast, the government and employers still expected men to work 'normal' hours, which were not designed for anyone with caregiving responsibilities – and, indeed, men's hours of paid employment in Britain were increasing at this time. In the European Community overwork was recognized as a problem, but attempts to impose a limit of 48 hours per week via the proposed Working Time Directive were bitterly resisted by the British government, which temporarily succeeded in delaying its implementation for 10 years.[65] It was argued that the two-and-a-half million employees regularly employed for more than 48 hours per week should be allowed the freedom to continue doing so.[66] The existence of pressures on male employees to work excessive hours was not admitted. Again, although it is known that the fathers of young children have tended to have the longest hours of paid employment, policy-makers did not acknowledge this as an issue for working women left 'holding the baby'.[67]

Policy-makers continued to regard only a minority of 'exceptional' women as in a position to compete on equal terms with men.[68] Not surprisingly, therefore, the majority of women remained in subordinate positions in the workforce. Women were still normally being recruited into low-grade jobs.[69] Women were still a minority of the self-employed.[70] By 1991 women had become 43 per cent of the total workforce but only 2 per cent of senior managers.[71] It was claimed that government-funded bodies had made insufficient efforts to recruit and train women.[72] Research showed the ways in which 'flexible' part-time employment also compromised women's careers.[73] Arguably, by persuading the mothers of young children to return to paid employment sooner than they would otherwise have done (rather than the considerable numbers of women and prime-age men who had been on the unemployment registers for some time by the late-1980s), the government was targeting a group who were likely to move into 'flexible' part-time employment[74] or out of paid work completely when the labour market contracted again.

Women's Employment Opportunities and Family Policy

Following the passage of the Sex Discrimination Act, governments continued to pursue childcare and community care and policies that reinforced women's unpaid caregiving role and financial dependency within the private world of the family. This also undermined any tendency toward equal opportunities for women in paid work.

During the 1980s family policy shifted away from helping the 'normal' family to function by providing various forms of assistance, and instead emphasized family (and community) responsibilities by taking those supports away (David, 1990, p. 119). The increased responsibility for providing welfare for the elderly, sick and disabled was allowed to rest largely on unpaid women workers. Between 1979 and 1989 there was also strong encouragement for women to look after their own children at home. From the late-1980s, however, amid official concerns about the 'demographic time bomb', official attitudes towards working mothers changed. For example, during the early-1980s, subsidized nurseries provided by employers were taxed by the government, which created a disincentive; but from 1988–89 childcare provided by employers was encouraged, as was private childcare provided for profit. However, as is shown in more detail below, the State's own role as a direct provider of work-related childcare did not significantly increase. Some changes and fluctuations took place in parental leave provision, partly as a result of pressure from Europe; but pressure on women to provide care for dependent adult relatives in 'the community' increased after 1975.

Equal Opportunities and Parental Leave

The 1975 Sex Discrimination Act outlawed discrimination on the grounds of sex or marital status, but not parenthood; and it was ruled at an Employment Appeals Tribunal that it was not illegal to sack a woman because she was pregnant.[75] However, later in 1975 the Employment Protection Act gave pregnant women who had been with the same employer for six months the right to six weeks' paid maternity leave, protection from dismissal for being pregnant and the right to return to a job up to 29 weeks after a confinement (Public General Acts, 1975).

The 1975 Employment Protection Act was later gradually eroded: the incoming Conservative government in 1979 (ironically with Britain's first woman Prime Minister at its head) increased the qualifying period for protection from unfair dismissal to 12 months and then to two years (Lowe, 1980). The 1980 Employment Act eroded mothers' right to reinstatement after childbirth by adding the loophole 'where it is reasonably practicable' and also allowed employers to offer women a different job (Lowe, 1980; Public General Acts, 1980; Pollert, 1981, p. 231). In 1986 the government produced two White Papers: 'Lifting the Burden' (Cmnd 9571, 1986) and 'Building Businesses . . . not Barriers' (Cmnd 9794, 1986). The second of these was a clear policy statement that the right to reinstatement of new mothers working in firms employing fewer than ten people should be withdrawn. No interested parties, such as the Equal Opportunities Commission, had been consulted and there was no evidence that the protection of women's employment after childbirth actually impeded businesses.[76]

In contrast with social policy in other countries, such as the Scandinavian nations, the British State made no attempt to encourage fathers to share the hard work of caring for small babies (Lowe, 1980). There were several attempts to introduce paternity leave for men,[77] including Greville Jenner's Equal Opportunities for Men Bill, which was supported by the Equal Opportunities Commission – but all of them were defeated.[78] Most employing organizations appeared unlikely to introduce paternity leave voluntarily. A survey of 400 public and private sector employers in 1973 had found that only 3 per cent gave paid paternity leave and 5 per cent gave unpaid leave. Even this was often minimal: for example, the BBC gave only two days (Lowe, 1980). The notion of paternity leave provoked a hostile reaction from some men in powerful positions, such as the judge in a divorce case who announced that 'a man ought not to give up work and turn himself into a mother figure or nanny at the expense of the State'.[79]

In 1990 a draft European Community Directive proposed that all women should have the right to 14 weeks maternity leave on full pay, plus paid time off for antenatal checks and also greater protection from dismissal irrespective of their length of service. It was further stated that where necessary jobs should be reorganized to protect the health of pregnant women.[80] The Secretary of State for Employment said that he had 'no plans to harmonize entitlement to maternity leave with the other EU countries' and that any pressure to do so would be resisted by the British government. Michael Howard, the Employment Secretary, claimed that the provisions would place 'unacceptable burdens on employers', and threaten jobs,[81] and that 'Member States should be free to make their own arrangements for maternity, in accordance with national traditions and practices'.[82] He even went to the lengths of persuading other countries to resist the Draft Directive.[83]

Instead, the Pregnant Workers Directive was agreed in November 1991 and adopted in December 1992. It had to be implemented within two years. It reintroduced a small amount of protection for pregnant women: for example, expectant mothers did not have to work nights if they got a doctor's certificate to say that this would be bad for their health; and they would not have to work with harmful substances. There was a clause that employers should assess the risks to pregnant workers and adjust the work environment where necessary. However, since most employers had never been pregnant and were not medical practitioners they may not have been qualified to do so. The main change from the earlier draft was that although pregnant women could now have time off for antenatal checks and 14 weeks maternity leave, there was now no mention of pay. Women were still only entitled to the statutory minimum maternity pay. The main improvement was protection from dismissal for reasons connected with pregnancy, irrespective of length of service. Britain took the credit for this 'progressive' legislation.[84]

Nonetheless, the government did encourage women employees to return to work after maternity leave, especially women public servants. Two reports issued in 1991 found that nearly half of women who took maternity leave were back in employment by the time their baby was 9-months old, many with the same employer. It was also shown that the public sector did more to encourage their employees to return to work after maternity leave and that public sector employees were twice as likely to return.[85] Some new mothers may well have been driven by financial necessity to return to paid employment before they were ready. Six weeks paid maternity leave was clearly insufficient: barely long enough for a woman to recover from the physical effects of the birth. After this there was a baby who was still too young to be accepted by many nurseries and child-minders except at a very high cost, because of the large amounts of care tiny babies require. Further, an increasing proportion of women were not eligible to even obtain this minimal amount of time off with pay.

Childcare Policy and Equal Opportunities 1979–1988

During the early-1980s the government did not treat childcare as an equal employment opportunities issue, although it was known that women with pre-school children were the group least likely to be in paid employment.[86] The Manpower Services Commission described childcare responsibilities as 'personal factors', not as a structural issue affecting most women for some part of their lives.[87] The government reaffirmed that it was not the role of the State to provide day care to meet the needs of working mothers.[88] In 1978–79, local authority day nurseries catered for a mere 1 per cent of the child population aged under five: a total of 27,800 places,[89] and by 1983 this had only risen by 317 places nationwide.[90] Between 1984 and 1989 the number of children attending local authority day nurseries fell by 4 per cent (Moss and Melhuish, 1991, p. 88). There was, however, an expansion in part-time nursery school provision, which would allow mothers to do at the most very short hours of part-time employment. Drawing on care by relatives on a 'grace and favour' basis, using the infant classes of schools for the 'rising fives' and childminders for pre-schoolers continued to be the main childcare strategies of working mothers.

In 1980, in the context of closure of day nurseries in the former cotton-weaving districts of Blackburn and Accrington, the Parliamentary Under Secretary for Health and Social Security took the opportunity to say that he thought that mothers were doing a more important job if they stayed at home.[91] Policy-makers continued to present the home as the best place for the daily care of most pre-schoolers; and State day care was still targeted at 'priority' groups whose poor health, housing or lack of a male breadwinner made it impossible for them to provide a 'normal' family life.[92] For other mothers, not in the priority groups, local authority day care was available for their pre-school children but at a much higher price. Between 1976 and 1977, childcare fees in some local authority day nurseries increased by around 120 per cent,[93] thus cancelling out gains that women might have made through the Equal Pay and Sex Discrimination Acts. From 1988, the cost of childcare was no longer included in the earnings disregard for lone parents on a benefit, which tended to increase the already growing number of single mothers trapped in poverty.[94]

Although childcare remained predominantly women's responsibility, husbands were the main source of childcare for 47 per cent of working mothers with pre-school children in 1980.[95] However, policy-makers, generally assumed that men were available to work whatever hours their employer demanded. According to Hilary Land, the erosion of the school-meals service meant that more women were obliged to be at home to provide a midday meal and spent more of the day ferrying children to and from school (Land, 1981, p. 7). Throughout the 1980s childcare was still seen as women's responsibility, without being acknowledged as an equal opportunities issue,[96] even though the patterns of women's participation in paid work indicate that the countries with the best childcare provision have the lowest dip in women's paticipation rates after the age of 22 to 23. This was to change to some extent after 1988.

Childcare Policy and Equal Opportunities from the Late-1980s

Some important modifications took place in government childcare policy after 1989, yet much remained the same. The main shift was that, as in previous labour shortages, childcare again became recognized as a labour market issue. This time the government encouraged the recruitment and retention of women with very young children. The main barriers to women's greater levels of participation were seen as being affordable childcare (including school-holiday programmes) and flexibility of employment. It was acknowledged that childcare was an expensive solution for working mothers of pre-schoolers. One study found that women were paying on average £85 per week for full daytime care.[97] From 1992 there was a limited but highly publicized expansion in State-sponsored provision of after-school and school-holiday programmes, to help the mothers of school-aged children to return to paid work.[98]

There was not a great deal of additional intervention or direct provision of childcare geared to the needs of working parents, however. Instead the government's energy was directed toward encouraging organizations in the public and private sectors to be 'family friendly' and either provide childcare or assist with women returners childcare costs.[99] Such appeals, however, were relatively ineffective overall. A survey of 96 organizations (650 were invited to participate) by the Industrial Relations Services found that very few had a childcare policy of any kind.[100] By 1992 it was announced that some additional after-school places were to be funded by the government via the Training and Enterprise Councils.[101] There was also an increased use of child-minders; but women still wanted more formal childcare provision.[102]

Politicians and employers had two choices: to leave jobs as they were but put 'flexible' arrangements into place for women; or change typical male working patterns away from long hours and continuous employment towards ways that were 'family friendly' and took account of men's responsibilities within the family. It was quite clear at the time that these choices existed, because of the existence of an international convention on workers with family responsibilities,[103] advice from experts on childcare within Britain and over-seas, which all advocated greater direct provision of childcare geared to the needs of working parents and modifying 'normal' workplace practices to en-able men and women to share domestic responsibilities. Peter Moss told a conference on women and work organized by the Department of Employment that family and childcare issues should not be marginalized as women's is-sues.[104] He argued that Sweden and Denmark's more generous State childcare and parental-leave policies should be a model for Britain if more women workers were to be recruited and retained.[105]

There were signs that policies allowing men to take a greater share of caregiving would have been acceptable in Britain. Fathers were already doing significant amounts of childcare. A Eurobarometer survey in 1990 showed that 40 per cent of men throughout Europe would prefer not to be employed full time while their children were small. A few firms such as ICI voluntarily made their parental leave provisions available to men as well as women.[106] However, in general, British politicians and most employers of male staff continued to treat working mothers and fathers very differently. It was assumed that many mothers did not want to return to work until their children were more than two years old and that women would rather have part-time employment than nurseries;[107] but fathers' preferences were largely ignored. This tended to be glossed over by politicians' habit of referring to 'parents' when they meant only mothers.

Not surprisingly it was revealed in 1991 that very few women managers (less than 20 per cent) aged between 20 and 40 have children, compared with 80 per cent of that age group in the overall female population of Britain.[108] In the clash between the desire to recruit women and the wish to retain traditional working patterns by women and men, much of the potential for equal opportunities had been lost.

Equal Opportunities and 'Community Care'

In addition to maintaining women's responsibility for small children, which conflicted with equal opportunities for women, governments throughout the 1970s and 1980s were closing and running down State institutions catering for the elderly and people with disabilities and expecting women to provide unpaid care 'in the community'. By 1981 nearly three times more bedridden and severely disabled people were being cared for in the home than in institutions (Walker, 1983, p. 106). One study showed that women provided 20 times as much care for this group as men (Walker, 1982, p. 27). Doctors and health professionals tended to assume that it was women's reponsibility to care for dependent relatives (Walker, 1984, p. 35). Women often felt obliged to be the main care provider because it was linked with their perceptions of themselves as women (Madden, 1972). A survey conducted by the Equal Opportunities Commission indicated that one-fifth of women aged between 40 and 50 had given up paid work to care for someone other than their husband – and that more than half of them had wanted to remain in employment (Land, 1981, p. 5).

Community care policies particularly affected women who had already taken a career break to care for children and who had often been back in paid work for only a few years, although pressure was also put on some younger single women to give up work to care for elderly parents.[109] Research done during the 1980s showed not only the loss of employment opportunities for carers but also the huge amounts of unpaid work required (Finch and Groves, 1983, p. 15; Walker, 1982, p. 26), their own loss of mobility, freedom and social life[110] and carers' greater vulnerability to poverty in their own old age.[111]

Despite the sacrifices expected of carers, most housewives in Britian were not granted the Invalid Care Allowance when it was first introduced in 1976.[112] Although the Sex Discrimination Act, passed only the previous year, had outlawed discrimination on the grounds of marriage, this did not apply to social security payments and married and cohabiting women, as well as divorcees in receipt of maintenance from ex-partners, were all disallowed from receiving the Invalid Care Allowance.[113] Only men (including married men) and single women carers could receive the benefit and, from 1981, it was also payable to non-relatives.[114] Married and cohabiting women were judged to be the dependents of male partners – even when the person requiring care was the husband – and were expected to provide high-quality care under these exceedingly difficult circumstances. In 1986 there were still only 11,000 recipients of the Invalid Care Allowance, whereas it was estimated that about 96,000 married and cohabiting women would be able to claim the benefit if the regulations were altered. The Invalid Care Allowance had been omitted from the scope of the European Community's 1978 Directive on the Equal Treatment of Women and so the British government could avoid inclusion of partnered women in the Invalid Care Allowance until Mrs Jacqueline Drake took her successful claim to the European Court[115] in June 1986. Even then, only 10 per cent of carers actually qualified and for those who did, the amount paid, although welcome, was too low to adequately compensate for having given up the opportunity of a full-time career in paid employment (Payne, 1991).

Vocational Training Opportunities and Job Creation Policy

1975–1988

In 1973 an offical report had recommended that women should only receive vocational training when the economy required their labour.[116] However, after 1975 it was in the field of training that the government claimed to be taking the most radical measures to overcome occupational segregation and sex discrimination and promote women's opportunities in paid work. Training was the only area of the 1975 Sex Discrimination Act which allowed for positive discrimination; and the government's claim to have an adequate equal opportunities policy rested heavily on improving women's access to training. Not only were all formal barriers removed to the inclusion of women on courses of training for what had traditionally been seen as men's work' but training providers, such as employers, the Manpower Services Commission (MSC) and the Industrial Training Boards, were allowed to run women-only courses in non-traditional areas of employment.[117] These courses were cited by the government as Britiain's major contribution to the United Nations Decade for women 1975–1985.[118]

The MSC's women-only schemes, such as the Wider Opportunities for Women scheme in 1978[119] and the New Opportunities for Women scheme, aimed at women returners, although useful, were only provided for a tiny proportion of the potential female workforce.[120] Even following a 'modest expansion' in 1980–81 following applications to the European Social Fund[121] there were only 1,495 women on women-only courses and in 1982 there were just 72 women trainees on such courses in London.[122] While it was admitted that women-only courses were provided on a very small scale, it was always qualified by an insistence that all other vocational training courses were equally open to women.[123] In fact, however, women continued to be under-represented on most training courses. The disparity was most evident in relation to government skill-centre training for the unemployed. In 1984 only 3 per cent of trainees nationally were women, allegedly because the skill-centres 'concentrated on traditional skills as opposed to skills that are more appropriate for women'[124](emphasis added). The Technical and Vocational Education Initiative similarly developed along 'traditional lines': the official spokesman stated that although it would embody equal opportunities for girls it would not guarantee that equal numbers would be catered for.[125] The proportion of women trained on training opportunities courses initially rose rapidly after 1975 to over 40 per cent (Wickham, 1982, p. 154) but slipped back to 35 per cent in 1982[126] and 31 per cent in 1984.[127] Overall there were very few women aged over 25 on training schemes.[128]

Job creation schemes for the unemployed, administered by the Manpower Services Commission, also catered predominantly for boys and men. One of the earliest schemes, the Job Creation Scheme, was criticized for being 'of vastly more benefit to boys than girls'.[129] Its successors showed similar patterns. Under the Special Temporary Training Programme (STEP) and the Community Enterprise Programme (CEP) the ratio of male to female entrants actually declined from 75:25 in 1978–79, 80:20 in 1979–80 and 83:17 in 1980–81.[130]

Under the part-time Community Programme (CP) which succeeded CEP and STEP, the proportion of women initially increased to 23 percent, but in 1984 the eligibility critieria were altered, to admit only the longer term registered unemployed and their spouses, which effectively barred women with employed male partners and single mothers.[131] The CP was an important part of the government's strategy to promote flexibility in wage levels by reducing young unemployed workers' expectations. Married women, however, would have been *better* off on CP because they were ineligible for unemployment benefit. The attractiveness of CP to married women therefore posed a threat to government policy. The Equal Opportunities Commmission expressed concern at the way married women's interests were being sacrificed;[132] and in 1985 a Mrs Chandler took a case against the Department of Employment, claiming that the changed conditions were a form of indirect discrimination on the grounds of sex and marriage. Her case was successful[133] but the Department appealed against it, arguing that it was a form of discrimination which could be justified, because married women with employed husbands did not need places on schemes for the unemployed.[134]

Occupational segregation remained endemic on training and job-creation programmes. Girls and women were primarily trained for low-paid and unpaid work. Of the Job Creation Programme it was said that 'girls typed, boys worked at lathes; girls did laundry, boys drove the tractor'.[135] Much the same was true of the later schemes, in which boys and men did mainly labouring work while girls and women did mainly caregiving. In 1975 the Manpower Services

Commission held women's individual choices responsible for the segregation, arguing that women had lower aspirations and chose shorter and more limited courses. In 1984 this view was expressed again, this time by Sir Keith Joseph who, in refusing to channel money into training young women for science and engineering in Science and Engineering Year, said: 'I do not believe that money is the problem: it is the attitude of parents and of girls themselves.'[136]

The evidence suggests, however, that it was employers and the government who were responsible for discrimination in training. On Manpower Services Commission work-experience schemes, small employers in particular were 'notorious for their maintenance of segregated work roles', and the Commission claimed to have no control over this (Wickham, 1982, p. 158), although it had the power to withdraw subsidized labour from discriminatory employers. In fact the Manpower Services Commission discriminated directly in terms of the quantity and type of work it offered to males and females. This was not surprising, since the Area Action Committees which administered the schemes had a total of only two women members compared with 72 men in 1977.[137] The Labour government refused to make any changes,[138] and so did the incoming Conservatives. In 1984 only 7 per cent of people on the successors to the Area Action Committees, the Manpower Boards, were women;[139] the Secretary of State for Employment argued that for this reason the Boards would 'bend over backwards to ensure that girls' needs were properly taken into account'.[140] Needless to say there is no evidence to suggest that this happened.

Late-1980s onwards

By the late-1980s it was said that because of the tightening labour market and a skill shortage it was important to train women.[141] Nevertheless a survey by the Equal Opportunities Commission in 1991 found that women were still discriminated against in terms of access to training. Among younger workers, men were 50 per cent more likely to get job-related training. Boys leaving school were still more likely to go into jobs that provided training and day release. Only one-third of those on day release were female. Women who were part-timers (42 per cent of all female employees) were much less likely to receive training than women full-timers or men. On Youth Training girls continued to be marginalized into traditional low-paid women's work. Because women were still concentrated in the lowest grades in the workplace, they tended to receive less training – and what training they did receive was still of shorter duration. Women have also tended to work for smaller employers, who have provided less training. It was also found that the skills and qualifications that women did possess were still under utilized.[142] In short, after a more than a decade-and-a-half of equal opportunities policies, the patterns of training for women had not changed at all.

Women aged 18 to 59 were eligible for entry to employment training if they had been registered as unemployed for at least six months. These requirements were waived in the case of women returners and single parents, and the latter could also qualify for a childcare allowance.[143] However, unemployed women were only half as likely as unemployed men to be receiving employment-related training. Sex stereotyping also flourished within Employment Training, in which more than half of all women participants were in administrative and clerical work in 1989–90 and a further fifth were in health, community and personal services. Men again were trained in a much broader range of occupations, forming 95 per cent of participants in several occupational groups.[144] In 1991 it was estimated that only about 3 per cent of Employment Training entrants were women returners.[145] Young women vocational trainees had been having their expectations trimmed by means of low training allowances: 'a training in dependency, low expectations and fatalism to prepare them for an unpromising future' (Buswell, 1992, p. 92). Despite this, during the mid-1990s the *Employment Gazette* regularly published statistics showing that the gap in terms of the numbers of women and men receiving training, and the duration of training, was closing markedly.

A continuing problem was that women's training, once obtained, tended not to be as highly rewarded as the same qualifications obtained by men. In 1995 a House of Lords Committee on Science and Technology found that women scientists still faced disadvantageous requirements for returning to work after having children. Although the numbers of women at undergraduate level had often become equal to those of men, women were still underrepresented at higher levels of seniority. Women professors were still a 'tiny minority' even in a subject like biology which was studied by large numbers of women.[146]

Women and Incomes Policy, 1975–1995

Equal Opportunities and Dependency within Marriage

Despite the adoption of the Sex Discrimination Act, women's economic dependency on a male partner was still not perceived by policy-makers as incompatible with equal opportunities. Indeed, the Act omitted social security, taxation, matrimonial and family law from its original scope.[147] In 1975 the Department of Health and Social Security made clear its continuing policy of regarding wives as dependents and husbands as breadwinners in a letter to the National Council for Civil Liberties:

> It is normal for a married woman in this country to be supported by her husband, and she looks to him for support when not actually working ... Indeed it continues to be a widespread view that a

husband who is capable of work has a duty to society as well as to his
wife to provide the primary support to his family (Lowe, 1980).

After 1975 the government continued to reinforce wives's economic dependence on husbands in a variety of material ways. Married men received a
significant tax allowance, whereas married women's usually lower pay was
taxed at a higher rate because their pay was aggregated with the husband's for
tax purposes. The government treated the household as a single financial unit,
while at the same time increasing women's poorer position within it. Married
or cohabiting women could not claim supplementary benefit in their own right,
even if their partner was unemployed. This ruling was changed in 1983, again
after intervention from the European Court, because it did not comply with
the 1978 Equal Treatment Directive.[148] However, the cohabitation rule, which
denied a range of State benefits to anyone with a partner deemed able to
support them, continued to be applied mainly to women. (Richardson, 1984,
p. 3).

Although the State had the power to take legal action against a man for
failure to maintain his resident partner and children[149] it was seldom applied.
Wives (legal and *de facto*) were generally left to foster the goodwill of their
partners to dispose them to share their incomes. Women's lack of economic
independence, whether they were completely or semi-dependent, often with
young children or other relatives dependent on them in turn, put women in a
difficult and vulnerable position within the family. It made it harder for women
to negotiate the more equal sharing of domestic work and caring. Unpaid
housework continued not to be included in national accounts;[150] it still had no
scope for promotion or pay rises, however well it was done; and unpaid work
experience has tended not to be rated as relevant or useful by employers when
women have attempted to resume a career in paid employment. This has had
implications for women's pensions and their consequent poverty in old age,
since the value of the 'non-contributory' element has been eroded.

Social policies that reinforce women's financial dependency within
relationships and women's primary responsibility for unpaid work and
caregiving have also contributed to women's marginality in the paid
workforce. This, in turn, has reinforced women's lower pay, so the process is
circular. Equal opportunities policies in Britain have barely begun to address
this issue.

Equal Opportunities and Equal Pay

Equal opportunities legislation has not provided most women with economic
equality or independence and women have remained the majority of the
working poor (for a more detailed discussion of working women's poverty in
Britain, see Chapter 8). This has partly been because of the move towards
more flexible working patterns for women, which has undermined any trend

towards equal pay and opportunities. Part-timers have suffered the most: their hourly earnings in 1995 were still only 58 per cent of men's hourly pay. Black women earned up to 23 per cent less than White women. There were more than five million women employed part-time in Britain in 1990 and their average hourly earnings were £3.95.[151] Nonetheless, even many women in regular full-time employment continued to be paid substantially less than men doing similar work because of the limitations in the equal pay legislation, which did not deal adequately with the pay of women in gender-segregated employment. The equal opportunities legislation was intended to deal with this by breaking down gender segregation in paid work, but it was relatively unsuccessful in even this limited aim. After 25 years of equal pay legislation, even full-time working women's average weekly rates of pay in 1995 were still only 72 per cent of men's.[152]

At the time of writing, the British government still has no plans to revise the Equal Pay Act to ensure that women in 'women's jobs' benefit from the legislation,[153] even though the Employment Department's spokesman in the House of Lords said that the government's analysis for the continuing inequality between men's and women's wages were that job segregation was the main cause.[154] However, in the mid-1990s there has been a great deal of pressure on unions from women within the trade union movement to make equal pay their top priority.[155] A combination of court cases and bargaining has been found to be effective in negotiations. Demands were made at the 1995 TUC annual congress by women trade unionists for a national minimum wage of £4.15 per hour. The lowest paid occupations, mostly employing women, were waitressing, childcare, bar work, laundry work, cleaning, catering and dental nursing, all paying below this amount.[156] According to the Low Pay Unit there were 58 occupations paying less than the Council of Europe's decency threshold.

The Equal Opportunities Commission has created a draft code of practice for employers on pay, which will eventually be used in court. The main aim of the draft code is to uphold the official intention of the existing legislation by reminding employers that sex discrimination is unlawful and trying to appeal to employers' interests, saying that a clear equal pay policy will help to motivate staff.[157] They want employers to have an equal pay policy in which they examine their pay practices, monitor the impact of pay policy, protect employees in 'non-standard employment' or on maternity leave; provide training and guidance for management, and discuss and agree the policy with trade unions.

As we have seen, British governments, both Conservative and Labour, have resisted – sometimes overtly and sometimes passively – measures that would provide women with genuine equal opportunities and equal pay. However, there is hope that further intervention on women's pay and opportunities at work will come from Europe in due course, helped by a strong, concerted campaign from within Britain. Without such action, the prospects for more just rewards for working women in Britain are poor.

Conclusions

Did the adoption of equal opportunities legislation represent a radical new departure in employment policies towards women in Britain, as policy-makers claimed? Or did it mainly serve to disguise an extension of policies that have treated women as a flexible reserve labour force? This chapter has tended to support the second view. Because of the limited definitions of equality at work and a relative lack of commitment to achieving greater equality between women and men, in the context of social and economic policies designed to promote greater *inequality*, equal opportunities laws were destined to produce few measurable results.

The concept of equal employment opportunities has contained both strengths and limitations. One positive feature has been that even in the restricted form adopted by Britain, composed mainly of anti-discrimination legislation, equal employment opportunities has established the principle that women are entitled to compete for a more equal share of the most attractive jobs in terms of pay, status and power. However, it has not challenged the existence of wide (and widening) inequalities between workers, but has merely aimed to disperse the members of the various target groups, including women, somewhat more evenly through the hierarchy. It has not introduced any major steps to revalue the unpaid and low-paid work done by most women, despite its essential nature. The lives of most women have remained untouched by equal opportunities legislation: they still do low status work and often do not earn enough to support themselves and their dependents with dignity (see Chapter 8). By contrast, women who have been the beneficiaries of equal opportunities policies and are able to earn an independent livelihood tend to have usually been obliged to adopt modes of working which have been created by and for men without domestic responsibilities. Many such women have coped either by remaining single or childless while others have struggled to compete with men and appear both capable and feminine, carrying out major responsibilities as wives and mothers. They have been expected to 'look like a woman, act like a man and work like a dog' (Korndorffer, 1992). In some occupations, such as the Civil Service, many women have succeeded in doing so – but these occupations have then become feminized and have lost relative pay and status (Cockburn, 1991).

Despite their largely voluntary nature, equal employment opportunities policies have performed an educative function for employers, some of whom have come to more fully appreciate women's versatility.[158] Some firms and public sector departments have appointed women as equal opportunities officers to advise management on how to break down gender segregation at work. However, equal opportunities in some cases have deepened antagonisms between male and female employees by appearing to represent an alliance between managers and women workers. That some women should prefer to work directly with management rather than through the unions is understandable since, as we have seen, male trade unionists have often colluded with employers in twentieth-century Britain in order to exclude women from the best jobs. However, whether it is groups of men or women workers who do deals, the longer term result is that employees are generally divided, weakened and less able to improve working conditions for all.

However, even the limited aims and possibilities present in the 1975 and 1983 equal opportunities legislation have been thwarted by a lack of commitment on the part of policy-makers to its basic principles. Many employers have continued to discriminate against women, generally without having incurred any penalty from the government. Equal opportunities policies have been subordinated to other policy objectives so that women's employment opportunities have been pursued only when these fitted in with the more dominant aims. Between 1975 and 1989, the economic recession and a government unwilling to 'intervene' in the 'natural' workings of the labour market created an unworkable situation for equal opportunities policies. After 1989, when there was greater demand for women workers, equal opportunites received more attention from government and employers alike. Nonetheless, even since 1989 the continued promotion of labour market 'flexibility', cuts in social services and the strong emphasis on family obligations have all undermined women's economic position. Reductions in social provision for the infirm and elderly have increased the amount of unpaid caring work performed largely by women. After 20 years of equal opportunities legislation, British women are still a secondary, marginal labour force – and still 'the domestic sex'.

Notes

1. Walker, D. J., 1975, *Sex Discrimination*, p. xiii. In theory the 1975 Sex Discrimination Act should have effectively compensated for a deficiency in the 1970 Equal Pay Act, which denied equal pay to women not doing the same work as a man. A major aim of the 1975 Act was to break down occupational segregation, so that men and women would be doing the same work and be entitled to the same pay.
2. For example, Beloff, 1976, *Sex Discrimination: the New Law*, p. iii, described the legislation as 'a milestone in the development of human rights in Great Britain'.
3. *Hansard*, Vol. 754, col. 227; Vol. 759, col. 231.
4. *Hansard*, Vol. 755, col. 625; Vol. 760, col. 649; Byrne and Lowenduski, 1978, 'The Equal Opportunities Commission' *Women's Studies*, No. 2, p. 145; Mackie and Patullo, 1977, *Women at Work*, p. 131.
5. *Hansard*, Vol. 756, col. 625.
6. *Hansard*, Vol. 766, col. 32: Prime Minister, Harold Wilson. Although social class was recognized as a major form of inequality by the Labour government of this period (so that, for example, there had been some positive discrimination measures to increase the numbers of working-

class children going into higher education during the 1960s), gender inequality was not perceived as sufficiently problematic to warrant remedial action by the State.

7. *Hansard*, Vol. 764, col. 27: Harold Walker, Parliamentary Secretary to the Department of Employment and Productivity.
8. *Fulton Report* on the Civil Service (Cmnd 3638, 1968).
9. *Hansard*, 5th series, Vol. 811, cols 256 and·272.
10. David, 1990, 'Women and "work" in the decade of Thatcherism' in I.Taylor (Ed.) *The Social Effects of Free Market Policies*, p. 119; Ann Oakley, 1981 *Subject Women*; Coote and Campbell, 1982 *Sweet Freedom*; Pascall, 1986, *Social Policy: a Feminist Analysis*. Barroness Seear and the National Council for Civil Liberties perceived equal opportunities as a solution to the problem of equal pay being deliberately undermined by employers who segregated their male and female employees.
11. *Hansard*, Vol. 856, col. 38: Mr Chichester-Clark.
12. House of Commons, 1972–3 No. 333, 'Special Report of the Select Committee on the Anti-Discrimination Bill', p. iii.
13. *Hansard*, Vol. 813, cols 128, 131, 132, 141, 172; Vol. 812, col. 350. These included: women were barred from certain posts because of the lack of women's toilets; that there was a need to conform with practices in private industry; women could not be appointed to areas where there were no female staff already; that women were 'unlikely to possess the appropriate qualifications'; and that women might be required to lift books weighing up to 28lbs. Oddly, leading policy-makers did not generally seem to think that women should be protected from having to lift toddlers, bags of shopping or buckets of water weighing more than 28lbs.
14. House of Lords, 1972–3, No. 104, 'Special Report on the Anti-Discrimination Bill', p. 3.
15. House of Commons Papers, 1973–3, No. 333.
16. Public General Acts.
17. The Equal Opportunities Commission was originally envisaged by the Conservative Party as being simply an educational and advisory body; however, when the Labour Party took office in 1974 it gave the EOC some limited powers to enforce the Sex Discrimination Act.
18. Home Office, 1978, *Sex Equality*, pp. 16–17; Lambert, 1984, *Equality at Work*, pp. 14–15.
19. Equal Opportunities Commission, 1982, *Proposed Amendments to the Sex Discrimination Act, 1975 and the Equal Pay Act, 1970 (as amended)*, pp. 8–10.
20. *Hansard*, Vol. 18, col. 144.
21. *Hansard*, Vol. 50, col. 157.
22. *Employment Gazette*, 1986, p. 447.
23. *Employment Gazette*, 1986, p. 43.
24. Equal Opportunities Commission, 1986b, *Briefing for MPs: 'The Sex Discrimination Bill, 1986'*.

25. Pregnant women were still protected against working with lead and radioactive substances. *Employment Gazette*, 1987, p. 115; 1988, p. 629. Women were also once again given the right to retire at 65, the same age as men: *Employment Gazette*, 1986, p. 131.
26. Jewson and Mason, 1986 'The theory and practice of equal opportunities', *Sociological Review*, **34**, 2, p. 314. For example, following the passage of the Act, examples were cited of State-owned industries which claimed to have an equal opportunities policy even though they had no women in senior positions: *Hansard*, Vol. 41, col. 55; Vol. 17, col. 437.
27. *Hansard*, 6th series, Vol. 33, col. 35.
28. Lambert, 1984, p. 14–15; Coussins, 1977, p. 71; EOC, 1982, Proposed Amendments to *the Sex Discrimination Act*, 1975 and the *Equal Pay Act*, 1970 (as amended); *Hansard*, 5th series, Vol. 985, col. 801; *Hansard*, 6th series, Vol. 65, col. 144.
29. It was never proposed to practise 'reverse discrimination' in favour of women. See Cmnd 5724, 1974, *Equality for Women* and Robarts, Coste and Ball, 1981, p. 20. This was despite the fact that the 1979 UN convention on the elimination of all forms of discrimination against women *expected* member states to pursue positive action until such time as equality was achieved: Cockburn, 1991, p. 31.
30. As Lord Justice Denning had succinctly expressed it in 1950 in a speech called 'The equality of women' at the Annual Conference of Marriage Guidance Councellors: '[the wife] in her sphere does work as useful as the man does in his . . . if his work is more important in the life of the community, hers is more important in the life of the family. Neither can do without the other. They are equals.'
31. *Employment Gazette*, 1986, p. 43.
32. *Employment Gazette*, 1987, p. 55: John Lee.
33. Equal Opportunities Commission, 1986a, *Building Businesses . . . Not Barriers: Implications for Women of the White Paper Relating to Part Time Workers and Maternity Rights*, p. 2.
34. *Hansard*, 5th series, Vol. 911, col. 819; Hakim 1995, 'Five feminist fallacies about women's employment', *British Journal of Sociology*, **30**, 3, pp. 429–56.
35. Daniel and Stilgoe, 1978; Bruegel, 1979, p. 13, *The Effects of the Employment Protection Act*; *Hansard*, 6th series, Vol. 21, col. 147.
36. Bullock, 1994, *Women and Work*, p. 19. 'Underemployment', a term now used by the ILO, refers to employment that under-utilizes workers, either in terms of the hours of paid work provided or the level of skill and responsibility needed. However, one indicator of the seriousness of women's position was the decline in women's labour force participation rates, which fell from 60 per cent in 1979 to 56 per cent in 1981. See Walby, 1983, p. 160.
37. Pollert, 1981, *Girls, Wives, Factory Lives*, p. 229; Wickham, 1982, The state and training programmes for women', in E. Whitelegg (Ed.) *The*

Changing Experience of Women, p. 154; *Hansard*, 6th series, Vol. 78, col. 616; Vol. 55, col. 299 (written answer to a question); Vol. 59, col. 92 (written answer).

38. *Hansard*, 6th series, Vol. 62, col. 166 (written answer); Vol. 75, col. 141 (written answer).
39. *Hansard*, 6th series, Vol. 78, col. 617; Cmnd 9794, 1986, p. 37. McDowell, 1992, 'Gender Divisions in a post-fordist era' in McDowell and Pringle (Eds) *Defining Women*, argues that 'It is too often assumed that mothers *want* part-time employment, and British governments have pursued this line of thinking. Part-time employment was not created in response to demand from women workers. See also Briar, 1992, 'Part-time work and the State in Britain 1943–1986', in Lundy, Lundy and Warme (Eds) *Part Time Working: Risks working Part Time: Risks and Opportunities*; Hakim, 1987, 'Trends in the flexible workforce', *Employment Gazette, November*, pp. 549–60.
40. Equal Opportunities Commission, 1980, *The Experience of Caring for Elderly and Handicapped Dependents*, para. 3.1.
41. In Britain in 1988 women who worked part-time were responsible for general domestic duties in 88 per cent of couples. Women who were in full-time employment (with a male partner also in full-time employment) were responsible for housework in 72 per cent of cases. Where neither was employed, women were responsible in 76 per cent of cases (British Social Attitudes survey, 1989). Looking after the children was a more popular activity among fathers than routine household tasks such as cooking, cleaning and laundry.
42. EOC, 1980, p. 3; Cmnd 9794. Employers have been prone to use temporary contracts as a way of avoiding statutory employment protection.
43. *Ibid*.
44. It was argued that: 'part-time employees, while contributing significantly to the development of the economy and to the flexibility of the productive system, are as a group still behind their full-time colleagues in regard to wage rates, access to training and promotions and the provision of other benefits. This is both economically self-defeating and socially unacceptable, not least when it reinforces other types of discrimination, such as that between male and female employees. It must be a prime object of policy in this area to eradicate such inequalities in the structure of employment.'
45. *Hansard*, 6th series, Vol. 80, col. 748: Alan Clark, Under Secretary of State for Employment.
46. EOC, 1980, p. 4.
47. *Employment Gazette*, 1983, p. 173.
48. Scottish Low Pay Unit, 1995, *New Rights for Part-time Workers*.
49. *Employment Gazette*, 1989, pp. 118–21, p. 662.
50. *Hansard*: Patrick Nichols, 31 October 1989.
51. *Employment Gazette*, 1992, p. 263.

52. It had been reconstituted several times since the war whenever there was a shortage of women workers and had also advised on the Equal Pay Act, the Sex Discrimination Act and the Employment Act.
53. *Employment Gazette*, 1990, p. 6.
54. *Employment Gazette*, 1989, p. 672.
55. For example, a package *Returning without Fears* aimed at women returing to work, with an audio-tape to go with the booklet, was advertised. It suggested ways of getting help from friends and family. The price was £24.95. The National Extension College produced an even more expensive set of 'resources': *Return to Work* (£76.60) and Return to the Office (£62.95), written by women returners themselves, also advertised in *Employment Gazette*, 1991, p. 365. *Employment Gazette*, 1991, p. 49 contained a report on a private, fee-paying service: CVs for women returners.
56. Confederation of British Industry (1991), *Discriminate on Ability: Practical Steps to add Value to your Workforce*. The ten-point plan for employers suggested developing an equal opportunities policy, setting an action plan, including targets, providing training for all, monitoring the existing position and progress made, drawing up clear and justifiable job criteria, offering pre-employment training and positive action training, considering the organization's image, considering flexible working, reviewing selection, training and promotion regularly, and developing links with local community groups and schools. It was the most comprehensive mailing of material on equal opportunities undertaken by the government: sent out to 36,000 employers with 50 or more employees; and nearly 3,000 employers were asked what action they had taken on it. The pack was issued to employers in March 1992: a wallet of loose-leaf sheets giving practical advice on equal opportunities based on sex and ethnicity. Of employers who were later interviewed, less than one-third remembered seeing the pack, and of those who did only one-third had used it. That means that about one-tenth of employers receiving the pack actually used it, and these were largely the ones who already had an active EO policy in place: *Employment Gazette*, 1991, p. 572. There was also a government-sponsored initiative: *Business in the Community*. See Perrons, 1996, in Out of the Margins.
57. *Employment Gazette*, 1991, p. 637; *Employment Gazette*, 1992, p. 262; *Employment Gazette*, 1992, p. 597. The Fair Play for Women initiative was established in April 1994 as a joint Employment/EOC project with participation from the Chamber of Commerce, TUC, CBI, TECs, local authorities and the voluntary sector to help women reach their full potential and 'enhance their contribution to the economy and the community'. So far it has sponsored research, conferences, workshops and publications, and participated in a variety of events and schemes. These have included a female firefighters' conference; research on Asian women in employment; a survey to identify good practices among employers and

an Employer Childcare digest. It had its first national conference in 1995 and further action was proposed.

58. In 1980 the National Whitley Council on the Civil Service found that women were receiving too few of the rewards for the work they did. Following this, in 1984 the Minister for the Civil Service set up a programme of action to set up equality committees, appoint equality officers and introduce positive measures for women (Cockburn, 1991, p. 53). This was eventually published as *Equal Opportunities for Women in the Civil Service: Progress Report 1990–91*. Research on attempts to address the remaining problems it identified was published in Equal Opportunities Division, Office of the Minister for the Civil Service, 1992, *Programme for Action to Achieve Equality of Opportunity for Women in the Civil Service*. This report describes a programme of action to give women working in the civil service a fairer deal which was launched by the Cabinet Office. 'There is still further scope for part-time working schemes and other ways of helping staff to combine a career with domestic life', it argued. It did not set targets for the civil service, but only frameworks and guidelines. It had action checklists for managers.

59. In 1991 it was revealed that since 1984 more women had been breaking into junior levels of management in the civil service as a result of flexible working and childcare provision. See *Equal Opportunities for Women in the Civil Service: Progress Report 1990–91*. Women's promotion rates also improved.

60. *Employment Gazette*, 1991, p. 637.

61. *Hansard*, 31 October 1989: Patrick Nichols.

62. BP were using a schools-link programme and talking of setting up a crèche in order to retain mothers, although they conceded that probably the best way to reduce the wastage of skilled women was to promote them: *Employment Gazette*, 1989, p. 404. *Employment Gazette*, 1992, p. 378, describes the workshop for managers on being 'family friendly'.

63. In the *Employment Gazette*, 1992, p. 261, Gillian Shephard, Employment Secretary, announced two new National Training Awards to reward the successful workplace training of women and ethnic minorities.

64. *Employment Gazette*, 1989, p. 143; *Hansard*, 10 February 1989: Patrick Nichols, Secretary of State for Employment.

65. *Employment Gazette*, 1992, p. 33.

66. *Employment Gazette*, 1992, p. 260.

67. *Employment Gazette*, 1992, p. 325. This was reported on the same page as news about top firms in terms of promoting equal opportunities for women.

68. For example, the *Employment Gazette* often featured young technical woman achievers working in typical male fields such as defence.

69. *Employment Gazette*, 1989, p. 662.

70. *Employment Gazette*, 1990, p. 296 reported that women accounted for 35 per cent of the places on the Enterprise Allowance scheme. *Employment*

Gazette, 1990, p. 419, reported that women were just under one-quarter of the self-employed.

71. *Employment Gazette*, 1991, p. 637.

72. In 1990 Joanna Foster of the Equal Opportunities Commission had criticized training and enterprise councils for not appointing more women senior managers. She argued that the lack of training of women was responsible for Britain's poor economic performance.

73. *Beyond the Career Break: a study of profesional and managerial women returning to work after having a child*, Institute of Manpower Studies Report No. 223. Based on a survey of nearly 800 women, it showed women's concerns about slipping behind on the career ladder if they took a break.

74. *Employment Gazette*, 1990, p. 47: According to Patrick Nichols of the DE, using Labour Force Survey data in the spring of 1988, more than 31 per cent of mothers of a child aged under two were in part-time employment but only 12 per cent were employed full-time.

75. Hepple, 1981, *Employment Law*. A minority at the Employment Appeals Tribunal said that a true comparison should be between a man and a woman with a medical condition that would lead to absence.

76. Equal Opportunities Commission, 1986a, pp. 8–9; Department of Employment, 1985, *Unfair Dismissal Law and Practice in the 1980s*, Research Paper No. 53.

77. *Hansard*, 6th Series, Vol. 6, col. 593 (verbal answer to a question by Renée Short).

78. *Hansard*, 5th series, Vol. 961, col. 1494.

79. *Spare Rib*, July 1979; Patullo, 1983, *Judging Women*, p. 25.

80. *Employment Gazette*, 1990, p. 477; *Hansard*, 24 July 1990.

81. *Employment Gazette*, 1991, p. 241.

82. *Employment Gazette*, 1990, p. 477; *Hansard*, 24 July 1990.

83. It was estimated that it would cost up to £500 million per year to implement or 2 per cent of the annual wages bill. At the same time as resisting improved maternity leave for women and other progressive measures, the government was claiming to be one of those leading the adoption of EEC directives! *Employment Gazette*, 1990, p. 487; *Employment Gazette*, 1992, p. 33.

84. *Employment Gazette*, 1992, p. 521.

85. Equal Opportunities Commission and Department of Employment, 1991, *Maternity Rights in Britain: First Findings*; *PSI Maternity Rights: the experience of women and employers*.

86. Department of Employment, 1974, *Women and Work: a Statistical Survey*, Manpower Papers Series.

87. Manpower Services Commission, 1976, *Training Opportunities for Women*, para. 2.2.

88. *Hansard*, 5th series, Vol. 979, cols 411–13: Sir George Young, Under Secretary of State for Health and Social Security.

89. *Hansard*, 5th series, Vol. 942, col. 828; Vol. 958, col. 191.
90. *Hansard*, 6th series, Vol. 65, col. 9446 (written answer).
91. *Hansard*, 6th series, Vol. 979, col. 417.
92. *Hansard*, 5th series, Vol. 923, cols 525 and 592 (verbal answers to questions).
93. *Ibid.*
94. Payne, 1991, *Women, Health and Poverty: an Introduction*, p. 75. Eligibility rules expect claimants to be ready for work the next day and are asked whether they have made childcare arrangements. If not they are likely to lose their entitlement to benefit.
95. Equal Opportunities Commission, 1988.
96. For example, there was a refusal by the Secretary of State for Employment to provide crèches at skill-centres despite the low numbers of women trainees. See *Hansard*, 6th series, Vol. 52, col. 484 (written answer); Wickham, p. 154.
97. Institute of Manpower Studies, 1992.
98. *Employment Gazette*, 1992, p. 361 reported the addition of out-of-school and school-holiday schemes which it was hoped would particularly benefit women who wished to start work when their children began school. Employment Secretary Gillian Shephard set up a new 12-member working group on women to bring 'fresh ideas' to women's issues and raise their public profile. *Employment Gazette*, 1992, p. 259 reported that their first task was to advise on childcare: especially after-school care and school-holiday programmes through the TECs, using school premises in the main. They expected new premises to start appearing later in 1992. They were also to report on what was already available, such as the 'kids' clubs' network.
99. *Employment Gazette*, 1992, had a cover-page photo of a nursery and caption: 'Child's play: the family friendly firm'. *Employment Gazette*, 1990, p. 372 reported that two workplace nurseries were set up in autumn 1990 to cater for civil service 'parents' of children aged six months to five years (one in Liverpool and one in London). *Employment Gazette*, 1989, p. 271 reported that 'family friendly' firm ICI had extended their maternity and parental leave provisions. DVLC Swansea won the 1994 Working Mothers Association Employer of the year with its holiday-play scheme and workplace nursery, enhanced maternity, paternity and adoption leave, child-rearing leave, flexible working hours and elderly care support.
100. *Employment Gazette*, 1990, p. 582.
101. *Employment Gazette*, 1992, p. 321.
102. *Employment Gazette*, 1991, p. 322.
103. International Labour Organization Convention No. 153 on 'Workers with family responsibilities'.
104. *Employment Gazette*, 1990, p. 422.
105. *Employment Gazette*, 1990, p. 422. In Denmark there was 95 per cent

female labour force participation; and the equivalent of £10 million per year spent on childcare. Denmark also took the lead within Europe in the sharing of unpaid caring work within households. Swedish childcare policy was also held up as an example to Britain. In Sweden mothers and fathers were able to share up to 15 months parental leave at any time until the child reached the age of eight. Parents were also entitled to reduce their working day to six hours until the child reached eight years of age. Employers paid a 2 per cent levy towards the cost of childcare.

106. *Employment Gazette*, 1989, p. 271.
107. *Employment Gazette*, 1990, p. 422.
108. National Economic Development Office, 1991, *Women Managers: the Untapped Resource*. Only 1 per cent of top managers and 4 per cent of senior and middle managers were women.
109. The National Council for Single Women, 1974 *The Wages of Caring*.
110. Equal Opportunities Commission, 1980, *The Experience of Caring for Elderly and Handicapped Dependents*, para. 3.1.
111. Walker, 1982a, 'Dependency and old age', *Social Policy and Administration*, **16**, 2, p. 124; Graham, 1983, 'Caring : a Labour of Love', in Finch and Groves.
112. *Welfare Rights Bulletin*, No. 72, 1986.
113. *Hansard*, 6th series, Vol. 6, cols 589–90.
114. *Hansard*, 23 June 1986, cols cols 21–6.
115. *Hansard*, 6th series, Vol. 83, col. 605.
116. House of Commons Expenditure Committee, 6th Report, 1973: *The Employment of Women*; Wickham, 1982, pp. 151–2.
117. *Hansard*, 5th series, Vol. 979, col. 227.
118. *Hansard*, 6th series, Vol. 73, col. 138 (written answer): Alan Clark, Secretary of State for Employment.
119. *Hansard*, 5th series, Vol. 980, col. 391 (verbal answer).
120. *Hansard*, 6th series, Vol. 65, col. 144 (written answer).
121. *Hansard*, 5th series, 1991, col. 980, col. 391 (verbal answer).
122. *Hansard*, 5th series, Vol. 65, col. 144 (written answer).
123. *Hansard*, 5th series, Vol. 905, col. 977.
124. *Hansard*, 6th series, Vol. 74, col. 766.
125. *Hansard*, 6th series, Vol. 38, col. 693 (verbal answer).
126. *Hansard*, 6th series, Vol. 27, col. 15 (verbal answer).
127. *Hansard*, 6th series, Vol. 61, col. 384 (written answer).
128. *Hansard*, 6th series, Vol. 27, col. 15 (written answer).
129. 7th Report of the Expenditure Committee, *Job Creation Scheme*, May 1977, para. 67.
130. Youthaid, 1982, CEP is Working p. 2; Hansard 6th series Vol. 27 col. 15 (verbal answer).
131. Youthaid, 1982, p. 51.
132. *Hansard*, 6th series, Vol. 68, cols 178–80 (written answer).

133. Equal Opportunities Commission, 1986c, *Indirect Discrimination Brief*, 326, June, p. 12.
134. Official Journal of the European Communities, 28 May 1985, No. C129/19 and 20. Christine Crawley had brought the matter to the attention of the EEC in a written question on 29 January 1985(Q.No.1770/84). The answer given by Mr. Phieffer on behalf of the EEC on 15 March was that investigations would take place as to whether the changed eligibility criteria for the Community Programme constituted indirect discrimination on the grounds of sex or marriage.
135. 7th Report of the Expenditure Committee, 1977, *The Job Creation Scheme*, para. 100.
136. *Hansard*, 6th series, Vol. 55, col. 726.
137. *Hansard*, 5th series, Vol. 931, col. 67.
138. *Ibid.*
139. *Hansard*, 6th series, Vol. 58, col. 95 (written answer).
140. *Hansard*, 6th series, Vol. 38, col. 692.
141. *Employment Gazette*, 1989, p. 662.
142. *Employment Gazette*, 1991, p. 7.
143. *Employment Gazette*, 1989, p. 672.
144. Equal Opportunities Commission and Department of Employment, 1991.
145. *Employment Gazette*, 1991, p. 37; *Hansard*, 13 November 1990: Michael Howard.
146. *Morning Star*, 23. August 1995.
147. This was the Women's Liberation Campaign for Legal and Financial Independence, 1975.
148. Leeds Women and Social Security Group, 1983, *The State of Women's Benefits*.
149. *Hansard*, 5th series, Vol. 923, cols 635–6.
150. *Hansard*, 5th series, Vol. 902, col. 664.
151. *Employment Gazette*, 1991, p. 363.
152. Lucy Hyndley, *Unison*, October 1995, p. 4.
153. *Employment Gazette*, 1992, p. 360.
154. The other causal factors according to the Department's spokesman were (in order of importance): levels of skill and experience, job characteristics, family commitments and, finally, a residual element of discrimination. It can be seen here that discrimination was still defined extremely narrowly by this leading official spokesperson.
155. *Unison*, October 1995.
156. *Morning Star*, 14 September 1995.
157. Equal Opportunities Commission, 1995c, *Draft Code of Practice on Equal Pay*.
158. Cockburn, 1991, p. 37 points out that employers were also aware that to appear progressive would enhance a company's public image.

Chapter 8

Twentieth-Century Work and Welfare Policies: Have they Worked for Women?

How do we judge whether twentieth-century employment policies have worked for women? Indicators could be said to include power, status, autonomy, freedom of movement and financial security. Although it is by no means the only important factor in a working woman's life, material wellbeing is the platform on which she can start to build other projects and fully develop her capabilities. Financial rewards and economic security and independence are often closely associated with status and .autonomy, but also have the advantage of being easier to measure at a macro-level than other indicators that policies are working in women's favour. At present, although there have been and still are major differences between women based on ethnicity, sexuality, able-bodiedness and class, most women are linked by economic insecurity. Governments, employers and unions have used and continue to treat women differently on the grounds of sex; and continuing inequalities of income between women and men have been the result.

Although feminists throughout the period have tended to diverge over the question of how to deal with women's double exploitation and poverty which result from the combination of low paid and unpaid work (Dale and Foster, 1986, p. 124) most of the measures for which women have campaigned have had the basic aim of guaranteeing women a degree of financial autonomy. A major concern of first- and second-wave feminism has been on how women's economic independence might be achieved through improving their pay and opportunities within the full range of paid employment. Other feminists have campaigned for benefits that would provide a guaranteed regular income to caregivers and raise the value attached to the unpaid work done mainly by women (Rathbone, 1926), and women's economic dependence within marriage has been extensively critiqued and regarded as a denial of full citizenship.[1]

Some of the measures for which twentieth-century feminists campaigned have been achieved. Major changes have taken place in employment and income-maintenance policies between 1905 and 1995; and governments have claimed that the aims of many of these have been to improve women's financial situation. Yet how much benefit have working women obtained from these developments?

This chapter begins by assessing recent evidence to see whether employment and benefits policies have radically altered women's access to an adequate and reliable livelihood. Many of the findings are depressing. At the beginning of the century, economic dependence and/or poverty were the norm for women. In the 1990s women are still poor and often in enforced dependency. A range of government policies that contribute to women's material position is examined, to see which of them have improved the situation, which are ineffective and which have served to make matters worse. The chapter ends by examining a series of alternative policies that could work in women's economic interests and some strategies for achieving them.

Participation and Poverty

'Give us labour and the training that fits for labour,' said Olive Schreiner in 1911. At that time only 32 per cent of women and girls aged over ten were officially in paid work.[2] By 1994 the official economic activity rate for women of working age in Britain was 70 per cent,[3] and the 1993 Census of Employment found that women were almost half (49.2 per cent) of those in employment. Despite regional variations and differences based on ethnicity[4] women's total participation is projected to continue to grow faster than men's up to the year 2006.

However, despite having become half of the paid workforce, and having access to a range of benefits not available at the beginning of the century, women are still more likely than men to be poor, and their poverty is more severe. Women's relative poverty has implications for their power, status and quality of life and affects important life decisions. The share that women have had of direct income – wages and benefits paid directly to women – increased only from 15 per cent to 22 per cent between the end of the nineteenth century and the late-twentieth century (Lewis and Piachaud, 1992). In 1991 the largest group of women – those married with children – had an average direct income of only £60 per week, compared with £223 for married fathers (Esam and Berthoud, 1991, pp. 2–3). This suggests that a high proportion of wives and mothers are in full or partial financial dependency. The average direct incomes of all women over 30 were less than half of those of men in 1992.[5]

We do not know precisely how many financially dependent wives are poor in the sense of lacking access to goods and services seen as normal in a society, as mainstream poverty studies have traditionally looked at total household income and not at the distribution within families of income and resources.[6] However, we do know that many women are poor and have unequal access to resources even within relatively affluent households and some wives who separate from relatively well-paid men become financially better off on supplementary benefit.[7] It is often difficult to make generalizations about resource allocation within households, because families assume so many forms, for example, because of sexuality, ethnicity or religious beliefs. However, this is precisely why governments' assumptions that women are normally catered for within 'the family' are so damaging to women's economic position. Despite men's formal obligation to maintain their dependents, the State has provided no safeguards for women in families where resources are not shared equitably (Esam and Berthoud, 1991).

The treatment of women in employment and social security policy has assumed that men are not only willing to support their wives but are also *able* to do so. As Hermione Parker, 1993, has pointed out, in 1992 the average male wage of £268 per week was considerably lower than the £416 pre-tax income required to provide a two-parent family with two dependent children in the North of England with a 'modest but adequate' standard of living. This means that a high proportion even of those men who are willing to share their resources equitably are not in a position to keep a wife and children out of poverty. Indeed, despite the partial financial dependency of wives and mothers who are employed part-time, it is these women's small earnings that often keep the family just out of poverty.

Although State benefits are often more reliable than 'housekeeping money' from a partner; and even though single parentood provides an escape from extreme poverty for some wives, 'unsupported mothers' and their children throughout the century have been particularly likely to be poor. Their poverty has been more visible than that of wives and easier to count. In the first decade of this century, 61 per cent of adults on poor relief were women; whereas by the last decade women still made up 60 per cent of supplementary benefits recipients (Lewis and Piachaud, 1992, p. 27). A majority of single parents were found to be in poverty in the 1980s whether or not the parent was in employment (Graham, 1987). One-parent families by the mid-1990s had an average income of only £164.60 per week (1995 Family Spending Survey, Gentral Statistical office).

Policies about the place of lone parents – whether in paid work or at home with the children – have fluctuated throughout the century. Current policy in Britain, as in the USA, is to 'help' lone parents back to work (Millar, 1992, p. 156). However, lone mothers who move off benefit are often no better off unless they move into relatively well-paid full-time paid work, which means a heavy workload and little time to spend with their children.

Older women are poorer than older men (Payne, 1991, p. 45). Only 15 per cent of women obtain a full State pension in their own right; and the relatively few women who have an occupational pension receive an average of only £30 per week, compared with £61 received by men.[8] Employed women's position as a 'secondary labour force' with fewer perks, such as occupational pensions, coupled with lower lifetime earnings and greater unpaid caring responsibilities provide a woman with fewer opportunities to provide for her own old age (Groves, 1992, pp. 205–6), yet in 1995 it was still legal under the Sex Discrimination Act to discriminate against women in terms of pensions.

Income inequality increased faster during the 1980s in Britain than in almost any other country. The highest 10 per cent of income earners became 58 per cent better off, while the bottom 10 per cent became worse off. By 1990 12 million people were in or close to being in poverty, compared with 5 million a decade earlier (Millar and Glendinning, 1992, p. 3). Black women were poorer than white women (Bhavnani, 1994, p. 28). A redistribution of incomes has taken place from poorer to richer, from Black to White people and from women to men.

Women's Poverty and Dependence: Contributory Factors

Lower Rates of Pay

On first sight the wages gap seems to have closed markedly. In 1906, women's average earnings were 43.7 per cent of men's (Roberts, 1988, p. 26) and few women outside the textile trades earned sufficient even to keep a single woman in 'reasonable decency'. Women's average hourly rates of pay by 1994 were 79 per cent of men's[9] but there were great disparities within this: for example, research has found the hourly earnings gap between Black and White women to be as much as 23 per cent (Bhavnani, 1994, p. xiii) and the average hourly earnings of women part-timers were only 59 per cent of those of men working full-time (EOC, 1995d). The differences betweeen men's and women's weekly take-home pay were more considerable because of women's shorter hours of paid employment. By the early 1990s full-time women workers still earned less than two-thirds (64 per cent) of men's average weekly earnings and on average men earned £90 per week more than women. The gap between men's and women's annual and lifetime earnings (which are more significant) remains even greater, partly because women spend far fewer weeks and years in paid employment and more in unpaid work; although even single and childless women earn less than men (Joshi, 1987, p. 130). The pay differential is wider in Britain than in most EC States.[10] Women in the 1990s are the majority of the working poor. More than half of British women working full-time (and 81 per cent of women part-timers) earned less than the European decency threshold of £178 per week or £4.76 per hour in 1990 (Payne, 1991; Buswell, 1992, p. 87).

International evidence shows that strong and properly enforced equal pay legislation makes a difference in closing the 'gender gap' in hourly rates. During the 1970s the legislation did serve to partially close the gap in average hourly earnings. However, British governments have brought in equal pay legislation and amendments largely under duress, which has reduced the effectiveness of the 1970 and 1983 Acts. Leading policy-makers have continued to claim that government 'intervention' to reduce income inequality (for example, through a national minimum wage) will destroy jobs and job prospects;[11] and that the gender gap in wages will decrease automatically as a result of policies of encouraging enterprise and individual initiative. The Equal Opportunities Commission has requested that the European Commission re-examine Britain's equal pay legislation and has also put forward a draft code of practice on equal pay for employers – but this can only work within the existing legislation.[12] However, the number of women who are low-paid is predicted to increase in the rest of the 1990s (Dex, Lissenburgh and Taylor, 1994). This is partly because of reductions in women's hours of paid employment which have undermined most of the beneficial effects of equal pay legislation.

Unequal Hours of Paid Work

At the beginning of the century women who were officially part of the paid workforce generally spent long hours in paid employment. Since the Second World War there has been a particularly strong tendency in Britain for women's hours of paid work to be reduced. Women have shorter average hours of paid work than their European counterparts, whereas men have *longer* hours than average. This disparity has been overtly encouraged by government policy, but without any acknowledgment that this contributes to women's relative poverty. Indeed, we saw in Chapter 7, the creation of part-time employment since the 1980s has been couched in the language of equal opportunities for women. A complicating factor is that Black women, who tend to receive lower hourly pay, are more likely than White women to work full-time. In some ways this suggests that White women are more privileged to be able to work part-time, although the cost (as it has been for relatively privileged women in the past) is financial dependency.

Even women employed full-time have shorter hours in paid work than men. In spring 1995, full-time employees worked an average of 44 hours per week; but 28 per cent of males were regularly employed for more than 48 hours, while more than half of women full-timers had less than 40 hours paid work. Part-time employees, 87 per cent of whom are women, worked an average of only 18 hours per week for wages.[13] By 1995 almost half (47 per cent) of women workers were employed part-time. More than two million part-timers earned too little to pay National Insurance and so did not qualify for unemployment or sickness pay, or for a full State pension (EOC, 1995d). Again there are differences based on ethnicity, with Black women likely to be in longer hours of employment than White women (Bahavnani, 1994, p. xi), presumably partly to compensate for lower hourly rates of pay.

'Flexibility': Women's Irregular and Discontinuous Employment

The economic position of working women in the twentieth century has been affected not only by lower pay, but also by the fact that earnings have been irregular and discontinuous, providing little opportunity to save or make plans. Policy-makers have tended to give the impression that women's chequered patterns of employment have been mainly a result of women's lifecycle, arising from their position as wives and mothers. In fact, the evidence shows that British governments have played a large part in *ensuring* that this was so, for example, through the marriage bar between the wars and the shortage of reliable and affordable childcare.

Women's access to better paid employment has depended a great deal on fluctuations in government recruitment policies. Policy-makers have blatantly used women as the largest group of marginal reserves (smaller groups of reserves have included older workers, school-leavers and people with disabilities) and continue to do so. At a time when the labour market has been 'slack', women, especially wives and mothers, have had more restricted access to paid work; and in two world wars and the postwar boom (and in the current demographic situation) wives and mothers have been actively recruited.

Even in the 1990s, when the demand for women workers is increasing, about half of women workers are marginal, secondary or peripheral in the sense that their work is casual, seasonal or temporary. Outworking (homeworking) in the 1990s has been increasing. Homeworkers are often particularly poorly paid (Lonsdale, 1992), and a high proportion are Black women (Bhavnani, 1994). Contracting out of services by the Civil Service and the National Health Service since the early 1980s has vastly increased the numbers of workers, especially women, who are in insecure casual and part-time employment, most of which has no career prospects. Some women workers now have no fixed hours of employment and are 'on call'. The percentage of women on temporary contracts has been found to be twice as high as that of men (EOC, 1988). Only 20 per cent of mothers with dependent children are in full-time employment. Even well-qualified women returning to the paid workforce after having a 'career break' are apt to become part of the secondary labour market. Part-time employment, despite having become 'normal' for mothers, is still seen as 'atypical' or 'non-standard': caregiving is regarded as exclusively a women's issue, men are presumed to have a domestic helper and no childcare responsibilities and their situation is treated as the norm in employment policy.

The expectation that many male workers will be geographically mobile does not only impact on the women co-workers who are expected to compete on these terms, and whose families are unlikely to be willing to relocate on demand. It also affects the pay levels of working wives who are expected to interrupt their own work and career plans in order to accommodate their husbands' jobs. The EC has been attempting to control employers' expectations that workers must be prepared to be mobile, but the British government has so far resisted these controls, although there has been some modification of mobility clauses as part of recent equal opportunities initiatives in some of the higher grades of the civil service.

Occupational Segregation

It has become conventional to distinguish between horizontal and vertical gender divisions at work. The term 'horizontal occupational segregation' is used to describe the continuing preponderance of women in some jobs and men in others. In some ways, however, the term is a misnomer, since women's jobs generally have lower pay and status than men's jobs requiring similar levels of skill, training and responsibility, and it tends to create a vertical hierarchy of occupations. It is therefore perhaps more accurate to distinguish between inequalities of pay and status *between* and *within* occupations.

It is clear that in general, occupations, industries and workplaces that are numerically dominated by men will probably enjoy significantly higher pay and status that those in which women predominate. Establishments that employ mainly women are three times as likely to have low-paid workers than those that employ mainly men.[14] Segregation between occupations also exists on racial as well as on gender lines, however, and, for example, Black women are more likely to work in the health services and less likely to be employed in clerical work than White women (Bhavnani, 1994, p. 71). Women in general are more likely to do 'manual' than 'mental' work, however (Cockburn, 1991, p. 64).

There are no longer formal distinctions made by governments between 'men's jobs' and 'women's jobs'. However, women are still crowded into a narrow range of occupations (although not the same ones) just as at the beginning of the century. Occupational segregation actually increased after the 1970 Equal Pay Act, as employers were able to avoid equal pay by separating the women from the men and reclassifying their jobs. For women workers it can be difficult and uncongenial to work in areas that men have traditionally seen as their preserves – and this may also help to explain why young women have continued to enter low-paid 'women's jobs' in Britain and other OECD countries.[15] It has also been found that even when women do manage to move upwards through the ranks of previously male-dominated occupations, such as the civil service, these come to be seen as 'feminized' and lose pay and status (Cockburn, 1991).

Within occupations employing both men and women, men almost invariably occupy the lion's share of the more senior positions. Throughout the twentieth century there has been strong and largely successful resistance by governments, employers and men in unions to women managing men. Athough in the 1990s there has been a great deal of publicity given to increases in the numbers of women moving into management, particularly in the State sector, women are still not normally put in authority over men – and when women do achieve seniority, they mainly manage other women. Women are now receiving more job-related training than before,[16] but qualified women usually earn less than qualified men.[17] So far, however, the numbers of women moving up through the occupational hierarchies have been too small to have any measurable effect on women's average incomes.

Hidden Unemployment

Women campaigned at the beginning of the twentieth century to have female unemployment recognized by the State. Although some progress has been made in counting jobless women, the extent of British women's unemployment is still hidden because of the benefit regulations that fail to count most jobless partnered women and solo mothers. However, the 1995 Labour Force Survey showed that nearly one-and-a-half million women would 'like a job' compared with less than one million men. Nevertheless, the government claims that British women's unemployment is lower than men's.[18] There are also unknown numbers of women part-timers who are under-employed: they would take more paid work if they could obtain a suitable job and good quality, affordable childcare.

Benefits Regulations

Many of the benefits available today were not available at the beginning of the century: particularly old age pensions, child benefit and benefits for lone parents, widows and the unemployed. Although the sums allowed have provided for only a very basic living standard, they have generally been reliable, and for many mothers State benefits have compared favourably, as a source of livelihood, with the kinds of jobs available – and some husbands. Benefits have tended to make up a larger proportion of women's than men's incomes. Even so, there are two major problems that largely affect women: aggregation of couples' income for benefits assessment purposes and the loss of benefits as income rises. Many hard-working women, especially mothers, do not receive either a living wage or a benefit, apart from child benefit. There are some moves towards the disaggregation of incomes for benefits purposes, however, largely as a result of rulings from the EC, and partnered carers for frail or disabled people can now obtain a carer's allowance if they have been obliged to give up their paid work in order to provide care (Esam and Berthoud, 1991; Payne, 1991). However, this has not been extended to provide an income for partnered women.

Mothers without a male partner can now obtain a small but regular income from the State, which has enabled young single mothers to keep their children instead of having them adopted (Lewis, 1992). However, the abatement rates are such that lone mothers are likely to be trapped in poverty (Millar, 1992). The cohabitation rule is still enforced and in practice is still applied mainly to women. The aim is to force women and their children into financial dependence on a male sexual partner capable of supporting them; but lone mothers often form relationships with men who are themselves on a State benefit, in which case the benefit for the entire 'family' is paid to the man. Having her income transferred into the name of a male partner can be disastrous for a mother who has learned the difficult task of managing on a very tight budget (Campbell, 1984).

Unpaid Domestic Labour

Women looking after children and a home have been and still are described by the British government as 'economically inactive'. Unpaid housework is not measured in national and international accounting systems, or rewarded as work at all even though much of it is more necessary than much paid work and no economy could function without it.[19] Research in Australia has shown that unpaid household labour accounts for about half of all productive activity (Ironmonger, 1989). Contrary to popular belief, time spent on housework does not appear to have been diminishing (Bittman, 1991; Hartmann, 1981), or to have been substantially redistributed. Although responsibility for unpaid work is not the only reason for women's poverty, it is an important contributory factor, especially at stages in a woman's life when she is doing large amounts of caregiving. For much of the century a majority of women have obtained their keep through doing unpaid domestic work supplemented by low-paid employment.

Childcare has been treated by policy-makers as mothers' responsibility throughout the century and, not surprisingly, so it has remained. In a recent large-scale study of childcare sponsored by the Department of Employment, women were still the 'responsible adult' in 98 per cent of cases and in 92 per cent of cases they bore the financial responsibility for finding substitute care if paid care was required (Corti, Laurie and Dex, 1994). Governments have provided day care for children to assist mothers in earning a living only at times of exceptional demand for women's labour and in stigmatized cases, and this still seems to be the case. In response to the shortfall in the number of young workers in the early-1990s, the government has provided payments to childminders to help some women returners.

Nevertheless, fathers have provided significant amounts of back-up care outside their hours of full-time employment since the Second World War and now, along with other family members, are the chief source of childcare while mothers are working (Martin and Roberts, 1984; Corti, Laurie and Dex, 1994). Increases in the hours of paid employment in the English-speaking countries make it more difficult for men to spend time with their children and harder for women to earn an adequate income. Feminists in the 1990s, unlike their counterparts in the 1920s and 1930s, now argue that men should take greater responsibility for bringing up their children. This view is also widely accepted in policy-making circles in many nations of the European Community, to the extent that the British government is coming to be seen as something of a laggard in its assumption that domestic responsibilities, including childcare, are a problem for women and not men.

In Britain in the 1980s Heather Joshi (1987) calculated that women lose up to half their lifetime earnings as a result of unpaid caregiving – and that if the loss of pension rights is included, the cost is higher still. Research carried out in the 1990s has shown that for women, 'career breaks' tend to mean downward occupational mobility. In 1991 almost one in seven adults provided care 'in the community' (either inside or outside their own home) for a sick, frail, elderly or disabled person. Although total proportions of male and female carers are now very similar and both male and female carers are poorer than non-carers,[20] women provide more hours of unpaid care and are more likely to be involved in caregiving before the age of 60, when they would otherwise be in paid work; and this affects women's ability to stay out of poverty (Glendinning, 1992). Many caregivers are single women who are totally reliant on their own earnings, and who therefore become particularly vulnerable to poverty in their own old age.

Results of Women's Poverty and Dependence

Women's economic dependence on men is still not seen as a problem by leading British politicians despite having been extensively critiqued by feminists throughout the century.[21] Much of women's poverty, especially that of lone mothers, is still regarded by policy-makers and many poverty researchers as being the result of the absence of a male breadwinner.

Women nevertheless suffer both through relative and absolute poverty. Disparities in income between husbands and wives mean that women have an incentive to put up with unsatisfactory conditions within marriage (Wilson, 1987, p. 138), especially when there are children whose material standard of living would fall if the marriage ended. Cases have been cited of women remaining in or returning to violent relationships because of economic pressures (Kempson, Bryson and Rowlingson, 1994). As during the interwar period (Spring Rice, 1939; Orwell, 1959) women also reduce their own consumption of food in low-income households when there is not enough money to feed the rest of the family and pay the bills, with serious implications for their own nutrition and long-term health.[22]

However, others also suffer when women lack an adequate and reliable income, since it is primarily the amount of money the woman of the house has at her disposal that determines whether the family is warm, well-fed and properly housed and clothed, especially in low-income households (Wilson, 1987, pp. 135–54). Women appear to feel an obligation to manage the housekeeping money and make it go round rather than seeing it as being for their own consumption; and women's earnings are also absorbed into household expenditure (Morris and Ruane, 1989). By contrast, male spending on social activities is a protected area, often even after job loss.[23] Women's spending on social activities for themselves is very small. This is not to deny that many breadwinner partners do share their income but there is currently no protection for the dependents of those who do not share, or do not do so equitably (Esam and Berthoud, 1991, pp. 8–9).

Which Past and Present Policies could have Worked for Women?

Although the overall impact of twentieth-century employment policies on the economic differences between men and women has been small, some policies have had a more beneficial impact on women's living standards than others. It seems important to assess which past and current measures have made a difference and which could form an important part of future policy. Chapter 9 examines the potential for State action to build on and improve the more successful policies. Chapter 10 looks at what new additions could be made to these policies to form a feminist agenda for working women from the 1990s.

Equal Pay Legislation

During the 1970s the Equal Pay Act was moderately successful in reducing the 'gender gap' in hourly earnings (see Chapter 6), even though it only covered women doing the same job as a man. From the late-1970s, there were no appreciable further reductions in the pay gap between men and women, even after the 'equal value' amendment (see Chapter 7). The stubbornness with which women's hourly rates have remained stuck at about four-fifths of men's is partly the result of deficiencies in the legislation itself. The British system still largely relies on individual women to bring claims for equal pay for the same work or work of equal value and it is made very difficult for women to do so effectively. The potential exists for the legislation to be further amended and for class claims to be made possible, so that entire categories of workers could have their pay scales revised on the basis of their levels of skill, training and responsibility. This would allow female-dominated groups, such as nurses, to apply for comparable worth with male-dominated groups, such as the police. It was estimated that the short-lived New Zealand Employment Equity Act would have halved the gender gap in hourly earnings by this means. Indeed, in countries such as Sweden where there has been effective 'comparable worth' legislation, women's average hourly rates have become established at 90 per cent of men's. By contrast, in the USA, where equal pay legislation has been even weaker than in Britain, women's hourly pay has remained at only two-thirds of men's (Briar, 1994).

During most of the twentieth century, before the 1980s, the wages of the lowest paid workers – in practice, mainly women – were protected to some extent by Wages Councils. These have now largely been dismantled, which may provide a partial explanation of why the 'gender gap' has not been further reduced. However, the fact that they existed for so long and had some effect demonstrates that there can be a role for the State in fixing minimum wages which, provided they are set at a reasonable level, have some potential for safeguarding women's living standards.

Equal pay laws are unlikely to completely remove the pay inequalities between women and men, but they have the potential to significantly reduce the gender gap in hourly pay. However, these can be easily undermined by other policies, such as encouraging part-time employment for women or allowing employers to argue that unequal pay can be justified on 'commercial' grounds. In order to have a major effect on women's relative take-home pay and lifetime earnings, equal pay legislation needs to be situated in the context of an interlocking framework of policies geared towards improving women's financial position.

Equal Opportunities Legislation

Women's legal right of access to the full range of occupations previously reserved for men was resisted by governments, employers and men (and some women) in unions for a large part of the century. Yet gaining this much-vaunted right has made surprisingly little difference to women's economic position. The country with the strongest equal opportunities legislation in the English-speaking world, the United States, has the widest average wage differential between women and men. A minority of women have benefited from equal opportunities legislation, but the average woman worker has not. Although it is important to preserve the liberal rights which have been gained under this legislation, it is unwise to expect it to work in the interests of most women on its own.

State Benefits

Women do not necessarily receive an adequate or secure income from either the labour market or the marriage market. State welfare benefits have the potential to compensate for the vulnerable economic position of women and especially mothers. However, benefits, because of the specific regulations in Britain, have usually excluded most women and have tended to trap those who are recipients in poverty. Nevertheless, there have been exceptions to this rule. State benefits have been found to be most effective in lifting women out of poverty and providing economic independence when women have been allowed to keep their benefit as well as wages from employment (Spalter-Ross, Burr and Hartmann, 1995). The system of separation allowances for the wives of men in the armed forces during the First World War is a good example. (Braybon, 1981; Braybon and Summerfield, 1987). Widows have been made better off than most unpartnered women (provided they did not remarry) because they were allowed to work and retain their State pension.[24] The reliability of State benefits, compared with either the paid workforce or marriage, can provide a secure base for mothers, which has been one of the reasons for the popularity of universal family allowances among women (Walsh and Lister, 1985). Statutory paid maternity leave provides another example of a benefit that works for women, because it protects women's physical wellbeing while doing essential upaid work *and* safeguards their jobs (McRae, 1991).

State-funded Childcare

Childcare has been provided directly by the State, to varying degrees, through most of the century. Mothers have usually found local authority day nurseries better and more reliable than childminders. The subsidized places made available to the children of low-income householders have also allowed some mothers, especially sole parents, to work full-time for pay. However, the demand for day nursery places in Britain has greatly exceeded supply both in war and peace (Hunt, 1966; Summerfield, 1984). In peacetime, local authority day care has catered for only about 1 per cent of the child population aged under 3 (McRae, 1991). This is far lower than in many other countries, including Britain's economic partners in Europe. In France, for example, State care for pre-schoolers and school-age children has been and still is far more widely available than in Britain (Dex, Walters and Alden, 1993). The low level of provision of affordable childcare in Britain results in an accentuated 'twin peaks' pattern of participation in full-time paid employment by mothers. Two-thirds of married mothers and four-fifths of solo mothers of pre-schoolers still make unpaid caregiving their primary task (McRae, 1991).

During and after the Second World War, State policy was to encourage most working mothers to rely on their own private arrangements, which in practice has meant using relatives and partners when they are willing and available, and childminders. Since the 1970s many women wishing to pursue a career have had to pay high fees for private nursery places. The current policy trend is to encourage 'family friendly firms' to fill the unmet need for childcare. There are certain problems with this. First, because the policy is to encourage rather than require businesses to take account of workers' domestic responsibilities, only some employers, usually the larger ones, provide any sort of assistance. A high proportion of women workers are found in small firms. Second, much 'family friendliness' takes the form of allowing women unpaid time off to deal with domestic work commitments, rather than the provision of services such as childcare to help women engage in paid work. Third, even within large 'family friendly' organizations, not all the workforce is catered for. Often women in the full-time career workforce, who are probably White and middle class, are catered for while women in the part-time jobs and the cleaners (who are more likely to be Black) are less likely to have access to such facilities. At the same time, 'family friendliness' often does not extend to the male career workforce, because domestic responsibilities are still generally seen as women's issues. This allows employers to continue to see women as a distinctive and more expensive workforce. Finally, 'family friendliness' is most likely to occur in the future, as it has in the past, when there is a shortage of skilled workers.

Summary: Why are Women still Poorer than Men?

The State has not solved the problem of gender inequality at work and in many ways has exacerbated it. It is nevertheless clear that in a number of policy areas, women are better off when the State 'intervenes' directly, than when the market is allowed to govern the distribution of income, goods and services. The 'free' market often discriminates on the grounds of gender and ethnicity, avoids equal pay and does not provide non-contributory benefits, so any further erosion of the State benefit system would place mothers and their children in an even more precarious financial position. Further, the market provides childcare only for mothers who can pay or those whose skills are regarded by their employers as worthy of the investment in crèche facilities. The effects of a move towards a 'market-led' approach are illustrated by the gendered results of compulsory competitive tendering for services formerly provided directly by the State. In a study of 39 local authorities and four private contracting firms by the Equal Opportunities Commission, it was observed that between 1989 and 1993 female employment fell by 22 per cent and male employment by 12 per cent. The remaining workers often had to perform the additional work for the same or lower pay. More women than men were made temporary employees. This affected their maternity leave and holiday entitlements. The already low pay of women cleaners was further reduced and many women, who had their hours of paid work cut below the 16 hours needed to qualify for employment protection were thus obliged to take on several part-time jobs to maintain their income. Trade-union membership declined. The quality of working life was reduced for women by the intensification of work, income insecurity and worsened conditions. Despite this, all the organizations studied had equal opportunities policies or statements.[25]

Some major improvements in women's lives have certainly been brought about by social policy. Women have moved out into the public sphere, including the paid workforce, in greater numbers. It is now easier for women to leave unsatisfactory marriages and *de facto* relationships; contraception and safe abortion are easier to obtain and so women have gained a certain amount of sexual freedom. Yet in terms of women's economic position relative to that of men, which is a most fundamental and far-reaching form of inequality, not a great deal of change has occurred during the twentieth century. Further, the outlook is gloomy for the twenty-first century for women in Britain. This is partly because British governments still refuse even to recognize the two most basic factors that contribute towards women's relative – and sometimes absolute – poverty.

The first factor is women's enforced dependency on men, for example, through the aggregation of couples' incomes for benefits assessment purposes. All human beings are *naturally* dependent at some stage in their life cycle, such as in early childhood and frail old age; and adults also sometimes become dependent through ill health or severe disability. However, the majority of adult women (often with children dependent on them) are still forced into a socially constructed *economic* dependence on a male sexual partner. The presumption built into a range of social policies that women's financial needs are being met by their partners and that men's incomes are shared equitably within households has been a major factor in denying women an adequate direct income.

The second factor has been the lack of value or financial support given by governments in Britain to the essential work of caring and domestic labour that is still done predominantly by women as well as the continued undervaluing of the paid work women already do. Entry to paid work, even on a full-time basis, does not necessarily bring women, especially those with children, out of poverty. As a result, despite a long-term impovement in legislation and benefits provision, in the 1990s the 'underclass' of people denied full citizenship because of poverty is mainly composed of women and children. Unless these issues are addressed, women and children will still be poor and the costs of their poverty will be borne not only by themselves but by future generations.

Women have largely won political equal rights during the twentieth century and although these have not had as major an effect as feminists would have wished, women would undoubtedly wish to keep them. In the same way, if women are to obtain economic equality and independence, while this may not remove all gendered social inequality, it will be a major improvement to be safeguarded and built on. Like political equality, economic independence is in many ways a necessary precondition for full citizenship.

Notes

1. Perkins Gilman, 1898, *Women and Economics*; Rathbone, 1926, *The Disinherited Family*; Comer, 1974, *Wedlocked Women*; Barrett and McIntosh, 1982, *The Anti-Social Family*; Delphy, 1984, *Close to Home*; Delphy and Leonard, 1992, *Familiar Exploitation*; Pateman, 1992, 'The Patriarchal Welfare State', in McDowell and Pringle (Eds) *Defining Women: Social Institutions and Gender Divisions*; Lister, 1993, 'Tracing the contours of women's Citizenship', *Policy and Politics*, **21**, 1, pp. 3–16.
2. Roberts, 1988, *Women's Work, 1840–1940*, p. 22. Roberts nevertheless points out that much of women's paid work as well as unpaid work was not counted.
3. Department for Education and Employment, 1995, *United Nations Convention on the Elimination of all forms of Discrimination against Women:*

Third Report of the United Kingdom of Great Britain and Northern Ireland, p. 62.

4. For example, although Afro–Caribbean women have the highest labour force participation rates, women of Pakistani or Bangladeshi origin were considerably less likely to be in paid employment than other ethnic groups (Bhavnani, 1994, p. xi).
5. Equal Opportunities Commission, 1995e, *Some Facts About Women*.
6. Jenkins, 1991, 'Poverty measurement and the within household distribution: agenda for action', *Journal of Social Policy*, **20**, 4, pp. 457–48. For example, Mack and Lansley (1985) in *Poor Britain*, p. 189, argue that although lone parents are more at risk of poverty than two-parent families, women *in general* are not more at risk of poverty than men.
7. Pahl, 1980, 'Patterns of money management within marriage', *Journal of Social Policy* **9**, 3, pp. 313–35; Graham, 1992, 'Budgeting for health: Mothers in low income households', in Glendinning and Millar, p. 217; Millar, 1992, 'Lone mothers and poverty', in Glendinning and Millar, p. 155. In one large study Vogler (1989) found that only a fifth of households pooled income equally and that in most cases the men had a larger share of resources.
8. Equal Opportunities Commission, 1995d, *The Inequality Gap*.
9. *Hansard*, 26 January 1995.
10. 1994 EC Commission's Memorandum on Equal Pay COM(94)6Final.
11. *Hansard*, 7 March 1995: Philip Openheimer.
12. Equal Opportunities Commission, 1995b, *Request to the Commission of European Communities by the Equal Opportunities Commission for Great Britain in Relation to the Principle of Equal Pay*; Equal Opportunities Commission, 1995c, *Draft Code of Practice on Equal Pay*.
13. *Employment Gazette*, May 1995.
14. Millward, 1995, *Targeting Potential Discrimination*, p. vii, citing the 1990 Workplace Industrial Relations Survey which was based on a representative sample of 2000 workplaces.
15. In 1901, 88 per cent of women worked in female-dominated occupations and by 1971 the figure was still 84 per cent: Pateman, 1992, 'The patriarchal welfare state', p. 231; Bruegel, 1983, 'Women's employment, legislation and the labour market', in Lewis (Ed.) *Women's Welfare/Women's Rights*. See also Organization for Economic Cooperation and Development, 1985, *The Integration of Women into the Economy*.
16. *Employment Gazette*, October 1995.
17. Corti and Dex, *Employment Gazette*, 1995, p. 115.
18. Department for Education and Employment, 1995, *United Nations Convention on the Elimination of all Forms of Discrimination against Women: Third Report of the United Kingdom of Great Britain and Northern Ireland*, p. 63.
19. Waring, 1988, *Counting for Nothing: What Men Value and What Women are Worth*; Mahijani, 1992, *From Global Capitalism to Economic Justice*

points out that socialist as well as capitalist countries have failed to measure unpaid household labour in national accounts.

20. Corti and Dex, *Employment Gazette*, 1995.

21 Perkins Gilman, 1898, *Women and Economics*; Rathbone, 1926, *The Disinherited Family*; Comer, 1974, *Wedlocked Women*; Barrett and MacIntosh, 1982; *The Anti-Social Family*, Delphy, 1984, *Close to Home*.

22. Graham, 1993, *Hardship and Health in Women's Lives*, p. 160, cites evidence that women in low-income households are likely to have dietary deficiencies of vitamin C and iron even when the men and children of the house do not; Payne, 1991, *Women, Health and Poverty: an Introduction*.

23. Morris, 1984, 'Redundancy and patterns of household finance', *Sociological Review*, **32**, 3, pp. 492–523; Whitehead, 1981, ' "I'm hungry, Mum": The politics of domestic budgeting', in Young, Walkowitz and McCullagh (Eds) *Of Marriage and the Market: Women's Subordination in International Perspective*.

24. For example, in Sweden there are higher levels of participation in paid work by solo mothers than in the UK because Swedish mothers are able to keep most of their benefit when entering the labour market.

25. Equal Opportunities Commission, 1995a, *The Gender Impact of CCT in Local Government: the Summary Report*.

Chapter 9

Can State Policies Work for Women?
A Theoretical Discussion

The purpose of feminist theory is to provide explanations of the causes of women's subordination, oppression and exploitation, and to bring about change. The kind of change proposed depends on the analysis of the causes of the problem. This theoretical discussion thus has two simple aims. The first is to explore the question of why State employment policies in twentieth-century Britain have reaffirmed women as a marginal and secondary labour force and as 'the domestic sex'. This raises the major question of whether it is realistic to expect government policies to improve the financial situation and status of working women. The second aim of the chapter is therefore to explore the question of whether a 'woman-friendly' State is a theoretical possibility and under what circumstances this might occur in practice. The chapter ends with a discussion of some alternative principles that could inform future policies and benefit working women (and most men).

Explaining the Gendered Policies of the State

Women's subordination in paid and unpaid work has not 'just happened'. Governments in a myriad of ways have helped it to happen and continue to do so. Nor will this situation disappear of its own accord. If we are to break the patterns of gender discrimination at work through social policy it is essential to have a theoretical understanding of the forces in society that are most influencial in maintaining gender inequality at work via the State. The State need not be intrinsically either friendly or hostile to working women: it merely reflects dominant interests and alliances in society. I therefore examine the question: Who benefits from the impoverishment of working women? This form of categorization is helpful and widely used (Bryson, 1992), but needs to incorporate a recognition that some groups are in a stronger position than others to promote their interests at the level of the State.

There is no overall agreement among theorists about who benefits from (or indeed whether anyone benefits) and who has most influence on policies affecting working women, and I will therefore briefly summarize a range of views, drawn mainly from the academic disciplines of social policy, sociology and economics. Despite the ubiquitous and persistent nature of gendered employment and family policies the majority of mainstream writers in these fields have largely ignored these patterns. Critical theorists, particularly Marxist and Marxist–feminist writers, have attempted to fit an explanation of working women's exploitation around a pre-existing analysis of class in a capitalist society. Both these theoretical perspectives have already been critiqued by feminists in the fields of sociology and social policy during the 1980s (Pascall, 1986; Walby, 1986). Nevertheless feminists have differed in their views about whose interests are served by sexist State policies, and feminist theory in this area is still developing.

Gender Inequality at Work Benefits Everyone or No One*

Everyone benefits

Government economic and social policy-making, like the academic discipline of economics, has been largely based on economic liberalism during most of the twentieth century.[1] Such a theory tends to assume that individuals exercise free will in choosing their career paths and that for the most part society as a whole benefits from these choices. The model individual, rational, economic man is seen as maximizing his satisfaction by ruthlessly pursuing his self-interest within the market place. Inequality is viewed as useful because it is thought to encourage competition, although systemic gender (and other) inequalities tend not to be fully recognized. In fact, women's subordination in paid work has often been presented by British politicians as the result of free but irrational career choices by girls and women.[2] Institutional pressures shaping women's economic decisions have been largely overlooked.

The family, which is the main site of non-market work, is ignored by most liberal economists, but there is an implicit (and occasionally explicit) assumption that it is governed by altruism and cooperation, not by competitiveness and self-interest.[3] This is also presumed to be in the public interest. There is also an assumption that the benefits are equitably shared within the family, which is perceived as a single unit (although not primarily an economic unit). When its members arrive home from paid work they are no longer viewed as individuals. The links between the non-market activities of women and the market activities of 'rational men' are usually overlooked. The years of self-sacrifice that are invested, usually by women, in bringing individuals to maturity and caring for them when they are sick or old are for the most part ignored (Bunkle and Lynch, 1992; Hyman, 1994).

Mainstream academic social administration and official policy documents have also operated within an implicit functionalist framework. For most of the century, gendered employment and family policies have been presented by policy-makers as complementary and in the interests of both women and of men.[4] The employment policies of the State have been portrayed as benevolent, or at least neutral or pluralist, and as functioning on behalf of society as a whole.[5] They are characterized by a lack of adequate recognition of the pervasiveness and persistence of economic inequalities based on gender, class or ethnicity, and hence of conflicts of interest.

No one benefits

Since the 1970s it has become more fashionable to claim that no one benefits from gender inequality at work. It has been assumed that employers disadvantage themselves if they discriminate against women and that their economic interests lie in creating a more diverse workforce and making best use of the available talent. However, employers have continued to reinforce most women's disadvantaged position even while claiming to promote equality of opportunity. Equally, husbands can be seen as having an interest in the larger household income and financial security that results from wives' progress in a career. Politicians have couched policies, including discriminatory ones, in the language of equality.

Although it is relatively easy to point out the inaccuracies and inconsistencies in this set of views, it remains by far the most powerful and is the main viewpoint espoused by leading politicians, civil servants and employers. Some feminists also assume that in due course employers will come to fully appreciate women's abilities and occupational segregation will diminish.[6] It represents a major obstacle to genuine change via the State. This is because whether everyone or no one is thought to benefit from women's subordination in paid and unpaid work, the policy implications are much the same. If everyone benefits from gender inequality at work then no change is required. By contrast if no one has an interest in its continuation then it is an anachronism that will in time inevitably cease to exist. In neither case, according to this view, is radical intervention via the State required.

Gender Discrimination Benefits Capitalism and the Capitalist State

During the late 1970s and early 1980s critical social policy theory strongly influenced the academic discipline of social policy although its impact on government policy-making was smaller. It was based on neo-Marxist political economy, which is above all a conflict theory with an historical analysis of patterns of exploitation at work – and which also developed a sophisticated critique of the policies of the Welfare State (Ginsberg, 1979; Gough, 1979). The State was portrayed as acting primarily in favour of the dominant interests in society, despite having degrees of autonomy (Althusser, 1971). Many British feminists shared the ambiguous position with neo-Marxists at the same time critiquing the Welfare State and defending it from increasing attacks by the new right.[7]

However, there have been analytical problems, which have led to feminist critiques of this body of theory (Hartmann, 1979; Delphy, 1984; Walby, 1986; Cockburn, 1991). Marxist analyses have tended to place their main emphasis on patterns of class inequality at work (Gough, 1979); and writers in this tradition have also been primarily concerned with the male-dominated sphere of production for the market rather than non-market production within the family (Pascall, 1986, p. 235). Problems have arisen partly because of Marxist and Marxist–feminist analyses of capitalism itself: the system is assumed to be 'gender blind', which makes it difficult to explain systematic discrimination against women. So debates that took place during the 1970s were keen to see whether and in what ways women's unpaid and low-paid insecure employment could be explained in ways that fitted with this understanding of the nature of capitalism. For example, the 'domestic labour debate' attempted to discover whether women's work in the family was unproductive, reproductive or productive for capitalism.[8] Similarly the 'reserve army debate' was concerned with the question of whether women formed an industrial reserve army, like the unemployed, again of benefit to capitalism.[9] Once it became clear that the value to capitalism of women's insecure employment and unpaid house-work could not be proved, and once feminists began to assert the benefit to working-class men of working women's position there was a loss of interest in the topic by male writers of the left, although the problems for women remained real.

As with the liberal and functionalist ideas described in the previous section, there was an assumption that no one gains from the exploitation of women *as women*. This body of theory has contained an underlying assumption that patriarchy (where it was recognized at all) is merely ideology rather than an economic system (Beechey, 1979, p. 66); and that the systematic subordination of working women is caused chiefly by the influence of sets of old-fashioned ideas that will gradually disappear even without any intervention. Again, an important, although now less powerful set of ideas has assumed that no radical strategies to alter patterns of exploitation and oppression of working women are required.

Men Benefit from Gender Inequality at Work

Since the 1980s, increasing numbers of writers have argued that gender inequalities at work can be explained primarily in terms of their benefits to men. Authors have included socialist, radical and materialist feminists, conservatives and some male writers in the field of gender studies. Radical feminists have tended to argue that men in general have benefited from the subordination of women but with the exception of Catherine McKinnon (1979) most have chosen not to concentrate specifically on gender divisions at work. However, other writers have argued that not all men benefit equally or in the same ways.[10] Some materialist feminists (and some conservatives) have blamed organized labour; some have pointed out the benefits of gender divisions to men both as husbands and co-workers; and in the 1990s there is increasingly a recognition that capitalist employers are also patriarchal. However, pointing out the vested interests of groups of men is not enough on its own to explain the policies of governments. Groups must have sufficient power, either on their own or in alliances in order to influence the policies of the State.

Benefits to husbands (legal or de facto)

Some feminists have focused on the material benefits to husbands of women's unpaid household labour in producing washed and ironed clothes, cooked meals, a clean, comfortable home, cared-for children and a range of personal and sexual services for the man of the house.[11] This unpaid assistance by women results in career enhancement for the married man, from which he reaps the benefits in terms of higher pay and status over time, whether or not the marriage lasts; whereas women tend to experience downward occupational mobility as a direct result of the time and energy spent on household work during marriage (Joshi, 1989, pp. 168–70). While wives may manage the household money during marriage, they do not receive a wage themselves for the housework they do. This results in a massive reduction in lifetime earnings and, partly because of the rising divorce rate, increasingly often to poverty in later life. Christine Delphy (1984) concludes that patriarchy is an economic system, or mode of production, and that the marriage contract is a work contract through which men extort unpaid work from women. Although her work has been critiqued, mainly for her attempt to argue that all women (including those who remain unmarried) constitute a class because of their relationship to the 'domestic mode of production', her analysis of marriage stands up to scrutiny.[12] Whereas Delphy adapts and transforms Marxist economic theory, Pateman (1988) adapts political science theory to argue something similar: that marriage is part of a 'sexual contract'.[13] While men with dependent or semi-dependent wives lose in terms of aggregate household income, they gain personal power in the home and relative freedom from household responsibilities. When women obtain part-time employment, this if anything reinforces women's domestic role. The benefits to men of working women's domestic responsibilities are considerable and have been the subject of campaigns by working men in the past.[14] What is less clear is why working-class men have been able to secure these gains via the State under capitalism, when it might be expected that women could have been used instead to displace men in the paid workforce.

Male co-workers benefit

Working men's organizations have colluded with employers at the level of the State to disadvantage women at work relative to men. First- and second-wave feminist writers have focused on the ways in which men as co-workers have acted to limit women's competition in men's jobs and the better paid positions within occupations.[15] Working men are seen as benefiting in several ways. First, women still seldom compete with men for the best positions. This is often because equal opportunities policies, such as part-time employment and career breaks, in fact increase women's unpaid workload. This then makes it difficult for them to compete with male co-workers who have the unpaid assistance of their wives.[16] Second, much of women's paid work, like unpaid work; is designed to service, support and add value to men's paid work, clerical work being the most obvious example. Third, women are recruited into the jobs which men least like to do, especially work that is low-paid, boring and de-skilled, thus freeing men to do work that is higher status, more varied and provides greater autonomy. In general men enjoy greater physical mobility at work, while women are more confined and subject to greater surveillance (Cockburn, 1985, p. 10).

It is clear that working men both as husbands and as fellow-workers have a vested interest in restricting women's ability to compete in the paid workforce. Whether working men would have the power, as mere employees, to enforce the prioritization of men if employers genuinely wished to encourage competition for the best jobs is much more questionable. The evidence in this book and elsewhere shows that in their negotiations with unions and governments, employers have *allowed* men in the paid workforce to systematically exploit their female colleagues. The task here therefore is to question why this should be so.

Employers as men *benefit*

There is now growing evidence of employers' practices of prioritizing men for the best available jobs, although women have proved time and again between the First World War and the present day the ability to do the whole range of men's jobs just as well and more cheaply than men.[17] Most employers prefer male workers and put them at the head of the queue for the positions in organizations that both men and women workers regard as the most attractive: those jobs with the highest pay, security, skill, status and promotion opportunities (Reskin and Roos, 1990). Suitably qualified women are allowed access only after the available men have been appointed. Government policies have played a major part in assisting this process. The evidence in earlier chapters shows that this happens in war and peace, in booms and slumps. All that changes is the availability of the more attractive jobs: not who fills the best ones.

The benefits to employers of working women's subordination are not immediately apparent and employers' discriminatory practices are difficult to explain. This is partly because the problem is still inadequately theorized. Accepted exisiting bodies of theory – whether liberal, socialist or the numerous strands of feminism – all assume that employers' main interest lies in making money and that gender and race are irrelevant to capitalism.[18] Because of this unshakeable theoretical assumption it is presumed that employers, given the opportunity, will employ whoever proves to be the best value, irrespective of gender or race. First-wave feminists, writing before working women had been given the chance to prove themselves in men's jobs on any significant scale, avoided this question, out of concern that any admission of employers' preference for men would be interpreted as meaning that women were inferior workers. Second-wave feminists have also been relatively slow to address this question. Of those who have, most have assumed that employers' preference for men stems from the fear of male workers' reaction to being displaced by women.[19] Since existing theory cannot explain the systematic prioritizing of men by employers who, according to accepted theory, have nothing to gain and much to lose by discriminating, the gendered employment policies of employers and the State under capitalism have been overlooked or treated as if they were temporary or aberrant rather than endemic.

A few writers have focused attention on employers' regular, ongoing patterns of gender discrimination. Reskin and Roos point out that employers' and managers' preference for men overrides the extra cost. They claim this is because of the force of custom and because hiring is often done by biased subordinates. The fact that other employers are also biased means that patriarchal employers are not undercut (Reskin and Roos, 1990, pp. 36–7). However, this does not adequately explain why capitalists, *if* they are primarily motivated by profits, should consistently act against their own financial interests.

Other explanations have been put forward. Cockburn (1991) has suggested that under capitalism, controlling the workforce and thus providing stable conditions for making a profit is a major consideration. Employers prefer married men, especially at senior levels, and provide longer hours of employment to men with young children, who have the main financial responsibility to maintain their families. By contrast, wives are employed at low pay and/or for short hours and so lack economic independence. In this way both men and women workers are more easily controlled.[20] Presumably, however, if domestic roles were reversed, there would still be a controlling effect on men and women, so this alone does not explain working women's subordination. Nor does it explain why to such a significant extent employers in their own workplaces and at State level have been so keen to maintain existing forms of family life, with heterosexual relationships and subordinate wives. However, Cockburn utilizes the work of Pateman (1988) to argue that employers are party to a 'sexual contract'. Most employers are not only men but also husbands who themselves benefit considerably from having wives (Cockburn, 1991, p. 77). In addition, (although this need not have been the case) owners and managers have granted even the lowest grade male workers their domination of women in the home and the workplace (Cockburn, 1991, p. 62). In the process they have created a more collaborative relationship between male employers and working men.

It may be also be suggested by way of partial explanation that capitalism is a social as well as an economic system. Most employers and managers are men, with a strong tendency to recruit and promote 'in their own image' (Kanter, 1976). Employers sell not only their product but also their public image. Adkins (1995) suggests that with the decline of manufacturing and the growth of the service industries, employees are increasingly on public display and often *become* the product that they are selling. So they are both employed and marketed in ways that fit with prevailing sex stereotypes (Adkins, 1995).

However, it is hard for employers to always preserve a hierarchical sexual division of labour *and* maximize profits. Sometimes, maintaining a gendered workforce wins. Can the social aspects of a system such as capitalism consistently override its economic imperatives? Is this a challenge to the notion that socioeconomic systems in the last analysis are determined by their economic base, or is capitalism a patriarchal *economic* system? This is an area for continuing debate.

Materialist Feminism: From Dual Systems to Patriarchal Capitalism

The strand of feminist theorizing which has arguably made the greatest contribution, since the late 1970s, to an understanding of the ongoing patterns of gender divisions at work is known as materialist feminism. It has represented an attempt to reconcile socialist feminism, which saw patriarchy as mere ideology and subordinate to the capitalist economic system, with radical feminism which perceived patriarchy as older and more pervasive than capitalism, but was in danger of presenting patriarchy as static, universal and ahistoric (Pringle, 1992). Materialist feminist research since the 1980s has shown that patriarchal relations in the workplace are constantly changing and modifying and take different forms in different places, time and occupations and yet hierarchical divisions based on gender have been maintained (Game and Pringle, 1983; Walby, 1986; Bradley, 1989; Cockburn, 1991). This has demonstrated that it is possible to examine both the long-term patterns of power relations as well as the shifts and changes that occur.

Theoretical difficulties have remained, however, which have resulted mainly from the portrayal of capitalism and patriarchy as separate or dual systems. During the late 1970s and 1980s patriarchy was treated by materialist feminists as both external to capitalism and autonomous from it (Hartmann, 1979; Delphy, 1984; Walby, 1986 and 1990). Some feminist writers thus theorized capitalism, represented by employers, as keen to use women workers to displace men, if it was not for the resistance of patriarchy, as represented by working men's organizations.[21] This viewpoint assumed that working men's organizations were mainly responsible for patriarchal relations at work, and that men in the stronger unions were usually powerful enough to override the wishes of employers. In fact, however, there is some evidence that employers have discriminated against women even in occupations where there were no unions.[22] An unintended consequence of this persective is that feminists could find themselves allied with the political right, whose policies usually make working women worse off.

While there is truth and justice in pointing out that working men have striven to impede women's progress, it doubtful whether they have had the power to defeat employers at the level of the workplace or the State. An earlier version of the 'dual systems' theory by Hartmann (1979) argued that patriarchy and capitalism operated together, which fits with other evidence of collusion between employers and working men. However, capitalism itself was still presented as concerned with creating wealth rather than the subordination of women, so it does not address the issue of employers' willingness to give up the opportunity to allow women to compete effectively with the male elite of workers (Hartmann, 1979). Increasingly since the late 1980s feminists writing about women and work have suggested that sexual divisions at work are a central feature of capitalism rather than external to it and that gender is as important as class for analysing the capitalist system.[23] It is clear that the capitalist system – and the State under capitalism – is not solely concerned with profitability and competitiveness and that maintaining the 'sexual contract' appears to be a central and sometime overriding feature of capitalism. Patriarchy is coming to be seen as woven through all social relationships including the employer/employee relationship.[24] For example, some writers are now paying attention to the ways in which employers expect their women employees to conform to heterosexual notions of 'attractiveness' at work (Adkins, 1995); and the ways in which firms have encouraged 'suitable' heterosexual relationships to develop at work (Martens, 1995). In short, capitalism is coming to be recognized as a patriarchal social and economic system.[25] Capitalism may thus be redefined as a dynamic and shifting patriarchal socioeconomic system, which controls and exploits subordinate men by giving them privileges relative to women, including the ability to control and exploit women in the paid workforce, through heterosexual relationships and in the family. In this system both men and women, and their children, are constrained by women's economic dependence on men. In these circumstances, the most revolutionary action working men could take would be to refuse to be bribed and instead to work alongside women to change the system.

The State or the Market?

Since the late 1970s there have been considerable reductions in the 'welfare' aspects of the State, including the 'social wage' and the liberalization of labour markets. If the employment policies of the State have subordinated working women, does this mean that women will be better off as a result of the rolling back of the State? Although this book provides evidence of discrimination against women workers at State level, it is usually the case that when State intervention is reduced, women become even worse off.

It is often assumed that the market does not discriminate on the basis of gender or ethnicity. However, the 'free' market reinforces and perpetuates inequalities, particularly at times of high unemployment. The more unrestricted its activities, the greater is the potential for extremes of exploitation and abuse of women workers and other disadvantaged groups. This is partly because a move away from State intervention towards greater freedom for the market tends to widen financial inequalities generally, including those between men and women. However, this is also because employers tend to be patriarchal, so that when the equally patriarchal but more visible and account-able Welfare State backs out and labour markets are liberalized, working women become yet more vulnerable.

Without State intevention, how can gender discrimination be prevented? It is precisely because the market values – or fails to value – people according to apparently non-market criteria such as their gender, skin colour, social class and sexual orientation that ensuring that all waged workers receive fair treat-ment and an adequate income requires a good deal of bureocratic regulation. In a dynamic and flexible labour market it is hard to monitor discrimination. The private sector is less democratic, accountable and open to public scrutiny than the public sector. Governments, although considerably less accountable to women than they might be, are nevertheless elected on the basis of 'one person one vote'; whereas 'consumer sovereignty' rewards firms on the basis of '£1 one vote', giving women, who on average are poorer, fewer votes than men. Women thus appear to fare best in economic terms under centralized, corporatist systems, especially when they are well represented in decision-making positions (Cockburn, 1991). Despite the recent assertions that there are 'limits to social engineering' to reduce gender inequality (Hakim, 1995), Britain has not even begun to explore where those limits might lie and its governments have for the most part done more to perpetuate than to reduce gender inequality. In countries such as Sweden where there is a strong State with more control over employers' practices, the 'gender gap' in paid and unpaid work is much smaller than in 'market liberal' nations such as the United States and Britain.[26]

Even in the English-speaking countries, some State policies have ben-efited women. Whereas the State provides a 'social wage' of subsidized health care, housing, childcare and transport, which are of particular benefit to women, the market does not. While employers, especially at times of high unemployment, tend not to recognize or reward 'non-market' activity, perfomed mainly by women, the State has made a small start in this direction. Lone mothers receive a State benefit which enables them to live independently of men, albeit frugally.[27] The payment of child benefit provides all mothers of young dependent children with at least a small reliable income; and even though it has not changed women's larger share of poverty there is scope for these benefits to be expanded. Equal pay legislation, which was bitterly op-posed by employers, has had some impact on the hourly wages gap, even though the narrowing of the weekly wages gap has been slowed by the increase in part-time employment. Equal opportunities legislation has been relatively ineffective in raising women's pay and status, but has nevertheless established important principles. Combined with longer term changes such as the vote, married women's property rights and easier divorce, these policies have im-proved women's social standing to some extent, although without having provided the genuine choices that come from economic equality and inde-pendence. Despite considerable variations, patriarchal capitalist, but more democratic, governments have allowed women to make small and fragile gains. Finally, the State provides an arena for struggle and united action by women and other disadvantaged groups, which the market cannot (Sharp and Broomhill, 1988).

The Patriarchal Capitalist State: Hidden Problems and Potential

One of the obstacles to positive change for working women has been that politicians have tended to obscure the multitude of ways in which employment and family policies subordinate and exploit working women. They tend to futher claim that it is impossible or inappropriate for the State to 'intervene' to undo the effects of discriminatory policies. Key issues affecting women's standard of living have been removed from the political arena and treated as routine administrative matters, thus disguising some of the realities of power (Maguire, 1992). The role of the State under patriarchal capitalism has been to 'intervene' only when parts of the labour market or some families become 'dysfunctional'. In fact, this usually occurs when the ordinary daily forms of exploitation in paid jobs and the home break down – for example, when abuses of power occur in paid work or in the home – and social policies usually try to restore the conditions for paid or unpaid working relationships, minus the extreme forms of abuse. First, therefore, it is important to expose the ways in which discriminatory social policies have been disguised and to open up the hidden potential for change.

The Hidden Problem of State Discrimination against Working Women

Long-term systematic discrimination against working women is not admitted by policy-makers; nor does it figure in most social policy textbooks. It has not become 'common knowledge'. Indeed, social policy has been portrayed by policy-makers and most historians and mainstream social policy writers as acting in women's interests.[28] Beverley Thiele (1992) has described a number of ways in which political thought and language has been and continues to be used to conceal the stark fact of sex discrimination by the State. These include pseudo inclusion, dualisms, naturalism, appropriation and reversal. They illustrate some of the 'tricks of the trade' which have been practised by policy-makers in Britain and similar nations (Thiele, 1992, p. 32) and which are evident in this book.

Direct exclusion of women from policies designed for men has transparently affected working women's financial position especially in the earlier part of the century. However, women have not simply been 'left out' or overlooked from employment policies. During much of the century women have ostensibly not been barred from most training and employment. Instead, they have often subsequently experienced 'pseudo-inclusion' in ways that produce marginalization and disadvantage, as with the interwar Anomalies Regulations where, having been admitted to the National Insurance scheme, women paid contributions but did not receive benefits if they married – as most women did. Throughout the century, women have been treated as marginal reserves of labour, experiencing pseudo-inclusion as 'substitutes' in the better paid, male-dominated occupations only when there has been a shortage of suitably trained men. 'Dualisms' have also set up separate roles that are viewed as complementary and equivalent, when in reality women's roles have been auxilliary and supportive to those of men. The postwar policy of promoting women's 'dual role' has had results that are no different from those of 'separate spheres'.

Even policies of promoting equal treatment for men and women at work still produce unequal outcomes when the realities of most women's domestic responsibilities are wilfully ignored by the British equal opportunities legislation. We have also seen the use of generic and inclusive language increasingly being used to disguise discrimination. For example, discussion by policy-makers of the caring responsibilities of 'parents' almost invariably refers to mothers, since fathers are increasingly expected to work hours that are incompatible with parenting.

When domestic responsibilities are recognized, however, this involves treating women as 'other', or 'atypical' workers, and men as the norm, which almost invariably involves payment of 'atypical' wages for women. The resulting economic inequality between men and women is then treated as if it is the result of 'nature' or biology and as such requires no further explanation. By a further sleight of hand, 'naturalism' has in recent years equated childbearing not only with childcare but also with 'community' care for the elderly, sick and disabled and for healthy adult men by women. Finally, by a process of 'appropriation and reversal', what women have demanded has been taken and altered. For example, women's 'right to work' demanded by feminists at the beginning of the twentieth century has increasingly become an *obligation* to work in de-skilled, dead-end jobs which still do not pay a living wage. Although to a great extent employment policies towards working women have been implicit and hidden it is undeniable that, as Pateman (1992, p. 232) puts it, 'the State has confirmed rather than ameliorated our social exile'.

The Hidden Potential of the State for Overcoming Discrimination

Women's position as a secondary workforce and as the domestic sex has been reinforced, as we have just seen, by what governments do. But working women's subordination is also maintained by what governments normally *refuse* to do. Just as the State's own discriminatory practices are hidden, its powerful potential to overcome inequalities is also concealed. Policy-makers have often given the impression that governments do not have the power or the resources to alter the basic facts of working women's relative poverty and lowly status. Further, it is presented as being unnecessary and undesirable for the State to 'intervene' unduly in the 'natural' workings of the two areas in which women work: the 'free' labour market and the 'private' family.

In reality the State has enormous powers to intervene in market and non-market work. These are glimpsed only occasionally, usually during severe labour shortages or threatened social unrest. At such times governments have used their powers to take over and run private industry, conscript and direct both male and female workers into paid work in any part of the country, require women to work at nights, prevent workers from leaving their jobs, provide 24-hour nurseries and subsidized British Restaurants, give married mothers an adequate income based on the numbers of dependents and pay generous benefits, considerably higher than prevailing wages, to unemployed women workers. Since governments are able to acquire and use such powers at times of national emergency it seems logical to suppose that the State is also capable of providing women employees and domestic caregivers with more equal, adequate and reliable incomes and higher status in more 'normal' times. In Chapter 10 I discuss the kinds of alliances that might be formed to transform employment policy in peacetime and the specific kinds of policies around which these might form.

Alternative Policy Principles

Much of social policy-making takes place outside the 'political' arena. Political decision-making by elected politicians is routinely shaped by established principles and guidelines which inform ongoing administration and the drafting of new legislation by civil servants. These sets of ideas and policy principles, variously described as ideology, hegemony and conventional welfare discourses, have a major ongoing effect on policy outcomes (Bryson, 1992, p. 30). They are often used to set limits on what is seen as politically feasible. However, to bring about significant improvements in women's lives, these principles have to be challenged.

One of the factors that has divided working women and men – and has divided women among themselves – has been the established practice by governments of treating certain policy principles as opposites and alternatives, from which people are obliged to choose. This use of either/or dichotomies has been described as a central feature of patriarchy (Morgan, 1977). Currently these choices include work versus welfare, individual freedom versus collective responsibility and equality versus difference. Yet it is possible to have all these in ways that could unite women, and give men the impetus to work with women, while addressing the causes of working women's inequality and poverty. By this means it would be possible for women to have full economic as well as political citizenship rights, and so to have established the necessary preconditions for social equity.

Work and Welfare

Two main principles have informed the relationship between work and welfare policies in the English-speaking nations. First, to a large extent 'work' and 'welfare' have been mutually exclusive. With few exceptions since the 1830s, welfare benefits have not been paid to people who are in paid employment.[29] This principle was designed particularly to give male workers incentives to enter paid employment and so become 'independent workers'.[30] By contrast, women, especially wives and mothers have tended to be treated as the dependents of men – and again, with minor exceptions, State welfare has generally been paid directly only to mothers without a male provider. Once a person starts paid work or enters a heterosexual relationship they normally lose their entitlement to benefit.[31]

Second, as with other dualisms, the work/welfare dichotomy has regarded State welfare benefits as inferior and, far as possible, has made benefits lower than income from work. The principle of 'less eligibility' which was introduced in the 1934 Poor Law Amendment Act and still informs benefit provision in Britain, New Zealand, Australia and the United States, ruled that recipients of State benefits should always be worse off than waged labourers. 'Less eligibility' is in fact based on a view of human nature that is unsupportable, especially regarding women, because it assumes that without economic incentives, people will not work. In fact, women perform huge amounts of essential work without any financial reward,[32] and men also do substantial amounts of unpaid work in the home and community. Policy-makers are able to overlook this flaw in the argument by choosing to regard the unpaid work done mainly by women in the private sphere as not being real work.

However, there have been some problems with the work/welfare divide. It has not only impacted on the living standards of claimants and low-paid workers, but it has also to some extent undermined policy-makers' intentions. Instead of creating incentives to move into paid employment, this dichotomy creates a poverty trap, as male and female low-paid employees, but especially employed lone mothers, are often no better off than beneficiaries of the State, once work-related expenses such as childcare and transport are taken into account. Not surprisingly, solo mothers in Britain have a relatively low labour force participation rate. Because there has also been considerable ambivalence on the part of policy-makers about whether 'unsupported' mothers should be at home caring for their children or out in the paid workforce, fewer efforts have been made to force mothers (compared with fathers) into paid work from benefits – although the threat is ever-present. However, efforts to force solo mothers into economic dependence on a man via the 'cohabitation rule' have been stronger, often with disastrous financial consequences for women. Oddly, this policy also acts as a potential disincentive for women to enter stable heterosexual relationships (Spicker, 1988, p. 25) but encourages separation and divorce, promiscuity and same-sex relationships. In fact the work/welfare dichotomy creates disincentives for people to enter and remain in paid employment and 'normal' family relationships. This, however, may help to reduce the opposition to pressure for the removal of this fundamental principle.

A combination of work *and* welfare, for women and for men, would be an effective way of solving several of these problems. This is discussed in more detail in Chapter 10. Briefly, however, benefits would then provide a platform rather than a pit for those moving into the paid workforce, and welfare would not be assessed according to relationship status. If everyone was paid an adequate living allowance, irrespective of whether they were in paid employment, effectively some acknowledgment would be made of the unpaid work of both women and men. It would also help to overcome the long-standing division between feminists over whether mothers should receive a carers' benefit in order to stay at home with their children or whether all women should compete in the paid workforce. The principle of work *and* welfare for women and men would help to overcome the gender stereotyping of domestic and caring work and to continue the struggle for equality for women in the paid workforce. Finally, it is an issue that is already proving popular with men and could provide the basis for united action.

Equality and Difference

As with work and welfare, women have also been led to believe that we have to choose between equality and difference. Equality-versus-difference has become a major area of contention, especially in the United States (Phillips, 1992) and this dichotomous view is encouraged by social policies. Both 'equality' and 'difference' are encouraged by government policy, but separately and both in ways that disadvantage women. For example, being 'equal' in the workplace usually entails working hours that are incompatible with childcare. Being 'different' tends to mean part-time employment and the lack of prospects or a living wage. However, equality and difference are not opposites or even incompatible. In fact, the opposite of equality is inequality, whereas difference could coexist perfectly well with political and economic equality. To accept that women have to choose between 'equality' and 'difference' when women are inevitably different from men in some ways automatically disadvantages women (Scott, 1992, p. 260). The political notion of equality includes and depends on the acknowledgment of difference (Scott, 1992, p. 261). Further, differences based on factors such as gender or race should not lead, as they do now, to economic inequality (Phillips, 1992, p. 209). However, British policy-makers and employers have made gender differences count more than they need to. Women should not have to pay economic penalties for difference and we should not have to choose between equality and difference.

'Being equal' is, under current legislation and employment practice, usually interpreted as meaning that women have to be more like men in order to obtain the same rewards. In fact, British 'equality' legislation has never been designed to promote equality, but rather to give individual members of designated groups better opportunities to compete and so become unequal. A first stage was to remove the formal barriers to competition and promote equal treatment. However, equal or 'sex blind' treatment in paid employment can actually damage the prospects of women whose unpaid work responsibilities and lack of support make it difficult for them to compete effectively (Joshi, 1989, p. 157). A second step, used extensively in the United States and to a lesser extent in the other English-speaking nations, has been to discriminate in favour of disadvantaged groups – or treat them unequally – for a period of time until occupational segregation had been broken down and the target groups become more equally represented throughout occupational hierarchies. This, too, has had little impact in reducing economic inequalities. This is partly because governments do not take account of the ways in which gender inequalities continue to be constantly renegotiated and recreated (Game and Pringle, 1996, p. 190). There is a further problem: the more unequal the system, the more bitter will be the opposition to 'interlopers' from those occupying, or expecting that they will occupy, the most prized places in occupational hierarchies. There are in any case no guarantees that even if target groups do obtain some of the top positions, they will behave substantially differently from the White middle-class males who have created and shaped these positions.[33] The longer term challenge, therefore, is to promote 'vertical equity' by reducing economic inequality more generally (Bryson, 1992, p. 64). At present, however, the trend is in the opposite direction and it will require a strong and unified opposition to reverse it.

Gender inequality, by contrast, simply means that women because they are women are denied or given less of what men are allowed (Phillips, 1992, p. 205). Economic inequality between women and men arises from the fact that the average woman does a combination of more unpaid work and less paid work, as well as receiving lower rates of pay in employment.[34] It is less about essential gender difference than the lack of value given both to women and to women's work under patriarchal capitalism.[35] There are nevertheless significant inequalities between women.[36] Black women are the poorest and often have the least attractive jobs (Bhavnani, 1994, p. 170); middle-class White women have gained most from 'equality' policies since the 1970s. There are also inequalities between men.[37] These are real and illustrate the fact that past and present discrimination by the State and employers has not taken place exclusively on the grounds of gender. Nevertheless, there is considerable inequality between the economic positions of the average woman and man which stems directly from the ways in which gender differences such as the women's ability to bear children have been treated by governments and employers.

Policy-makers have generally treated women as different and inferior. The main measure of value is money – and it is significant that women have been classed and paid as doing 'work of national importance' when making munitions of war but not when raising children. Women are currently encouraged by higher pay to move out of traditional female occupations such as teaching and nursing into the armed forces.[38] Contrary to the official view, both first- and second-wave feminists have at times claimed that women are different from and superior to men. This has been a useful political strategy for overcoming women's internalized feelings of inferiority which stem from living under patriarchy and in building a strong women's movement (Walby, 1990). However, in reality we do not know how much of women's and men's typical behaviour is socially constructed, how much of women's 'niceness' is the result of oppression and how far this would change if women obtained genuine equality. In recent years a number of feminists have also expressed the fear that any statement of women's 'difference' will be taken by conservatives as a case for separate spheres that will be used to further ghettoize working women into low-paid and unpaid work, because they fuel the assumptions that women lack ambition, not that women are victims of discrimination.[39] The notion of difference needs to be used with caution, with full recognition of the ways in which it can be misused.

Can the notion of women's 'difference' from men actually help to produce greater economic gender equality (Meehan and Sevenhuijsen, 1991)? There is a case for treating women as a group differently to compensate for the effects of past sex discrimination (positive action), and to take account of biological difference: for example by providing paid maternity leave. This is not the same as treating women and men differently in order to reinforce inequality. There is also still a case for diversity and autonomy. There is no reason why diverse groups, linked by common interests, should not assist demands for economic equality. Women *as women* have long experienced discrimination at work and it is women who have a material interest in changing that experience.

Individual Freedom and Collective Responsibility

Recent social policy directions have been strongly informed by neo-liberalism, which promotes individual freedom and individual responsibility. Politicians using this perspective have argued that the Welfare State takes both away. Consequently publicly funded institutions, services and cash transfers have been replaced by 'community care', reductions in the 'social wage' and more stringently tested benefits. In many ways, these policies have detracted from most women's and other low income groups' ability to exercise individual freedom and choice. In particular, however, allowing freedom to competitive individuals in the public sphere of the market incurrs hidden costs for women in the private non-market family unit. The reality is that individual responsibilities do not tend to fall on the same individuals who enjoy their freedom.

However, it is not necessarily the notions of either individualism or liberty *per se* that are problematic to women. The problem is that women have been placed in a situation where it is difficult to exercise freedom and choice in any real sense. Women have largely obtained negative equal rights freedom which has removed formal barriers,[40] but have still not obtained positive, enabling freedom. In particular, most women have still not gained the secure economic base that is a precondition for personal freedom. To millions of women whose personal living standards are hidden behind the façade of 'household income', and who cannot obtain a State benefit in their own right, individual assessment would be a major improvement.[41]

In some respects critics of the Welfare State are correct in their assessment that it removed individual liberty. Individual decisions whether to seek, accept or change jobs or to enter or leave personal relationships are in reality profoundly mediated by the current benefits system as well as hidden within family relationships. However, the more residual and selective the Welfare State is, the more intrusive and restrictive it becomes. Arguably the most humanitarian and effective way to promote genuine freedom for all women and men would be to provide universal benefits, paid to individuals not households, irrespective of employment or family circumstances and geared to the cost of living. This would have the additional advantage of attracting the support of both women and men, libertarians and socialists (Purdy, 1994).

Conclusions

Could State employment policies work for women? I have argued that capitalism is patriarchal and that discriminatory employment policies result from collusion between employers and working men. However, the system is not static: it is constantly changing and so alliances can also shift. If this is true, the State under capitalism is not inevitably patriarchal, but has been discriminatory only because of the combination of patriarchal forces acting upon it. Moreover, there is more scope for improving the conditions for working women via the State than the market. I have identified a number of principles that would form the basis for policies that could work for women. The challenge is to find a mix of policies that will bring about this level of equality and attract widespread support from working women and men.

Notes

* An earlier version of some of the material in this chapter was published in Briar, 'Explaining women's position in the workforce: a social policy analysis': Morrison *Proceedings of the 6th Conference on Labour, Employment and Work*, Victoria University of Wellington, March 1995.
  1. Although economic liberalism has to some extent waxed and waned during the century and has been modified at times by social democratic policies, it has been the major influence on social and economic policies in

the English-speaking nations. 'Economic man' is used as a generic term, although men dominate most market activity.

2. There has been at times an implicit assumption on the part of policy-makers that women make a 'rational' choice if they invest their energy in supporting their husbands' careers; but the rising divorce rate would remove even the superficial plausibility of this argument.

3. Folbre and Hartmann, 1988, 'The rhetoric of self interest and the ideology of gender', in Klamer, McCloskey and Solow (Eds) *The Consequences of Economic Rhetoric* put forward a critique of economists such as Becker, 1973, 'A theory of marriage, part one', *Journal of Political Economy*, **81**, pp. 813–46 and 1974, 'A theory of marriage, part two', *Journal of Political Economy*, **82**, pp. 1063–93 and theorists who do not directly address the issue of non-market labour.

4. As Cockburn, 1985, *Machinery of Dominance*, p. 223, points out, 'complementarity is structured in such a way as to produce inequality'.

5. Many texts in the social administration tradition, especially up to the late 1970s, defined social policy in ways that assumed the benevolence of the State and a common public interest. This analytical framework has allowed policies which have excluded women from earning an adequate living to be presented as 'protecting' women. Just one example is: 'Policies are ways of meeting needs, of satisfying our wants or achieving our purposes', Tim Booth, 1979, *Planning for Welfare – Social Policy and the Expenditure Process*, p. ix.

6. For example Reskin and Roos, 1990, *Job Queues, Gender Queues*. See also the literature on 'family friendly' firms.

7. This shift to liberalism is in some ways unfortunate for women, since all disadvantaged groups are relatively better off in economic terms under a system which is more egalitarian and has a more extensive 'social wage'.

8. For example, the 'domestic labour' debate that took place during the 1970s was concerned with whether domestic labour was unproductive, reproductive or productive in its benefit to capitalism. See Dalla Costa and James, 1972, *The Power of Women and the Subversion of the Community*; Fine and Harris, 1976, 'Controversial issues in Marxist economic theory', *Socialist Register*, pp. 141–78; Seccombe, 1974, 'The Housewife and her labour under capitalism', *New Left Review*, **83**, pp. 3–24. For feminist critiques, see Walby, 1986, pp. 16–20, and Bradley, 1989, *Men's Work, Women's Work*, pp. 56–7.

9. Beechey, 1977, 'Some notes on female wage labour in capitalist production', *Capital and Class*, **3**, pp. 45–66 saw married women as a 'reserve army' of great value to capitalism at times of labour shortage, because once they are no longer required their upkeep will be met within the family rather than by the State. However, the degree of sex segregation in the labour market led writers such as Bruegel to suggest that in peacetime (that is, when there is not a severe shortage of male workers) only women in mixed occupations are likely to be used as a 'reserve army of labour'

and to point to the fact that in recessions there are higher levels of job loss from mixed occupations than from single-sex jobs. Bruegel, 1979, 'Women as a reserve army of labour: A note on recent British experience', *Feminist Review*, **3**, p. 16; see also Milkman, 1976, 'Women's work and the economic crisis', *Review of Radical Political Economy*, **8**, 1.

10. See, for example, Beechey, 1979, 'Patriarchy', *Feminist Review*, **3**, p. 66. Other writers dislike the term and refuse to use it at all.

11. Delphy, 1984; Novitz, 1987, 'Bridging the gap', in Cox (Ed.) *Public and Private Worlds*; Dex, 1987, in *Women's Occupational Mobility* and Delphy and Leonard, 1992, *Familiar Exploitation* have all shown that wives returning to paid work experience downward occupational mobility. A number of studies have shown that wives have the main responsibility for unpaid work. Finch, 1983, in *Married to the Job*, showed that wives also often provide considerable direct unpaid help with their husbands' careers, even to the point of substituting for him where necessary; and although she argued that by this means capitalist employers obtain two workers for the price of one, it is also possible to argue, as Delphy does, that there are substantial benefits to the husbands in whose name the work is generally carried out.

12. For further discussion of this point see Walby, 1986, pp. 37–42. Delphy's 1984 work had already addressed the issue of the exploitation of ex-wives by ex-husbands. In Delphy's later work with Leonard, 1992, she also comments on the domestic exploitation of single women by male relatives other than husbands.

13. Pateman, 1988, *The Sexual Contract*. This argument is taken up by a number of writers including Joshi, 1989, and Cockburn, 1991.

14. For example on the family wage see Hartmann, 1979; Barrett, 1980, *Women's Oppression Today: Problems in Marxist Feminist Analysis*; Land, 1981, 'The Family Wage', *New Statesman*, 18 December, pp. 16–18.

15. For example, Drake, 1917, *Women in the Engineering Trades*; Rathbone, 1926, *The Disinherited Family*; Hartmann, 1979; Walby, 1986; Cockburn, 1991; Game and Pringle, 1983, *Gender at Work*; Reskin and Roos, 1990; Adkins, 1995.

16. Cockburn, 1991, found that although career breaks and part-time work put paid to women's promotion prospects, interestingly men praised these strategies as enhancing working women's progress.

17. Reskin and Roos, 1990, *Job Queues, Gender Queues*, present evidence from a range of occupations that this process has continued since the 1970s. Research by Adkins, 1995, also shows that employers discriminate in favour of working men.

18. It has not only been liberals, Marxists and Marxist–feminists who have assumed that capitalism is not patriarchal, but 'dual systems' theorists such as Hartmann, 1979, and Walby, 1986, also assumed that capitalism was 'gender blind'.

19. Walby, 1986; Reskin and Roos, 1990, 'Bringing the men back in: Sex

differentiation and the devaluation of women's work', *Gender and Society*, **2** (March), pp. 58–81.

20. Cockburn, 1991, argues that 'Employers will sometimes forgo immediate profit in the interests of increasing their long-term control over the labour force, and in doing so will act in ways that are at odds with their apparent capitalist goals in order to maintain sexual divisions.' See also Game and Pringle, 1983, p. 22.

21. The notion of a 'dual system' in conflict between working men and employers over women's labour is most clearly advanced by Walby, 1986, *Patriarchy at Work*.

22. Martens, 1995, unpublished paper, Sociology Department, University of Lancaster, cites the example of the exclusion of women from banking before the Second World War.

23. Cockburn, 1991, p. 61; Adkins, 1995; Game and Pringle, 1996, 'Gender at Work', in Argyrous and Stilwell (Eds) *Economics as a Social Science*, p. 189.

24. Joan Acker, 1989, 'The problem with patriarchy,' *Sociology*, **23**, 2, pp. 235–40 argues that patriarchy need not be seen as an autonomous system.

25. Briar, 1987; Calasanti and Bailey 1991; Adkins, 1995. Eisenstein, Z. (1979 and 1984) also had an analysis of capitalist patriarchy but was criticized by Walby, 1986, for then analysing the capitalist and patriarchal elements of the system as though they were separate. Young, 1981, *Women and Revolution*

26. Adams and Winston, 1980, *Mothers at Work*; Ruggie, 1984, *The State and Working Women*; Calasanti and Bailey, 1991; Bryson, 1992; Hyman, 1994, *Women and Economics*, p. 185.

27. Kay Saville Smith (1987) 'Women and the State' in Cox (Ed.) *Public and Private Worlds*; Pateman, 1992, 'The patriarchal welfare state', in McDowell and Pringle (Eds) *Defining Women*, p. 234.

28. For example, most historians of the Welfare State uncritically accept that 'protective' legislation was designed to safeguard women's interests, not to make it harder for women to compete with men in paid work. See, for example, Fraser, 1973, *The Evolution of the British Welfare State*.

29. Family allowances have been paid regardless of employment status, but have been too low to be seen as a threat to employment incentives. An exception was the introduction of the Family Income Supplement during the 1970s.

30. Using a sliding scale of welfare benefits to supplement low wages under the Speenhamland System was said to create disincentive to seek employment and was discredited by the 1832 Poor Law Commissioners. This is different from the kind of universal benefit described in Chapter 10, because the universal basic income would not be phased out as a person's income increased.

31. Widows have been an exceptional case because they have been able to do paid work and keep their pension. Because of this, widows' labour force

participation rates have been higher than those of divorced or never-married mothers. However, they have lost that pension if they remarried.

32. Oakley, 1974, *The Sociology of Housework*, and Bittman, 1991, *Juggling Time*, have found that full-time mothers of pre-schoolers often work around 100 hours per week. Hartmann, 1981, 'The family as the locus of gender, class and political struggle: the example of housework', *Signs*, **6**, 3, found that husbands were a net drain on wives' time and energy.

33. Swasti Mitter, 1994, *New Left Review*, **205**, May/June, p. 101, reminds us that there are no guarantees that ambitious women are innately more compassionate than men.

34. The average woman has to work 50 per cent longer than the average man to obtain the same level of income according to Glendinning and Millar, 1991, 'Poverty: the forgotten Englishwomen. Reconstructing research and policy on poverty', in McLean and Groves (Eds) *Women's Issues in Social Policy*.

35. For example, in same-sex relationships, the more employment-oriented partner has been found to distance themself more from unpaid household responsibilities. This can be seen as a result of geater power of individuals in full-time, well-paid employment. See Habgood, 1992, 'On his terms: Gender and the politics of domestic life' in du Plessis, Bunkle, Irwin, Laurie and Middleton (Eds) *Feminist Voices*, Auckland, Oxford University Press.

36. For example, Lewis, 1992, p. 10, cites the differences between the lone mother and the professional woman in a dual career couple who can pay for a nanny.

37. Collinson and Hearn, 1994, for example, argue that there are major differences between men based on disability, class and sexuality.

38. According to Reskin and Roos, 1990, p. 39, women were attracted into the United States military by the fact that they could earn 40 per cent more than in civilian employment.

39. Milkman, 1986, 'Women's history and the Sears case', *Feminist Studies*, **12**, 2, pp. 375–400, argues that we have to be careful when and how we assert women's difference; Scott, 1992, p. 257; Lewis, 1992, maintains that we need to firmly establish equality (including equality for men to have parental leave) before we can start making claims based on difference. Phillips, 1992, p. 207, argues that although it is important to value women, it is important not to perpetuate feminine stereotypes.

40. Political liberalism is concerned with equal rights for citizens and social justice: Phillips, 1992, p. 206. Although it is often seen as reformist, many feminists have pointed to its 'radical potential': Eisenstein, 1981, *The Radical Future of Liberalism*.

41. Eisenstein, 1981, argues that individualism for women is radical because it would entail economic independence from men.

Chapter 10

What Could Work for Women? Policies and Strategies

Much of the evidence in this book could create an incapacitating sense of despondency. For the most part government policies have not improved working women's economic position relative to that of men. Morover, this situation cannot easily be changed. Compromises between male employers and employees at state level have effectively excluded women from full citizenship. However, it is vital to have an agenda for radical change that is different from the one currently proposed by the right. Otherwise, most women in the twenty-first century will continue to be poor, marginal members of the paid workforce who are financially insecure and semi-dependent on men. Worse still, in the current political climate, especially once the temporary demographic changes are past, without a popular agenda for change and a strategy for making it a reality, women are also likely to lose even the limited gains that have been made: access to benefits for sole mothers, family allowances, equal pay and opportunities legislation and reproductive choice.

This final chapter sets out an agenda for change based on the principles of combining work and welfare, equality and diversity, and individual freedom and collective responsibility. Of the combination of specific policies to be discussed, only one is new in the sense that it has not yet been adopted by any country, despite having been discussed for much of this century in many nations: the concept of universal basic income. Because of its relative unfamiliarity it is described below in more detail than the other policies that should accompany it. Universal entitlement to an adequate basic income combined with more effective pay and opportunities legislation would for the first time give women economic independence, genuine choices and a stronger basis for full citizenship. Finally, without understating the difficulties involved, the chapter explores which strategies and alliances might lead to the adoption of policies that could work for women.

Towards Citizenship for Working Women

The concept of citizenship has been a focus of feminist theorizing since the late 1980s. The concept of citizens' rights is derived from political liberalism and so is reformist rather than revolutionary. Nevertheless, the legitimacy of the liberal democratic State depends to a large extent on the equal treatment of citizens (Bryson, 1992, p. 65). This provides some leverage for feminists who want to create the conditions for more radical change, as well as for others concerned about a growing 'underclass' of people, especially women with children, living in poverty.

Citizens are those who are full members of a community (Marshall, 1963, p. 253; Spicker, 1988, p. 65). In fact, however, certain groups have long been denied citizenship (Young, 1989, pp. 251-74). Citizenship in ancient Greece was restricted to free men: only they could take part in public life and engage in political decision-making, whereas women and slaves were confined to the private sphere. This distinction between public and private worlds and the value ascribed to each has not dissipated. Women's position in the private sphere continues to be a primary mechanism by which women have been denied full citizenship (Phillips, 1992, p. 209). However, this reality is often obsured (Phillips, 1992, p. 216: 'Liberalism pretends we can be equal in the public sphere when our differences are overwhelmingly in the private arena.')

Citizenship has also traditionally been restricted to those with economic independence which, since the rise of capitalism, has usually meant dependence on a wage. For women, there have been three main sources of an income: men, benefits and wages (Lewis, 1992). The first two do not confer full citizenship. Even in the 1990s only a minority of women earn an adequate independent living from paid employment and so most women have also effectively been denied full citizenship. Again, the political significance of the gender division of labour has been ignored by most democratic theorists' (Pateman, 1992, p. 227).

Some forms of State welfare have nevertheless confirmed citizenship, whereas others have denied it. Early twentieth-century recipients of Poor Law relief lost their status as citizens. National Insurance against unemployment, by contrast, was explicitly devised to give working men a 'stake in the system', by protecting their citizenship status even during periods when they did not have economic independence through a wage. The Welfare State in postwar Britain was said to have enhanced citizens' rights (Lewis, 1992, p. 114) mainly by extending National Insurance cover – but in reality the 'two track' welfare system continued. Women have seldom qualified for National Insurance benefits. Women's State welfare continues to be based to a greater extent on the social security 'safety net' with its Poor Law history, greater selectivity and consequent intrusiveness.

According to Pateman, 1992, pp. 243 and 223, women received formal citizenship when the right to vote was won, but women have not yet gained *full* citizenship. Economic equality and independence does not automatically mean equality and full citizenship in all spheres of life. Women in the former Soviet Union and East Germany had greater economic equality and reproductive choice than women in the 'free' West, and the social wage made an important contribution to women's economic wellbeing – but without having gained full political representation, social equality or shared housework.

Economic independence is nonetheless a necessary precondition for full social citizenship.

Citizenship rights are closely linked to equality, which can and should encompass difference. It is thus not the case that women can only be citizens by adopting male patterns of work. Working women have demanded to have their capabilities and efforts in the paid workforce rewarded as highly as men's and to have their unemployment taken as seriously. On the other hand, women have also pressed for and continue to demand welfare rights *as women*, such as paid maternity leave, child benefit and the recognition of women's unpaid work. The question now is: What combination of work and policies could provide all women and men with at least the economic requirements for full citizenship?

Employment Equity

Paid work and welfare need not be seen as alternatives. The employment equity proposals discussed here are envisaged as being additional to a State welfare programme designed to abolish poverty and recognize participation by all citizens.

A National Minimum Wage

A statutory national hourly minimum wage for all employees (Cockburn, 1991, p. 228) would have a major impact on the average woman's earnings and would also benefit some male workers. If a basic income is also adopted it should not be used to subsidize low wages (Smail, 1985). Everyone engaging in paid employment should receive a proper reward for the work they do, otherwise there is a danger of creating a 'workfare' State.

Not all advocates of a universal basic income are in favour of a minimum wage, however, and some are prepared to trade off minimum wages in an attempt to obtain more support for basic income.[1] Potential supporters of basic income who tend to the political right hope that low-income earners will no longer object to low pay if they are subsidized by a basic income; whereas some supporters of basic income on the left hope that low-paid workers would be able to refuse poorly paid jobs, and that wages and conditions would be improved in order to attract workers. There are no guarantees, however, that this would be the case and it would be wiser to continue to press for minimum wage legislation in addition to basic income.

Pay Equity

There is scope for existing equal pay legislation to be improved and extended. British legislation has initially had some effect on the hourly rates of pay, but its 'equal value' provisions (since 1983) have been weak. Women are still penalized financially for working with other women (Millward, 1995). However, to eliminate gender segregation at work would be a massive task, given its widespread nature as well as the disruption and resistance desegregation would incur. Large numbers of women currently in female-dominated occupations do jobs that are equivalent in terms of skill, training, effort and responsibility to jobs done by men in male-dominated jobs, but receive lower pay. Legislative provision for class claims between occupations such as nursing and the police force would eliminate the discriminatory element (approximately half) of the gender gap in hourly earnings. This would be consistent with international trends. In the United States, the 1994 Fair Pay Act which introduced pay equity into the State sector, is seen as having been successful in remedying wage discrimination (Hartmann and Aaronson, 1994). In Europe in recent years, there have been greater moves to have gender-neutral evaluations of job content rather than to focus on the gender of the workers.

Equal Opportunities

Although the impact of equal opportunities and affirmative action policies on women's overall economic position have been minor, even in America, they are still important to secure women's equal representation in leadership and decision-making positions in employment and politics. The social policies of the State which have affected working women have largely been the outcome of agreements and compromises between White male employers, working men and senior politicians and civil servants. Until 'women-centred' women are fully represented in policy-making positions, there are no guarantees that women's interests will be fostered. However, in order for this to occur, the notion of equality of opportunity needs to be interpreted and more broadly applied.

The relative ineffectiveness of equal opportunities policies to date is mainly because of the narrowness of the legislation, underpinned by an unrealistic appraisal of the magnitude of gender discrimination at work. People working to implement equal opportunities policies have been expected to overcome huge obstacles with few resources (Briar, 1994). However, there is scope for equal opportunities policies to be extended and improved. First, anti-discrimination policies should be proactive not reactive. This means that instead of waiting for discrimination to occur and then putting the onus on the individual to prove it, the emphasis should be on recognizing that discrimination is systemic and thus giving organizations the responsibility to plan to overcome it. Second, organizations that remain top heavy with White males should be penalized and obliged to rectify the situation. Affirmative action for target groups should be mandatory for as long as these groups are under-represented (Cockburn, 1991, p. 228).

Childcare

The State in Britain, except at times of extreme labour shortage, does not admit any responsibility for providing childcare for the normal children of ordinary mothers (Pascall, 1986, pp. 79–83). Currently mothers' choices about whether to engage in paid work are still mediated by the availability of suitable care for the children. For employed mothers the extra job of finding enough reliable, good-quality, affordable childcare is often a continuing source of stress and anxiety. Since women currently still normally pay childcare fees out of their own lower earnings, this aspect of the 'social wage' is of particular importance in reducing economic inequality between women and men. Current policy is for the State to encourage firms to be 'family friendly', which provides no assistance to most mothers.

It is nevertheless possible for a change in policy direction to occur. Communally provided and State-funded childcare is more equitable, reliable and popular than private arrangements made by mothers and the demand for places usually exceeds the supply.[2] In Australia, where, until the late 1980s, policy had followed the British tradition, childcare geared to the needs of working parents was then introduced by a Labour government keen to stay in favour with women voters. There need be no conflict between the quality of childcare and its convenience for working parents. Childcare should be available for all pre-schoolers as well as after-school and holiday programmes for older children (Cockburn, 1991, p. 228). At the same time, however, parents should not be obliged to work excessive hours to earn an adequate income.

A Policy on Hours of Employment

Men's typical employment patterns are an equal opportunities issue for women. British men work longer hours than any others in Europe (Hewitt, 1993, p. 8). The 'normal' working day or week is designed for people who have no caregiving responsibilities. This creates problems for some men who would wish to spend more time with their children, for their partners who often get little relief from unpaid work, as well as for mothers who are expected to compete on these terms. Women, especially those working full-time, have already made major adjustments in adapting to men's patterns of paid work: there is now increasingly a case for working men becoming more like women (Marsh, 1991). This could be addressed partly by a maximum working week. There is already a 40-hour maximum working week in Sweden and there have been moves in the EC to introduce a maximum 48-hour week, which were resisted and delayed by Britain but subsequently overruled by the European court. Cockburn (1991, p. 228) suggests that a 30-hour week, similar to that in the public service in Denmark, should be a goal for Britain. Given these developments in continental Europe, it is likely that even Britain will eventually be obliged to put a ceiling on hours of paid employment.

There is a particularly strong case for gradually reducing the length of the 'normal' or 'typical' working *day*.[3] This would make it easier for single parents of school-aged children to combine paid and unpaid work and to allow partnered parents to share the care of pre-schoolers. Caregivers could then no longer be so easily sidelined into dead-end, part-time work and treated as 'atypical' employees. As an interim step, the model used in Sweden, where parents – both fathers and mothers – have the option of a shorter working day while their children are young could be appropriate. Currently in Britain the men who work the longest hours in paid employment are the fathers of young children. The financial demands on them at this stage in their lives are considerable and so at present many would oppose shorter hours.[4] Policies should therefore ensure that parents are not pushed into poverty by reductions in working hours. Combining a universal basic income with a shorter working week would ensure that this did not occur.

If men are given more time away from paid employment to spend with their families, there is no guarantee that all men will in fact spend their extra time in this way: Cockburn (1991, p. 101) is pessimistic about this and suggests that many men will use the additional time for their own leisure pursuits. However, the evidence is inconclusive. For example, in a large study by McRae and Daniel (1991) it was found that more than three-quarters of fathers took leave on or just after the birth of their children. One of the preconditions for the transformation of women's lives is that men must change; but men need to be given the opportunity to change and social policy is the obvious vehicle.

A Policy on Geographical Mobility

Many better paid jobs contain geographical mobility clauses that require staff to be willing to be transferred to other parts of the country or even overseas when asked to by the organization. This affects the careers of women as coworkers who, if they have families, usually cannot comply with such demands; but it also disrupts the paid work of wives, who usually do move to meet the requirements of their husband's jobs. Again, the European Community has been investigating the possibility of restricting employers' ability to impose mobility clauses but the British government has been resistant to such a policy.

Welfare that Works for Women

Feminists are divided over whether dependence on the State is preferable to dependence on a man. The State is a parsimonious surrogate husband, eager to pass the responsibility for maintaining a woman and her children over to a man, but it is a more reliable provider than many men and it is often easier for women to claim their rights to an income in the public domain of the benefits office than on an individual basis in the privacy of the home (Briar, 1992a; Pateman, 1992, p. 239).

Twentieth-century Britain and other English-speaking nations have had relatively residual Welfare States compared with the Scandinavian nations. Because of this many benefits are stigmatized. Selective benefits are justified on the grounds that the costs are lower and they go only to those who really need them. However, those who do not qualify for benefits often resent paying taxes on behalf of those who do receive income from the State. Solo mothers on benefits have been particularly scapegoated in recent years. Although the benefits system has been designed more to fit with men's relationship to the workforce than women's working lives, women are dependent for a greater proportion of their income on State benefits than are men (Pascall, 1986, p. 197). In Britain the only benefits that come close to being universal and hence unstigmatized are the family allowance and old age pensions which are both contingent on age. These benefits are also the most popular. The fact that those who are financially better off effectively lose their universal benefits through taxation does not appear to reduce their popularity. Even for the relatively well off, universal benefits represent a form of security to which they are entitled simply through citizenship. For the working poor, the majority of whom are mothers, they potentially represent a means to a dignified living.

The Universal Basic Income Concept

Although women are the majority of the poor, there are also large numbers of men living on low incomes. This section explores what is increasingly acknowledged as potentially being the most effective way of eradicating poverty. A full universal basic income would make all people currently on low incomes better off, and there would be some reversal of the recent redistribution which has taken place from the lower paid to the higher paid. In the process, it would also treat partnered women as individuals rather than as dependents.

Juliet Rhys William's 'social contract' scheme, intended as an alternative to the Beveridge scheme in the postwar era (see Chapter 6), would have provided a tax-free living allowance to every man and woman whether employed or not and irrespective of relationship status. There were to have been no adult dependents of either sex (Rhys Williams, 1943, p. 151). It would have provided an adequate income for every citizen, based on participation in and belonging to a society. In the process it would have resourced and rewarded domestic and caregiving work in the home and community. Although her scheme was not adopted, the ideas put forward by Rhys Williams have continued to be explored and developed by economists.[5] After more than 50 years it is clear that the Beveridge scheme has failed to meet its major objective of abolishing poverty, and it is becoming increasingly apparent that women are suffering most as a result. Even when women qualify, state benefits are low and the structure of the abatement levels keeps the recipients in poverty (Payne, 1991; Walker, 1993).

A universal basic income would not cure all social ills. But it would have some significant advantages for both men and women over the current wages and benefits system. First, because recipients would be entitled to work *and* welfare it would be the most effective means of abolishing poverty without destroying incentives to take paid employment.[6] Unlike negative income tax, basic income would be retained in full when beneficiaries started paid employment and so it would remove 'poverty traps'. Second, because it would be universal, it would not be socially divisive: it would not create a conflict of interests between claimants and tax payers (Rhys Williams, 1943, p. 205). Third it would not attempt to control men's or women's lifestyles. Unlike the proposals that were made during the 1970s for wages for housework, a universal basic income would not stereotype women as carers, since it would also be paid to men. It would promote both individual freedom and collective responsibility. Finally, it would be a major step toward the conferment of full citizenship on all individuals who currently do not have an independent income.

A full universal basic income would also have some distinct advantages to governments. The first would be administrative simplicity. It would create a single tax and benefits system. The universal grant would replace all current benefits and would act as a child benefit, student grant, carers' benefit, unemployment pay, disability allowance and retirement pension. Payments would be credited automatically. The only slight area of complexity is that there would be some people with special needs (through disability or advanced age) who could be entitled to extra help. However, there should be no intrusive investigations to determine entitlement. Another advantage from the government's viewpoint would be that such a measure would have a wide range of potential supporters. This would include not only beneficiaries, the low-paid and the anti-poverty lobby, but also many employers and better paid workers, because flexible ways of working would become more attractive.

Paying for a Universal Basic Income

The main problem that is usually cited in relation to a universal basic income scheme is that of funding (Hill, 1990, p. 164). In 1989 it was calculated that the replacement of all current benefits and tax allowances would yield an income almost as high as the unemployment pay level for every citizen, which would mean only having to levy a relatively small amount of additional taxation to bring basic income up to the current benefits level. However, many people would still require additions to their income beyond that, partly because of special needs but mainly because of housing costs. It was realized that continuing to pay the current housing benefit on top of Universal Basic Income (UBI) would be extremely costly (Atkinson, 1995). It was calculated that if UBI plus housing benefit was to be financed out of general taxation it could involve income tax rates too high to be seen as politically feasible in Britain in the 1990s and potentially liable to affect employment incentive among higher income earners (Smail, 1985; Parker, 1989; Atkinson, 1995). This could be problematic, not because paid employment is necessarily superior to unpaid work, but because *if* the universal benefits system was financed from income tax it would be uneconomic to alienate a large section of tax payers.

Many leading advocates of UBI in Britain during the late 1980s therefore chose to reduce their demands from a full basic income to 'citizens' income' which would not be sufficient to live on, but would require less expenditure.[7] A plethora of suggested schemes developed, including 'Partial basic income' (Parker, 1993); 'two tier basic income' (Smail, 1985); a citizens' income or basic income guarantee, payable to all, with supplements paid to those who would otherwise be in poverty, such as lone parents, people with disabilities, the elderly and the unemployed. Even if part-time employees were included, as Smail advocates, this would have the advantage of restricting income tax to the region of 34–40 per cent. However, such a partial scheme would conflict with the features identified as desirable for UBI by the same authors, such as administrative simplicity and unconditionality. People moving into full-time employment would lose the top tier of their income and so there might be an element of disincentive at that point. Even a partial or citizens' income would have certain advantages: for example, it would help to re-establish the principle of universality and citizenship. Nevertheless it would not provide income adequacy or security – and people cannot live on principles.

However, it is possible to fund a relatively generous full universal basic income, higher than current benefit rates, by using a different funding base. Robertson (1994) advocates replacing income taxes, except perhaps for those on very high incomes, in favour of an annual tax on the value of land (excluding buildings) and fuel consumption from coal, oil, natural gas and nuclear power but not power from renewable sources. He argues that this would be better for the ecosystem because it would tax 'bads' like depletion of fossil fuels instead of 'goods' like the desire to work. He also suggests a 1 per cent tax on financial transactions. Other writers have also acknowledged that a full basic income might be achieved by widening the tax base. Other sources of funding that might be examined could include taxes on wealth, company profits, financial transactions, pollution or unused assets. In the interests of reversing the widening inequality that has occurred it would be advisable to emphasize taxes, which would be redistributive.

There is general agreement among writers that any basic income scheme should be introduced gradually.[8] Basic income could be phased in either by starting with a small sum paid to all citizens and gradually extending it, or by initially targeting specific groups. If basic income was to be paid in full but initially targeted to specific groups, as Purdy suggests (1994, pp. 30–48), this might be done as an extended child benefit, which would continue to normally be payable to the mother. Alternatively, or as the next stage, a parental care allowance could be paid as a cash benefit to parents who were full-time care providers and those who were part time employees (Smail, 1985; Esam and Berthoud, 1991, p. 62). Several writers have put forward proposals for a small transitional basic income paid to all (Atkinson, 1995; Parker, 1989). This could involve replacing existing tax allowances with a small benefit. It would be deducted from other benefits and in the short run this would introduce an extra layer of administrative complexity. However, in the longer term the transitional benefit could be gradually increased until it replaced all other benefits and also provided a living allowance for people who currently do not receive an income from the State. In order for this to be achieved, workable costings would still be necessary. In the longer term a full guaranteed universal basic income would be technically possible in Britain. The main obstacle at present is policy-makers' belief that high levels of public spending on universal benefits are not desirable.

Benefits to Women of a Full Basic Income

The group who would benefit from a full basic income most would be partnered carers (mainly married women) with children who, for the first time, would be guaranteed an adequate income whether or not they were in paid work. Mothers or fathers who chose to stay at home with their children while they were small would not suffer the financial penalties they do now.

Once caregiving partners were freed from financial dependence, more choices would become available to women and men. Women in unsatisfactory relationships would be able to leave more easily than at present. At the same time, however, unpartnered women, including single mothers, would be enabled to form new relationships or cohabit without the stresses associated with becoming financially dependent on a partner. A guaranteed basic income would also provide financial independence to divorced women and free them from continued economic ties to ex-partners. Governments in the English-speaking countries assume that the remedy for the poverty faced by lone parents is for non-custodial parents (mainly fathers) to pay for the upkeep of the children (Millar, 1992, p. 157). This is often presented as a form of long overdue justice for women – making men face up to their financial responsibilities – when in fact it is a means of keeping women financially dependent on men even beyond marriage. The reality, however, is that most non-custodial or divorced fathers do not earn enough to maintain even one and certainly not two homes (MacLean, 1990). Nor do they remove custodial parents and their children from poverty. It is not even an efficient way for the State to redistribute income from men to women as, across OECD countries, the rate of non-payment is high and the administrative costs of collection are significant. A full basic income would spread the cost of raising the next generation of children across the whole community instead of facing individual parents with the entire cost. This would also have the effect of depersonalizing financial relations between ex-partners and so reducing long-term hostilities.

Women and men would also have more choices over whether and on what terms to undertake caring work in the community. Carers currently only receive a benefit if they are not in employment, which creates isolation and poverty. With a guaranteed basic income, carers would be able to take part-time employment, and perhaps share the work of caring with another part-time employee. There are indications that some men are already doing more unpaid caregiving work for the elderly and disabled, and suffering the financial penalties that currently accompany this work (Corti, Laurie and Dex, 1994). A universal basic income would make it easier for men to share caring responsibilities.

One major advantage to women would be the removal of barriers to entering paid employment. Although this would also apply to men on benefits, lone mothers in particular would benefit from being able to work part-time, spend some time with their children and still be out of poverty. Between 1977–79 and 1983–85 solo mothers' participation in paid work halved, while that of widows remained constant (EOC, 1988, p. 43), because employed single mothers faced a poverty trap of loss of benefit, which widows did not. Many wives currently give up work or remain out of paid employment if their husbands become unemployed, primarily because most of the wife's earnings would be deducted from the husband's unemployment benefit (Cooke, 1987, pp. 371–82). With a guaranteed basic income system and disaggregated benefits, wives and partered mothers would also be able to benefit from paid work and adult company in the workplace.

A universal basic income would provide income security to older women and men and allow people to retire from paid work when they were ready to do so. A tax-funded pension scheme similar to a basic income already exists for retired people in Denmark and could serve as a useful model. Universal Basic Income would reverse the redistribution from women to men which has occurred in the English-speaking countries with the reductions in taxation and benefits and the advent of 'community care'.

Advantages of a Partial or Transitional Basic Income for Women

A citizens' income, or a basic income guarantee would not meet most of the principles of a full universal basic income. However, a guaranteed partial income could nevertheless be of some benefit to women.

UK women benefit considerably from the current child benefit, even though it is not a large amount. Research has shown that the money is spent chiefly on children's food, clothes and shoes, school expenses and general household expenses and that mothers regarded the money as essential and appreciated the fact that the income was regular, reliable and paid directly to them.[9] Mothers assume responsibility for day-to-day spending on children, for planning when to get specific items and saving for specific costly items such as shoes and winter coats, as well as special occasions such as school outings, Christmas and birthdays. Mothers have used the fact that their child benefit was regular and reliable as part of their budgeting strategy.

The millions of women with small personal incomes and others dependent on them would be better off with even a partial citizens' income or basic income guarantee. It would enable partnered mothers in particular to manage better within their existing circumstances. It would help to make women's poverty less severe but would not eradicate it. However, these benefits would not provide economic independence particularly since the supplements to a partial or citizens' income would continue to be means-tested according to the joint incomes of couples. Many women therefore would continue to be trapped in relative poverty and partial dependence and thus denied full citizenship. A partial basic income might serve to obsure that fact. Further, just as wages from the part-time employment of wives reduces the demands on husbands' incomes without altering the division of domestic responsibilities, a partial basic income would probably have the same effect. A partial universal income should be therefore considered only as part of a feasible longer term strategy for a full UBI and not as an alternative to it.

The Potential for Change

If implemented, a combination of work and welfare policies as described above would probably be the most effective way of eradicating poverty, reducing inequality and promoting universal citizenship. However, government policies in the English-speaking world currently tend to be opposed to extending either State benefits or equality-at-work legislation: indeed, the challenge in recent years has been to prevent past gains from being taken away. The two major political parties in Britain are likely to oppose the adoption of a universal basic income (George and Howards, 1991; Jordan, 1992, pp. 115–23). Even the Liberal Democrats, who had been the only political party in Britain to support UBI, abandoned their proposal for a citizens' income in late 1994. The principles of universality, the notion that all citizens deserve a reliable income and that women should receive a living allowance regardless of their family status, are all in direct opposition to current mainstream government thinking. It would undoubtedly be argued by leading British policy-makers that a basic income would lead to the breakdown of the family and destroy work incentives. In fact, it could well improve the quality of family life because financial stresses would be removed, women could leave abusive relationships and negotiate better and more equal partnerships. The major political parties are allegedly in favour of full employment, which they regard as an alternative to welfare, although both parties have abandoned policies that could have brought the creation of enough secure jobs for all. It therefore appears unlikely that Britain will become the first country to adopt a universal basic income system, although Britain may follow if other European countries take a lead.

In parts of continental Europe the philosophical underpinnings of social policy differ from Britain's in some important respects. For example, some European countries do not regard the problems of combining paid and unpaid work as being exclusively a women's issue. The European Commission's Second Action Programme states that men and women should share family responsibilities so that women can play a more active role in the public world of paid work and political life. Policies are being encouraged across Europe which will make it possible for men to take a larger share of home responsibilities. Membership of the European Community has given some impetus to groups in Britain pressing for an improvement of the economic position of women since it became clear that European Community legislation can take precedence over the laws of its member nation states (Hall-Smith *et al.*, 1983). There are already some hopeful signs, such as the partial disaggregation of incomes for assessment purposes, partly as a result of cases brought to the European Court by British women (Esam and Berthoud, 1991; Payne, 1991). However, in the first half of the 1990s the British government's resistance to pressure from Europe to adopt policies such as a maximum working week and limits on mobility clauses has been disheartening. If Britain is again forced by legal action to amend its pay and opportunities legislation again, or to adopt a maximum working week, there will probably be another series of delays and loopholes. Real change requires a government commited to the principles of greater equality and citizenship for all. This in turn will only be brought about if there is large-scale, active, highly visible support for these principle among the voting population in Britain.

Forming Alliances

Feminism's overall impact on social and economic policy has been relatively small, arguably because of the combined power of patriarchal employers and male workers. In order to reverse the trend of the past decade-and-a-half towards widening inequalities it is necessary to mobilize as large and as broad an opposition as possible. The situation can change if new, strong alliances are formed to lobby for policies that would provide working women and men with financial security and equality (Pateman, 1992, p. 232). The combination of interests that has worked against women is powerful but not omnipotent. It has incured costs as well as benefits for those involved in it. Employers have wasted much of women's potential and male employees have divided and weakened working people by alienating women.

Building Bridges: Meeting the Needs of Diverse Groups of Women

Women have seldom been united. Early second-wave feminists, who were predominantly White, well-educated and from the richer nations of the world, assumed that the differences between women were relatively minor and so over time they alienated Black women, lesbians and women with disabilities. Women workers are not a homogenous group. Black women in Britain have suffered higher levels of unemployment, racial discriminantion and been confined to an even narrower range of jobs than their White counterparts. There are also huge differences in employment experiences between various ethnic groups of women often collectively described as 'Black', and State policies, although usually silent on issues of race have been described as institutionally racist as they are sexist (Phizacklea, 1988, pp. 43–4). Lesbians, though often less visibly 'different', often find themselves having to choose between 'being out' at work and risking penalties such as harrassment, loss of promotion or even dismissal, or remaining uncomfortably invisible in a heterosexist working environment. Women with disabilities have suffered higher levels of unemployment than either able-bodied women or disabled men.

The 'identity' politics that developed as a result of unacknowledged differences, though intended to be a source of pride, have tended to cause friction and mistrust between diverse groups of women (Cockburn, 1991, pp. 237–8). Work and welfare policies of governments and employers have also traditionally tended to divide and give different treatment to younger and older, married and single working women and to mothers and childfree women, thus fostering resentment. The working lives of many women, particularly the poorest, have remained as unaffected by the women's movement as by government's 'equality' policies – except that a sense of failure and discomfort about doing so much undervalued work has been added to their burdens. However, Hakim's (1995, pp. 429–56) suggestion that feminists should listen to women, the majority of whom want to stay at home with their children or say they prefer part-time employment, embodied an uncritical acceptance of preferences conditioned by shortages of adequate and affordable childcare, career paths or adequate welfare benefits, which mean that most women have few real choices (Ginn *et al.*, 1996). The challenge for social policy is to provide real freedom and positive choices for women and for men.

Although it would be naïve to assume that women have identical interests, they have enough shared economic interests to form a potentially powerful lobby group. Indeed, this has happened on occasions in the past, for example over equal pay (see Chapter 7). Most women have children and bring them up at huge financial costs to themselves because this work receives few supports from the State and even fewer from employers. Even if women choose not to become parents because of the costs in career terms, this is often a difficult and painful decision that few 'career men' have to make. Even women who never marry or have children still earn less than similarly qualified men. Gender discrimination at work, low pay and mothers' poverty are issues that potentially form a basis for partnerships between groups of women. In the process of making links, however, it is also necessary to celebrate diversity (Cockburn, 1991, p. 239).

Marriages of Convenience: Working with Working Men?

Since the 1980s feminists have become increasingly aware that gender inequality is only one form of social inequality. Morover, working women have not succeeded on their own in radically altering social and economic policies and may never do so. An alliance between organized labour and an autonomous women's movement that recognizes class inequality would be more effective, if one could be created (Pateman, 1992, p. 240). However, this raises the question of how feasible it is for feminists to work along with working men to bring about economic equality for women.

At times, alliances between feminists and trade unions have taken place, for example, during the almost century-long struggle for equal pay for women. However, many working men have been ambivalent about equal pay and at times have shared an interest with employers in resisting equal pay for work of equal value. Some husbands seem to be prepared to settle for a smaller household income rather than to see their wives economically independent. Men of all ethnic groups in the workplace were particularly negative about equal opportunities initiatives (Cockburn, 1991, p. 66; Snell, 1979, pp. 37–58). Unions have traditionally been male-dominated, and men are often still opposed to 'women's issues' dominating union agendas. It is possible that working men might prefer to remain worse off and continue to collude with employers against women.

Nevertheless, there are some hopeful signs. Women's participation in trade unions has grown as men's has diminished, especially among Black women. Many men are becoming discontented with long hours and poor conditions and are concerned at the contraction in secure employment. There is thus some scope for feminists and groups such as the workplace democracy movement to form alliances around issues that are in the interests of both women and men (Pateman, 1992, p. 241) but with certain provisos. There would still have to be an autonomous women's movement and respect for the diverse groups within it. Women's groups need to be fully represented in any discussions of policy. Gains that have been obtained so far for women via the State would have to be safeguarded and all new policies carefully checked by all interested parties.

Women workers in the past have been accused of 'dividing the working class' by not supporting their unions, while male employees have divided workers by making deals with employers to restrict women to the poorest jobs. Indeed, reinforcing gender divisions appears to be one means by which class inequality has been maintained. Men need to be prepared to work with women on a more equal basis and to lose some privileges relative to women in exchange for a stronger and more effective movement. In many ways the prospect of trying to reach such an agreement is daunting. However, with goodwill and an agreed set of principles and policies designed to benefit both diverse groups of women and most men, change is possible.

New Contractual Arrangements: Working with Employers?

Earlier in the century, a debate took place in which feminists were divided over whether to claim full equal pay and in so doing to side with the trade unions who had attempted to exclude them from a range of occupations, or to collude with employers by offering their services at slightly less pay in the hope of undercutting working men. Similarly in the 1990s, some women see the weakening of trade unions as creating new opportunities to negotiate directly with employers and so take jobs previously dominated by men. Employers also usually prefer to bargain with women individually. However, most women alone are in a weaker bargaining position than in unions. A few women do well, but the majority become worse off, especially in an economic recession. There are also other costs. Women also lose the basis for support and goodwill they might have had from unions. Further, throughout the century, employers have demonstrated a preference for men in the more sought-after jobs and this cannot be entirely explained by the activities of working men. The 'employment equity policies' suggested here would impose stronger State controls on employers' ability to discriminate. The 'welfare' policies outlined above would reduce women's dependence on a wage, which should therefore put women and men in a more favourable position in wage negotiations.

However, arguably such policies would also benefit employers in the long run. Employees who are in a position to be flexible and adaptable, who are not worried and preoccupied about childcare and/or paying the bills and are not exhausted will make fewer mistakes, produce better goods and services and will be in a better postion to meet the new demands of a changing work environment. Nonetheless, many, indeed most employers may not initially see their interests as lying in this direction, especially in the current political climate. Overcoming their resistance may still prove to be the biggest challenge.

Conclusions

The policies suggested here would doubtless be currently considered unreasonable by most leading politicans. There has been and still is substantial opposition from government to feminist pressure for recognizing or revaluing women's unpaid work (Lewis, 1992, p. 116) or viewing any non-market activity as valuable. However, all the gains that have been made by women and working people have, for some time before being accepted, been seen as out of the question'. One of the lessons of history is that with enough support, major changes can be accomplished. Shorter hours of paid work and a national minimum wage already have support from trade unions. We should not assume that measures involving higher taxation will necessarily be as unpopular with the voting population as they are with politicians. The 1995 Social Attitudes survey[10] shows a high level of support for the Welfare State, especially for universal services such as health and education, and strong support for higher levels of taxation on the better-off. This agenda does not have to mean a bureaucratic and controlling State. Indeed, although some of the 'work' policies would be more regulatory in some respects, the 'welfare' policies would be far less intrusive than at present – and far less stifling to initiative. Small-scale, local enterprises meeting local needs, including cooperatives, would be made more feasible by a basic income.

Alternative economic strategies that fail to take account of women's different work histories, economic needs and experience have often been criticized by feminists. However, it is possible to create an agenda that works for women and still improves the economic positions of other disadvantaged groups and most men. The question is whether men will be prepared to give up their relative privileges to support such a strategy.

Notes

1. Some see basic income as an alternative to demands for a minimum wage and as a potential trade-off. See, for example, Desai (1995), speaking at a conference on 'Citizens' income: Winning the argument' who argued that once poverty is eradicated by a basic income (and this argument can only be seriously considered if there is to be a *full* Universal Basic Income) there is no longer a viable case for a minimum wage.
2. However, childcare places should not be made available as a way to force solo mothers off benefits and into employment or 'workfare', as has happened in parts of the United States. Mothers should have genuine choices about when and for how long to leave their children.
3. As Pateman, 1992, in 'The patriarchal welfare state' points out, a shorter working week has been supported by men because it would give them more leisure. But a shorter working day would be of more benefit to parents of school-age children.
4. Many British workers do not currently appear to want shorter hours instead of increases in pay although the engineers' union has successfully campaigned for a shorter working week. This is probably because wages are lower in Britain than in most EC countries. Surveys in the 1990s have indicated that the largest group of workers, including women working part-time, when asked for their preferences in terms of reduced hours, have said they would like to take any decrease in hours as longer holidays

(Hewitt, 1993, pp. 70–2). Again this appears to be because many workers currently have no holiday entitlement or very little. However, this is to be addressed by the European Community Time Directive, which is to give all workers four weeks' annual leave by 1999, which the British government has been vigorously opposing. It appears likely that workers will be happier to reduce their daily hours of paid work if they have a guaranteed basic income and longer paid holidays.

5. These have included Meade, 1948, *Planning and the Price Mechanism*; Meade, 1972, 'Poverty in the welfare state', *Oxford Economic Papers,* **24**, 3; Parker, 1989, *Instead of the Dole: an Enquiry into an Integration of the Tax and Benefit System*; Parker, 1991, *Basic Income and the Labour Market*; and Parker, 1993, *Citizens' Income and Women*; and Atkinson, 1995, *Public Economics in Action: The Basic Income/Flat Tax Proposal.*

6. Although paid employment is not the only or necessarily best way of organizing work, a benefits scheme funded from taxation on earnings from paid work would have to be devised in a way that maintained incentives to enter and remain in paid employment.

7. In the process, the main British-based organization that had been campaigning for a universal basic income changed their name from the Basic Income Research Group to a Citizens' Income Research Group.

8. Robertson, 1994, p. 34, suggests three years' preparation, followed by ten years' phasing in, without creating large defecits and surpluses in any one year. Parker, 1993, p. 8, agrees that even a partial basic income would take many years to implement.

9. Walsh and Lister, 1985, *Mother's Lifeline*; Child Poverty Action Group; Walker, Middleton and Thomas, 1993, *Mostly on the Children: the Significance of Child Benefit in Family Budgets.*

10. *British Social Attitudes: the 12th Report*, 1995.

References

Books, Articles, Theses and Unpublished Papers

ABBOTT, E. (1907) 'Municipal employment of unemployed women in London', *Journal of Political Economy*, November.

ACKER, J. (1989) 'The Problem with Patriarchy', *Sociology*, **23**, 2, pp. 235–40.

ADAMS, C.T. and WINSTON, C.T. (1980) *Mothers at Work: Public Policies in the United States, Sweden and China*, New York: Longman.

ADKINS, L. (1995) *Gendered Work: Sexuality, Family and the Labour Market*, Buckingham: Open University Press.

ANDREWS, I.O. (1918) *The Economic Effects of the War on Women and Children in Great Britain*, New York: Oxford University Press.

ALTHUSSER, L. (1971) 'Ideology and ideological state apparatuses', in L. Althusser, *Lenin and Philosophy*, New York: Monthly Review Press.

ATKINSON, A.B. (1995) *Public Economics in Action: the Basic Income/Flat Tax Proposal*, Oxford: The Clarendon Press.

BALDOCK, C.V. and CASS, B. (Eds) (1988) *Women, Women, Social Welfare and the State*, Sydney: Allen & Unwin.

BARRETT, M. (1980) *Women's Oppression Today: Problems in Marxist Feminist Analysis*, London: Verso.

BARRETT, M. and MCINTOSH, M. (1982) *The Anti-Social Family*, London: Verso.

BEAUCHAMP, J. (1937) *Women Who Work*, London: Lawrence & Wishart.

BECKER, G. (1973) 'A theory of marriage, part one', *Journal of Political Economy*, **81**, pp. 813–46.

BECKER, G. (1974) 'A theory of Marriage, part two', *Journal of Political Economy*, **82**, pp. 1063–93.

BEDDOE, D. (1989) *Back to Home and Duty*, London: Pandora.

BEECHEY, V. (1977) 'Some notes on female wage labour in capitalist production', *Capital and Class*, **3**, pp. 45–66.

BEECHEY, V. (1979) 'On Patriarchy', *Feminist Review*, **3**, pp. 66–82.

BELOFF, M.J. (1976) *Sex Discrimination: The New Law*, London: Butterworth.

BEVERIDGE, W.H. (1909) *Unemployment: A Problem of Industry*, London: Longman Green.

BEVERIDGE, W.H. (1930) Unemployment: A Problem of Industry, London: Longman Green.

BHAVNANI, R. (1994) *Black Women in the Labour Market: a Research Review*, Manchester: Equal Opportunities Commision.

BITTMAN, M. (1991) *Juggling Time: How Australian Families Use Time*, Canberra: Office of the Status of Women: Department of the Prime Minister and Cabinet.

BLACK, C. (Ed.) (1915) *Married Women's Work*, London: Bell & Sons.

BOOTH, T. (1979) *Planning for Welfare: Social Policy and the Expenditure Process*, Oxford: Blackwell.

BOSANQUET, H. (1916) 'Women in industry', *Economic Journal*, **26**.

BOSTON, S. (1980) *Women Workers and the Trade Union Movement*, London: Davis Poynter.

BOWLBY, J. (1951) *Maternal Care and Maternal Health*, Geneva: World Health Organisation.

BRADLEY, H. (1989) *Men's Work, Women's Work*, Cambridge: Polity Press.

BRANSON, N. (1976) *Britain in the 1920s*, Minneapolis: University of Minnesota Press.

BRAYBON, G. (1981) *Women Workers in the First World War*, London: Croom Helm.

BRAYBON, G. and SUMMERFIELD, P. (1987) *Out of the Cage: Women's Experiences in Two World Wars*, London: Pandora.

BRIAR, C. (1987) 'Women and State employment policy, 1905–1985', unpublished PhD thesis, University of Sheffield.

BRIAR, C. (1992a) 'Women, economic dependence and social policy', in C. BRIAR, R. MUNFORD and M. NASH (Eds) *Superwoman Where Are You? Social Policy and Women's Experience*, Palmerston North: Dunmore Press.

BRIAR, C. (1992b) 'Part time work and the State in Britain 1943–1986', in L.P. LUNDY, K. LUNDY and B. WARME (Eds) *Working Part Time: Risks and Opportunities*, New York: Praeger.

BRIAR, C. (1994) 'Tracing the patterns: the development of EEO policies in New Zealand and overseas', in J. SAYERS and M. TREMAINE (Eds) *The Vision and the Reality*, Palmerston North: Dunmore Press.

BRIAR, C. (1995) 'Explaining women's position in the workforce: A social political analysis', in P. MORRISON (Ed.) *Proceedings of the 6th Conference on Labour Employment and Work*, Victoria: University of Wellington, Centre for Industrial Relations.

BRITISH SOCIAL ATTITUDES (1989) *Special International Report*, Aldershot: Gower.

BRITISH SOCIAL ATTITUDES (1995) *British Social Attitudes: the 12th Report*, Aldershot: Dartmouth Publishing House.

BROCKWAY, F. (1931) *The Anomolies Bill: Why its Rejection was Moved*, London: ILP.

BROWN, K.D. (1971) *Labour and Unemployment 1900–1910*, Newton Abbott: David & Charles.

BRUEGEL, I. (1979) 'Women as a reserve army of labour: a note on recent British experience', *Feminist Review*, **3**, pp. 12–23.

BRUEGEL, I. (1983) 'Women's employment, legislation and the labour market', in J. LEWIS (Ed.) *Women's Welfare/Women's Rights*, London: Croom Helm.

BRYSON, L. (1992) *Welfare and the State: Who Benefits?* Basingstoke: Macmillan.

BULLOCK, S. (1994) *Women and Work*, London: Zed Books.

BUNKLE, P. and LYNCH, J. (1992) 'What's Wrong with the New Right?' in C. BRIAR, R. MUNFORD and M. NASH (Eds) *Superwoman Where Are You? Social Policy and Women's Experience*, Palmerston North, Dunmore Press.

BUSWELL, C. (1992) 'Training girls to be low paid women', in C. GLENDINNING and J. MILLAR (Eds) *Women and Poverty in Britain: the 1990s*, Hemel Hempstead: Harvester Wheatsheaf.

BYRNE, P. and LOWENDUSKI, J. (1978) 'The Equal Opportunities Commission', *Women's Studies*, **2**.

CADBURY, E., MATHESON C.M. and SHANN, G. (1906) *Women's Work and Wages*, London: T. Fisher Unwin.

CALASANTI, T.M. and BAILEY C.A. (1991) 'Inequality in the division of household labor in the United States and Sweden: a socialist feminist approach', *Social Problems*, **38**, 1, pp. 34–53.

CAMPBELL, Bea (1984) *Wigan Pier Revisited*, London: Virago.

CHEW, D. NIELD (1982) *Ada Nield Chew: the Life and Writings of a Working Woman*, London: Virago.

CLARK, G. (1982) 'Recent developments in working patterns', *Employment Gazette*, **70**, p. 285.

COCKBURN, C. (1985) *Machinery of Dominance: Women, Men and Technical Knowhow*, London: Pluto Press.

COCKBURN, C. (1991) *In the Way of Women: Men's Resistance to Sex Equality in Organisations*, London: Macmillan.

COLLETT, C. (1898) The Extent and Effects of the Industrial Employment of Women', *Journal of the Royal Statistical Society*, June.

COLLINSON, D. and HEARN, J. (1994) 'Naming men as men: implications for work, organisation and management', *Gender, Work and Organisation*, **1**, 1, pp. 2–22.

COMER, L. (1974) *Wedlocked Women*, Leeds: Feminist Books.

CONFEDERATION OF BRITISH INDUSTRY (1991) *Discriminate on Ability: Practical steps to add value to your workforce*, London: CBI.

CONSTANTINE, S. (1980) *Unemployment in Britain between the Wars*, London: Longman.

COOKE, K. (1987) 'The withdrawal from paid work of the wives of unemployed men', *Journal of Social Policy*, **16**, 3, pp. 371–82.

COOTE, A. and CAMPBELL, B. (1982) *Sweet Freedom*, London: Picador.

CORTI, L., LAURIE H. and DEX, S. (1994) *Caring and Employment*, Employment Department Research Series No. 39, London: Employment Department.

COUSSINS, J. (1977) *The Equality Report*, London: NCCL.

COYLE, Angela and SKINNER, Jane (Eds) (1988) *Women and Work: Positive Action for Change*, London: Macmillan.

CROMPTON, R. and SANDERSON, K. (1990) *Gendered Jobs and Social Change*, London: Unwin Hyman.

CURRAN, M. (1986) *Selection and Stereotypes: Gender and Family in the Recruitment Process*, London HMSO.

DALE, J. and FOSTER, P. (1986) *Feminists and State Welfare*, London: Routledge & Kegan Paul.

DALLA COSTA, M. and JAMES, S. (1972) *The Power of Women and the Subversion of the Community*, Bristol: Falling Wall Press.

DANIEL, W.W. and STILGOE, E. (1978) *The Effects of Employment Protection Laws*, London: Policy Studies Institute.

DAVID, M. (1990) 'Women and "work" in the decade of Thatcherism', in I. TAYLOR (Ed.) *The Social Effects of Free Market Policies: an International Text*, London: Harvester Wheatsheaf.

DAVIDOFF, L. (1976) 'The rationalisation of housework', in D.L. BARKER and S. ALLEN (Eds) *Dependence and Exploitation in Work and Marriage*, London: Longman.

DEACON, A. (1977) *In Search of the Scrounger*, Leeds: Occasional Papers in Social Administration.

DELPHY, C. (1984) *Close to Home: a Materialist Analysis of Women's Oppression*, London: Hutchinson.

DELPHY, C. and LEONARD, D.L. (1992) *Familiar Exploitation*, Cambridge: Polity Press.

DEPARTMENT FOR EDUCATION AND EMPLOYMENT (1995) *United Nations Convention on the Elimination of all Forms of Discrimination against Women: Third report of the United Kingdom of Great Britain and Northern Ireland*, London, Department for Education and Employment.

DEPARTMENT OF EMPLOYMENT (1974) *Women and Work: a Statistical Survey*, London: Manpower Papers Series.

DEPARTMENT OF EMPLOYMENT (1985) *Unfair Dismissal Law and Practice in the 1980s*, London: Research Paper No. 53.

DE SCHWEINITZ, K. (1961) *England's Road to Social Security from the Statute of Labourers 1340 to the Beveridge Report of 1942*, New York: A.S. Barnes.

DESAI, M. (1995) Keynote speech at the Citizen's Income: winning the argument conference, London: Citizen's Income Research Group.

DEX, S. (1987) *Women's Occupational Mobility*, London: Macmillan.

DEX, S. and PARRY, S. (1984) 'Women's employment in the 1970s', *Employment Gazette*.

DEX, S., LISSENBURGH, S. and TAYLOR, M. (1994) *Women and Low Pay: Identifying the Issues*, Manchester: Equal Opportunities Commission.

DEX, S., WALTERS, P. and ALDEN, D.M. (1993) *French and British Mothers at Work*, London: Macmillan.

DRAKE, B. (1917) *Women in the Engineering Trades*, London: Fabian Research Department.

EISENSTEIN, H. (1984) *Contemporary Feminist Thought*, London: Counterpoint.

EISENSTEIN, Z.R. (1979) 'Developing a theory of capitalist patriarchy and socialist feminism', in Z.R. EISENSTEIN (Ed.) *Capitalist Patriarchy*, New York: Monthly Review Press.

EISENSTEIN, Z. (1981) (Ed.) *The Radical Future of Liberal Feminism*, New York: Longman.

EQUAL OPPORTUNITIES COMMISSION (1980) *The Experience of Caring for Elderly and Handicapped Dependents*, Manchester: EOC.

EQUAL OPPORTUNITIES COMMISSION (1982a) *Proposed Amendments to the Sex Discrimination Act, 1975 and the Equal Pay Act, 1970 (as amended)*, Manchester: EOC.

EQUAL OPPORTUNITIES COMMISSION (1986a) *Building Businesses . . . Not Barriers: Implications for Women of the White Paper Relating to Part Time Workers and Maternity Rights*, Manchester: EOC.

EQUAL OPPORTUNITIES COMMISSION (1986b) *Briefing for MPs: 'The Sex Discrimination Bill*, Manchester: EOC.

EQUAL OPPORTUNITIES COMMISSION (1986c) *Indirect Discrimination Brief*, Manchester: EOC.

EQUAL OPPORTUNITIES COMMISSION (1988) *Women and Men*, London: HMSO.

EQUAL OPPORTUNITIES COMMISSION (1995a) *The Gender Impact of CCT in Local Government: The Summary Report*, Manchester: EOC.

Equal Opportunities Commission (1995b) *Request to the Commission of European Communities by the Equal Opportunities Commission for Great Britain in Relation to the Principle of Equal Pay; Draft Code of Practice on Equal Pay*, Manchester: EOC.

EQUAL OPPORTUNITIES COMMISSION (1995c) *Draft Code of Practice on Equal Pay*, Manchester: EOC.

EQUAL OPPORTUNITIES COMMISSION (1995d) *The Inequality Gap*, Manchester: EOC.

EQUAL OPPORTUNITIES COMMISSION (1995e) *Some Facts About Women*, Manchester: EOC.

EQUAL OPPORTUNITIES COMMISSION and DEPARTMENT of EMPLOYMENT (1991) *Maternity Rights in Britain: First Findings*, Manchester: EOC.

ESAM, P. and BERTHOUD, R. (1991) *Independent Benefits for Men and Women*, London: Policy Studies Institute.

EUROPEAN COMMUNITY COMMISSION (1994) 'Memorandum on Equal Pay' COM 94 Final, official directive of the European Community.

FAWCETT, M. GARRETT (1918) 'Equal pay for equal work', *Economic Journal*, **27**, pp. 1–3.

FINCH, J. (1983) *Married to the Job*, London: Allen & Unwin.

FINCH, J. and GROVES, D. (Eds) (1983) *A Labour of Love: Women, Work and Caring*, London: Routledge.

FINCH, J. and SUMMERFIELD, P. (1991) 'Social reconstruction and the emergence of companionate marriage', in D. CLARKE (Ed.) *Marriage, Social Change and Domestic Life: Essays in Honour of Jackie Burgoyne*, London: Routledge.

FINE, B. and HARRIS, L. (1976) 'Controversial issues in Marxist economic theory', *Socialist Register*, pp. 141–78.

FOLBRE, N. and HARTMANN, H. (1988) 'The rhetoric of self-interest and the ideology of gender', in A. KLAMER, D. McCLOSKEY and R.M. SOLOW (Eds) *The Consequences of Economic Rhetoric*, Cambridge: Cambridge University Press.

FRASER, D. (1973) *The Evolution of the British Welfare State*, London: Macmillan.

GAME, A. and PRINGLE, R. (1983) *Gender at Work*, London: Pluto Press.

GAME, A. and PRINGLE, R. (1996) 'Gender at work', in G. ARGYROUS (Ed.) *Economics as a Social Science*, Sydney: Pluto Press.

GARDINER, J. (1976) 'Women and unemployment', *Red Rag*, **10**.

GEORGE, V. and HOWARDS, I. (1991) *Poverty Amidst Affluence: Britain and the United States*, Aldershot: Edward Elgar.

GINN, J., ARBER, S., BRANNEN, J., DALE, A., DEX, S., ELIAS, P., MOSS, P., Pahl, J. *et al.* (1996) 'Feminist fallacies: a reply to Hakim on women's employment', *British Journal of Sociology*, **47**, 1, pp. 167–73.

GINSBERG, N. (1979) *Class, Capital and Social Policy*, London: Macmillan.

GLENDINNING, C. (1992) ' "Community Care": the financial consequences for women', in C. GLENDINNING and J. MILLAR (Eds) *Women and Poverty in Britain: the 1990s*, Hemel Hempstead: Harvester Wheatsheaf.

GLENDINNING, C. and MILLAR, J. (1991) 'Poverty: the forgotten Englishwomen – reconstructing research and policy on poverty', in M. McLEAN and D. GROVES (Eds) *Women's Issues in Social Policy*, London: Routledge.

GOUGH, I. (1979) *The Political Economy of the Welfare State*, London: Macmillan.

GRAHAM, H. (1983) 'Caring: a labour of love', in J. FINCH and D. GROVES, *A Labour of Love: Women, Work and Caring*, London: Routledge.

GRAHAM, H. (1987) 'Being poor: coping and lone motherhood', in J. BRANNEN and G. WILSON (Eds) *Give and Take in Families*, London: Allen & Unwin.

GRAHAM, H (1992) 'Budgeting for health: mothers in low income households', in C. GLENDINNING and J. MILLAR (Eds) *Women and Poverty in Britain: the 1990s*, Hemel Hempstead: Harvester Wheatsheaf.

GRAHAM, H. (1993) *Hardship and Health in Women's Lives*, London: Harvester Wheatsheaf.

GRAVES, R. and HODGE, A. (1941) *The Long Weekend*, London: Readers' Union.

GREGORY, J. (1987) *Sex, Race and the Law*, London: Sage.

GROVES, D. (1992) 'Occupational pension provision and women's poverty in old age', in C. GLENDINNING and J. MILLAR (Eds) *Women and Poverty in Britain: the 1990s*, Hemel Hempstead: Harvester Wheatsheaf.

HABGOOD, R. (1992) 'On his terms: Gender and the politics of everyday life', in R. DU PLESSIS, P. BUNKLE, K. IRWIN, A. LAURIE and S. MIDDLETON (Eds) *Feminist Voices*, Aukland: Oxford University Press.

HAKIM, C. (1979) 'Occupational segregation: A comparative study of the degree and pattern of differentiation between men's and women's work in Britain, the United States and other countries', London: Department of Employment Research Paper, Department of Employment.

HAKIM, C. (1987) 'Trends in the flexible workforce', Employment Gazette, November, pp. 549–60.

HAKIM, C. (1995) 'Five feminist fallacies about women's employment', *British Journal of Sociology*, **30**, 3, pp. 429–56.

HALL-SMITH, V., HOSKYNS, K., KEINER, J. and SZYSZCAK, E. (1983) *Women's Rights and the EEC*, London: Rights of Women Europe.

HARRIS, J. (1972) *Unemployment and Politics 1886–1914*, London: Oxford University Press.

HARRIS, J. (1977) *William Beveridge: a Biography*, Oxford: Clarendon Press.

HARTMANN, H. (1979) 'The unhappy marriage of marxism and feminism: towards a more progressive union', *Capital and Class*, **8**, pp. 1–33.

HARTMANN, H. (1981) 'The family as the locus of gender: Class and political struggle: the example of housework', *Signs*, **6**, pp. 366–94.

HARTMANN, H. and AARONSON, S. (1994) *Pay Equity as a Remedy for Wage Discrimination: Success in the State Civil Service*, Washington DC: Institute for Women's Policy Research.

HARTMANN, S.M. (1981) *The Home Front and Beyond: Women in the 1940s*, Boston: Twayne.

HEPPLE, B.A. (1981) *Employment Law*, London: Sweet & Maxwell.

HERNES, H. (1987) *Welfare State and Woman Power*, Oslo: Norwegian University Press.

HEWITT, P. (1993) *About Time*, London: IPP/Rivers Oram Press.

HILL, M. (1990) *Social Security Policy in Great Britain*, Aldershot: Edward Elgar.

HOBSON, B. (1990) 'No exit, no voice: women's economic dependency and the welfare state', *Acta Sociologica*, **33**, 3.

HUNT, A. (1966) *A Survey of Women's Employment*, London: HMSO.

HUTCHINS, B.L. (1915) *Women in Modern Industry*, London: Bell.

HUTCHINS, B.L. (1917) *Women in Industry after the War*, Social Reconstruction Pamphlet No. III.

HUTCHINS, B.L. (1921) 'The present position of women industrial workers', *Economic Journal*, **30**, p. 246.

HYMAN, P. (1994) *Women and Economics: a New Zealand Feminist Perspective*, Wellington, Bridget Wiliams Books.

INSTITUTE OF MANPOWER STUDIES (c.1992) *Beyond the Career Break: a Study of Professional and Managerial Women Returning to Work After Having a Child*, London: Institute of Manpower Studies, Report No. 223.

IRONMONGER, D. (1989) 'Households and the household economy', in D. IRONMONGER (Ed.) *Households Work*, Sydney: Allen & Unwin.

JEFFREYS, S. (1985) *The Spinster and her Enemies: Feminsim and Sexuality*, 1880–1930, London: Pandora.

JENKINS, S. (1991) 'Poverty measurement and the within household distribution: agenda for action', *Journal of Social Policy*, **20**, 4, pp. 457–48.

JEWSON, N. and MASON, D. (1986) 'The theory and practice of equal opportunities', *Sociological Review*, **34**, 2, pp. 307–34.

JORDAN, B. (1992) 'The prospects for basic income', *Social Policy and Administration*, **22**, 2, pp. 115–23.

JOSHI, H. (1987) 'The costs of caring', in J. MILLAR and C. GLENDINNING (Eds) *Women and Poverty in Britain*, London, Harvester Wheatsheaf.

JOSHI, H. (1989) 'The changing form of women's economic dependency', in H. JOSHI (Ed.) *The Changing Population of Britain*, Oxford: Blackwell.

KANTER, R. (1976) *Men and Women of the Corporation*, New York: Basic Books.

KEMPSON, E., BRYSON, A. and ROWLINGSON, K. (1994) *Hard Times: How Poor Families Make Ends Meet*, London: Policy Studies Institute.

KLEIN, V. (1965) *Britains Married Women Workers*, London: Routledge & Kegan Paul.

KORNDORFFER, W. (1992) 'Look like a woman, act like a man and work like a dog', in C. BRIAR, R. MUNFORD and M. NASH (Eds) *Superwoman Where Are You? Social Policy and Women's Experience*, Palmerston North: Dunmore Press.

LAMBERT, D. (1984) *Equality at Work*, Manchester: EOC.

LAND, H. (1981) *Parity Begins at Home: Women's and Men's Work and its Effects on their Paid Employment*, Manchester: EOC/SSRC.

LEEDS WOMEN AND SOCIAL SECURITY GROUP (1983) *The State of Women's Benefits*, Leeds: Leeds Women and Social Security Group.

LEIRA, A. (1993) 'The "women friendly" welfare state? The case of Norway and Sweden', in JANE LEWIS (Ed.) *Women and Social Policies in Europe*, Aldershot: Edward Elgar.

LEWENHAK, S. (1977) *Women and Trade Unions: an Outline History of Women in the British Trade Union Movement*, London: Ernest Benn.

LEWENHAK, S. (1980) *Women and Work*, London: Fontana.

LEWENHAK, S. (1988) *The Revaluation of Women's Work*, London: Croom Helm.

LEWIS, J. (1983) 'Dealing with dependency: State practices and social realities 1870–1946', in J. LEWIS (Ed.) *Women's Welfare: Women's Rights*, London: Croom Helm.

LEWIS, J. (1984) *Women in England 1870–1950*, Brighton: Harvester Wheatsheaf.

LEWIS, J. (1992) *Women in Britain since 1945 : Women, Family Work and the State in the Post War Years*, Oxford: Basil Blackwell.

LEWIS, J. and PIACHAUD, D. (1992) 'Women and poverty in the twentieth century', in C. GLENDINNING and J. MILLAR (Eds) *Women ad Poverty in Britain: the 1990s*, Hemel Hempstead: Harvester Wheatsheaf.

LIDDINGTON, J. and NORRIS, J. (1978) *With One Hand Tied Behind Us*, London: Virago.

LISTER, R. (1993) 'Tracing the contours of women's citizenship', *Policy and Politics*, **21**, 1, pp. 3–16.

LONSDALE, S. (1992) 'Patterns of paid work', in C. GLENDINNING and J. MILLAR (Eds) *Women and Poverty in Britain: the 1990s*, Hemel Hempstead: Harvester Wheatsheaf.

LOWE, M. (1980) *Women's Rights: Homeworkers*, London: NCCL.

MACDONALD, J.R. (1912) *Margaret Ethel Macdonald*, London: Allen & Unwin.

MACDONALD, MRS J.R. (M. E.) and MRS PLAYER (*c*.1916) *Wage Earning Mothers*, London: Women's Labour League.

MACLEAN, M. (1990) 'Lone parent families: family law and income transfers', in *OECD, Lone Parent Families: the Economic Challenge*, Paris: OECD.

MACK, J. and LANSLEY, S. (1985) *Poor Britain*, London: Allen & Unwin.

MACKIE, L. and PATULLO, P. (1977) *Women Who Work*, London: Tavistock.

MADDEN, J.F. (1972) *The Economics of Sex Discrimination*, Lexington, MA: Lexington Books.

MAGUIRE, A. (1992) 'Power: now you see it, now you don't: a woman's guide to how power works', in L. McDOWELL and R. PRINGLE (Eds) *Defining Women: Social Institutions and Gender Divisions*, Cambridge: Polity Press/Open University Press.

MAHIJANI, A. (1992) *From Global Capitalism to Economic Justice*, London: Apex Press.

MANPOWER SERVICES COMMISSION (1976) *Training Opportunities for Women*, London: MSC.

MARSDEN, D. (1969) *Mothers Alone: Poverty and the Fatherless Family*, Harmondsworth: Penguin.

MARSH, C. (1991) *Hours of Work of Women and Men in Britain*, Equal Opportunities Commission, London: HMSO.

MARSHALL, T.H. (1963) 'Citizenship and social class', in *Sociology at the Crossroads*, New York: Doubleday.

MARTENS, L. (1995) 'Women in Banking', unpublished paper, Sociology Dept., University of Lancaster.

MARTIN, J. and ROBERTS, C. (1984) *Women and Employment: a Lifetime Perspective. The Report of the DE/OPCS Survey*, London: HMSO.

MARTINDALE, H. (1938) *Women Servants of the State*, London: Allen & Unwin.

MARWICK, A. (1976) *The Home Front: the British and the Second World War*, London: Thames & Hudson.

MARWICK, A. (1977) *Women at War 1914–1918*, London: Fontana.

MEADE, J. (1948) *Planning and the Price Mechanism*, London: Allen & Unwin.

MEADE, J. (1972) 'Poverty in the welfare state', Oxford Economic Papers, **24**, 3.

McDOWELL L. (1992) 'Gender divisions in a post Fordist era', in L. McDOWELL and R. PRINGLE (Eds) *Defining Women: Social Institutions and Gender Divisions*, Cambridge: Polity Press/Open University Press.

McKINNON, C.A. (1979) *Sexual Harassment of Working Women: a case of sex discrimination*, New Haven: Yale University Press.

McRAE, S. (1991) *Maternity Rights in Britain: the Experience of Women and Employers*, London, PSI.

McRAE, S. and DANIEL, W.W. (1991) *Maternity Rights in Britain: First Findings*, London: PSI.

MEEHAN, E. and SEVENHUIJSEN, S. (1991) 'Problems in principles and politics', in E. MEEHAN and S. SEVENHUIJSEN (Eds) *Equality, Politics, Gender*, London: Sage.

MIDDLETON, S. and THOMAS, M. (1994) 'How mothers use child benefit', in S. MIDDLETON, K. ASHWORTH and R. WALKER (Eds) *Family Fortunes: Pressures on Parents and Children in the 1990s*, London: Child Poverty Action Group.

MILKMAN, R. (1976) 'Women's work and the economic crisis', *Review of Radical Political Economy*, **8**, 1.

MILKMAN, R. (1987) *Gender at Work: the Dynamics of Job Segregation by Sex during World War II*, Urbana, IL: University of Illinois Press.

MILLAR, J. (1992) 'Lone mothers and poverty', in C. GLENDINNING and J. MILLAR (Eds) *Women and Poverty in Britain: the 1990s*, Hemel Hempstead, Harvester Wheatsheaf.

MILLAR, J. and GLENDINNING, C. (1992) '"It all really starts in the family": gender divisions and poverty', in C. GLENDINNING and J. MILLAR (Eds) *Women and Poverty in Britain: the 1990s*, Hemel Hempstead, Harvester Wheatsheaf.

MILLWARD, N. (1995) *Targeting Potential Discrimination*, Manchester: EOC.

MINISTRY OF LABOUR (1942) *Mobilisation of women power; Planning for part-time work*, London: HMSO.

MITTER, S. (1994) 'What women demand of technology', *New Left Review*, **205** (May/June), pp. 100–12.

MORGAN, R. (1977) *Going too Far: the Personal Chronicle of a Feminist*, New York: Random House.

MORRIS, L. (1984) 'Redundancy and patterns of household finance', *Sociological Review*, **32**, 3, pp. 492–523.

MORRIS, L. (1990) *The Workings of the Household*, Cambridge: Polity Press.

MORRIS, L. and RUANE, S. (1989) *Household Finance Management and the Labour Market*, Aldershot: Avebury.

MOSS, P. and MELHUISH, E. (1991) *Current Issues in Day Care for Young Children*, London: HMSO.

MUDIE-SMITH, R. (1980; originally published 1906) *Sweated Industries*, London: Bradbury Agnew.

NATIONAL COUNCIL FOR SINGLE WOMEN (1974) *The Wages of Caring*, London: National Council for Single Women.

NATIONAL ECONOMIC DEVELOPMENT OFFICE (1991) *Women Managers: the Untapped Resource*, London: Kogan Page.

NEWSOM, J. (1948) *The Education of Girls*, London: Faber & Faber.

NOVITZ, R. (1987) 'Bridging the gap', in S. Cox (Ed.) *Public and Private Worlds*, Wellington: Allen & Unwin/Port Nicholson Press.

OAKLEY, A. (1974) *The Sociology of Housework*, Oxford: Basil Blackwell.

OAKLEY, A. (1981) *Subject Women*, Oxford: Martin Robertson.

ORGANIZATION FOR ECONOMIC COOPERATION AND DEVELOPMENT (1985) *The Integration of Women into the Economy*, Paris: OECD.

ORWELL, G. (1959) *The Road to Wigan Pier*, London: Secker & Warburg.

PAHL, R.E. (1980) 'Patterns of money management within marriage', *Journal of Social Policy*, **9**, 3, pp. 313–35.

PAHL, R.E. (1992) 'Work and Employment', in L. McDOWELL and R. PRINGLE (Eds) *Defining Women: Social Institutions and Gender Divisions*, Cambridge: Polity Press/Open University Press.

PANKHURST, S. (1911) *The Suffragettes: The History of the Women*, London: Gay and Hancock.

PARKER, H. (1989) *Instead of the Dole: an Enquiry into Integration of the Tax and Benefits System*, London: Routledge.

PARKER, H. (Ed.) (1991) *Basic Income and the Labour Market*, London: Basic Income Research Group Paper No. 1.

PARKER, H. (Ed.) (1993) *Citizens' Income and Women*, London: Basic Income Research Group Paper No. 2.

PASCALL, G. (1986) *Social Policy: A Feminist Analysis*, London: Allen & Unwin.

PATEMAN, C. (1988) *The Sexual Contract*, Stanford, CA: Stanford University Press.

PATEMAN, C. (1992) 'The patriarchal Welfare State', in L. McDOWELL and R. PRINGLE (Eds) *Defining Women: Social Institutions and Gender Divisions*, Cambridge: Polity Press/Open University Press.

PATULLO, POLLY (1983) *Judging Women*, London: NCCL.

PAYNE, S. (1991) *Women, Health and Poverty: an Introduction*, London: Harvester Wheatsheaf.

PEDERSEN, S. (1989) 'The failure of feminism in the making of the Welfare State', *Radical History Review*, **43**, pp. 86–110.

PEMBER REEVES, M. (1913) *Round About a Pound a Week*, London: Bell.

PERKINS GILMAN, C. (1966; first published 1898) *Women and Economics*, New York: Harper & Row.

PERRONS, D., BRUEGEL, I. and HEGEWISCH, A. (1996) 'Britain in Europe: the deregulated, rotten apple in the Barrel?' paper presented to the ESRC seminar on the Economics of Equal Opportunities, London, 17 May 1996.

PHILLIPS, A. (1992) 'Feminism, equality and difference', in L. McDOWELL and R. PRINGLE (Eds) *Defining Women Social Institutions and Gender Divisions*, Cambridge: Polity Press/Open University Press.

PHILLIPS, G. and WHITESIDE, N. (1985) *Casual Labour: Unemployment in the Port Transport Industry*, Oxford: Clarendon.

PHIZACKLEA, A. (1988) 'Gender, racism and occupational segregation', in S. WALBY (Ed.) *Gender Segregation at Work*, Milton Keynes: Open University Press.

PILGRIM TRUST (1968; first published 1938) *Men Without Work*, New York: Greenwood.

PINCHBECK, IVY (1981; first published 1930) *Women Workers and the Industrial Resolution 1750–1850*, London: Virago.

POLLARD, S. (1991) *The Development of the British Economy 1914–1990*, London: Edward Arnold.

POLLERT, A. (1981) *Girls, Wives, Factory Lives*, London: Macmillan.

PRINGLE, R. (1992) 'Women and consumer capitalism', in L. McDOWELL and R. PRINGLE (Eds) *Defining Women: Social Institutions and Gender Divisions*, Cambridge: Polity Press/Open University Press.

PURDY, D. (1994) 'Citizenship, basic income and the State', *New Left Review*, **208**, pp. 30–48.

RAMDIN, R. (1987) *The Making of the Black Working Class in Britain*, Aldershot: Gower.

RATHBONE, E. (1917) 'The renumeration of women's services', *Economic Journal 1917*, pp. 56–8.

RATHBONE, E. (1926) *The Disinherited Family: a Plea for the Endowment of the Family*, London: Edward Arnold.

RESKIN, B.F. and ROOS, P.A. (1990) *Job Queues, Gender Queues: Explaining Women's Inroads into Male Occupations*, Philadelphia, PA: Temple University Press.

RHYS WILLIAMS, J. (1943) *Something to Look Forward to*, London: Macdonald.

RICE, M.S. (1981; first published 1939) *Working Class Wives*, London: Virago.

RICHARDSON, J. (1984) *Women and Welfare*, London: Labour Party.

RILEY, D. (1981) 'The Free Mothers: pronatalism and working women in industry at the end of the last war in Britain', *History Workshop*, **II**.

ROBARTS, S., COOTE, A. and BALL, E. (1981) *Positive Action for Women: the Next Step*, London, NCCL.

ROBERTS, E. (1984) *A Woman's Place: An Oral History of Working Class Women 1890–1940*, Oxford: Blackwell.

ROBERTS, E. (1988) *Women's Work, 1840–1940*, London: Macmillan.

ROBERTS, E. (1995) *Women and Families: an Oral History 1940–1970*, Oxford: Blackwell.

ROBERTSON, J. (1994) *Benefits and Taxes: A Radical Strategy*, London: The New Economics Foundation.

ROBERTSON, M. (1979) 'Social policy in relation to industry', in D.C. MARSH (Ed.) *Introducing Social Policy*, London: Routledge & Kegan Paul.

ROBINSON, O. and WALLACE, J. (1984) 'The growth and utilisation of part time employment in Great Britain', *Employment Gazette*, **92**, p. 396.

ROWNTREE, B.S. and STUART, F.D. (1921) *The Responsibility of Women Workers for Dependents*, Oxford: Clarendon Press.

RUGGIE, M. (1984) *Working Women and the State: a Comparative Study of Britain and Sweden*, Princeton, NJ: Princeton University Press.

SACHS, A. and HOFF WILSON, J. (1979) *Sexism and the Law*, New York: Free Press.

SAVILLE SMITH, K. (1987) 'Women and the State', in S. Cox (Ed.) *Public and Private Worlds*, Wellington: Allen & Unwin/Port Nicholson Press.

SCHMIDT, F. (Ed.) (1978) *Discrimination in Employment*, Stockholm: Almquvist & Wiskell International.

SCHREINER, O. (1918) *Women and Labour*, London: Fisher Unwin.

SCOTT, J.W. (1992) 'Deconstructing equality-versus-difference', in L. MCDOWELL and R. PRINGLE (Eds) *Defining Women: Social Institutions and Gender Divisions*, Cambridge: Polity Press/Open University Press.

SCOTTISH LOW PAY UNIT (1995) *New Rights for Part-Time Workers*, Glasgow: SLPU.

SECCOMBE, W. (1974) 'The Housewife and her labour under capitalism', *New Left Review*, **83**, pp. 3–24.

SHARP, R. and BROOMHILL, R. (1988) *Short Changed: Women and Economic Policies*, Sydney: Allen & Unwin.

SMAIL, R. (1985) 'A two-tier basic income and a national minimum wage', London: Basic Income Research Group Bulletin No. 4.

SMITH, D.E. (1915) *Wage Earning Women and their Families*, London: Fabian Women's Group.

SNELL, M. (1979) 'The Equal Pay Act and the Sex Discrimination Act: their impact on the workplace', *Feminist Review*, **1**, pp. 37–57.

SPALTER-ROSS, R., BURR, B. and HARTMANN, H. (1995) *Welfare that Works: The Working Lives of AFDC Recipients*, Washington DC: Institute for Women's Policy Research.

SPICKER, P. (1988) *Principle of Social Welfare*, London: Routledge.

STRACHEY, R. (1978; first published 1928) *The Cause: a Short History of the Women's Movement in Britain*, London: Virago.

SULLIVAN, M. (1992) *The Politics of Social Policy*, London: Harvester Wheatsheaf.

SUMMERFIELD, P. (1983) 'Women, work and welfare: a study of childcare and shopping in the Second World War', *Journal of Social History*, **16** (December), pp. 249–70.

SUMMERFIELD, P. (1984) *Women Workers in the Second World War*, London: Croom Helm.

TAWNEY, J. (1910) 'Women and unemployment', *Economic Review*.

THIELE, B. (1992) 'Vanishing acts in social and political thought: tricks of the trade', in L. MCDOWELL and R. PRINGLE (Eds) *Defining Women: Social Institutions and Gender Divisions*, Cambridge, Polity Press/Open University Press.

TILLY, L.A. and SCOTT, J.W. (1978) *Women, Work and Family*, New York: Holt Reinhart & Winston.

TILYARD, F. and BALL, F.N. (1949) *Unemployment Insurance in Great Britain 1922–8*, London: Thames Bank Publishing Company.

TITMUSS, R.M. (1976) *Essays on the Welfare State*, London: Allen & Unwin.

UNGERSON, C. (Ed.) (1985) *Women and Social Policy: a Reader*, Basingstoke: Macmillan.

VOGLER, C. (1989) *Labour Market Change and Patterns of Financial Allocation within Households*, Oxford: ESRSC Social Change and Economic Life Initiative.

WALBY, S. (1983) 'Patriarchal structures: the case of unemployment', in E. GAMARNIKOW (Ed.) *Gender, Class and Work*, London: Heinemann.

WALBY, S. (1984) 'Gender and unemployment', in D. Gallie (Ed.) *New Approaches to Economic Life*, Manchester: Manchester University Press.

WALBY, S. (1986) *Patriarchy at Work*, Cambridge: Polity Press.

WALBY, S. (1990) *Theorising Patriarchy*, Oxford: Basil Blackwell.

WALKER, A. (1982) 'Dependency and old age', *Social Policy and Administration*, **16**, 2, pp. 116–35.

WALKER, A. (1983) 'Care for elderly people: a conflict between women and the State', in J. FINCH, and D. GROVES (Eds) *A Labour of Love*, London: Routledge.

WALKER, A. (1984) *Social Planning: a Strategy for Socialist Welfare*, Oxford: Basil Blackwell.

WALKER, C. (1993) *Managing Poverty: the Limits of Social Assistance*, London: Routledge.

WALKER, D.J. (1975) *Sex Discrimination*, London: Shaw.

WALKER, R., MIDDLETON, S. and THOMAS, M. (1993) *Mostly on the Children: the Significance of Child Benefit in Family Budgets*, London: Centre for Research in Social Policy, Working Paper No. 218.

WALSH, A. and LISTER, R. (1985) *Mother's Lifeline*, London: Child Poverty Action Group.

WARING, M. (1988) *Counting for Nothing: What Men Value and What Women are Worth*, Wellington: Allen & Unwin/Port Nicholson Press.

WHITEHEAD, C. (1981) '"I'm hungry, Mum": the politics of domestic budgeting', in K. YOUNG, C. WALKOWITZ and R. MCCULLAGH (Eds) *Of Marriage and the Market: Women's Subordination in International Perspective*, London: CSE Books.

WICKHAM, A. (1982) 'The State and training programmes for women', in E. WHITELEGG (Ed.) *The Changing Experience of Women*, Milton Keynes: Open University Press.

WILLIAMS, M. (1972) *Inside Number 10*, London: Weidenfeld & Nicolson.

WILSON, E. (1977) *Women and the Welfare State*, London: Tavistock.

WILSON, E. (1980) *Only Halfway to Paradise: Women in Postwar Britain 1945–68*, London: Tavistock.

WILSON, G. (1987) 'Money: patterns of responsibility and irresponsibility within marriage', in J. BRANNEN and G. WILSON (Eds) *Give and Take in Families: Studies in Resource Distribution*, London: Allen & Unwin.

WRIGLEY, C. (1982) 'The Ministry of Munitions: a innovatory department', in Kathleen Burke (Ed.) *War and the State: the Transformation of British Government*, London: Allen & Unwin.

YOUNG, I. (1981) 'Beyond the unhappy marriage: a critique of "dual systems" theory', in L. SARGENT (Ed.) *Women and Revolution*, London: Pluto Press.

YOUNG, I. (1989) 'Polity and group difference: a critique of the idea of universal citizenship', *Ethics*, **99**, pp. 251–74.

YOUTHAID (1982) *CEP is Working*, London: Youthaid.

ZIMMECK, M. (1986) 'Jobs for the girls: the expansion of clerical work for women 1850–1914', in A. JOHN (Ed.) *Unequal Opportunities: Women's Employment in England 1800–1918*, Oxford: Basil Blackwell.

Government Sources

British Parliamentary Papers: Summary Tables on Occupation

Cd 8110 (1915) *Clerical and Commercial Employment*

Cd 8185 (1916) Health of Munition Workers Committee, Memorandum No. 4, *Employment of Women*

Cd 8186 (1916) *Health of Munition Workers Committee Memorandum No.5: Hours of Work*

Cd 8511 (1917) *Health of Munition Workers Interim Report*

Cmd 67 (1919) *Ministry of Reconstruction: Women's Advisory Committee on the Domestic Service Problem*

Cmd 135 (1919) *Report of the War Cabinet Committee on Women in Industry*

Cmd 164 (1919) *Civil Service Recruitment After the War*

Cmd 167 (1919) *Women in Industry*

Cmd 403 (1919) *Openings in Canada for Women from the United Kingdom*

Cmd 745 (1920) *Openings in Australia for Women from the United Kingdom*

Cmd 3508 (1929/30) *A Study of the Factors which have Operated in the Past and which Still Operate to Determine the Distribution of Women in Industry*

Cmd 3872 (1931) *Royal Commission on Unemployment Insurance*

Cmd 4185 (1931/2) *Royal Commission on Unemployment Insurance Majority Report*

Cmd 4346 (1932/3) *The Operation of the Anomolies Regulations*

Cmd 6301 (1941) *Calling up of Civil Servants*

Cmd 6307 (1941) *Interim Report of the Beveridge Committee*

Cmd 6182 (1940) *Hours of Employment of Women and Young Persons During the First Five Months of the War*

Cmd 6324 (1941–2) *Manpower*

Cmd 6548 (1943–4) *Manpower: Reallocation of Manpower between the Armed*

Forces and Civilian Employment during any Interim Period between the Defeat of Germany and the Defeat of Japan

Cmd 6568 (1945) *Reallocation of Man power between Civilian Employment duing the Interim Period between the Defeat of Germany and the Defeat of Japan*

Cmd 6650 (1944/5) *Report on the Post War Organisation of Domestic Employment*

Cmd 6886 (1945/6) *Civil Service National Whitley Council Committee on the Marriage Bar*

Cmd 7046 (1946/7) *Economic Survey for 1947*

Cmd 7895 (1950) *Statement on Defence*

Cmd 8146 (1950/51) *Defence Programme*

Cmd 9628 (1955/6) *The Employment of Older Men and Women*

Cmd 9703 (1955/6) *Technical Education*

Cmnd 902 (1959/60) *Scientific and Engineering Manpower in Great Britain*

Cmnd 1490 (1960/61) *Long-term Demand for Scientific Manpower*

Cmnd 1892 (1962/3) *Industrial Training: Government Proposals*

Cmnd 2800 (1964/5) Committee on Manpower Resources for Science and Technology *A Review of the Problems of Scientific and Technical Manpower Policy*

Cmnd 3102 (1966/7) *Interim Report of the Working Party on Manpower: Parameters for Scientific Growth*

Cmnd 3103 (1966/7) *Report on the Triennial Manpower Survey of Engineers, Scientists and Technologist and Technical Supporting Staff*

Cmnd 3417 (1966/7) *The Brain Drain*

Cmnd 3623 (1967/8) *Report of the Royal Commission on Trade Unions and Employers' Associations (The Donovan Report)*

Cmnd 3638 (1968) *'The Civil Service' (The Fulton Report Vol. 1)*

Cmnd 3760 (1967/8) *The Flow into Employment of Scientists, Engineers and Technologists*

Cmnd 5205 (1972/3) *Counter Inflation Policy*

Cmnd 5536 (1972/3) Department of Employment *6th Report of the Expenditure Committee*

Cmnd 5724 (1974) *Equality for Women*

Cmnd 9571 (1986) *Lifting the Burden*

Cmnd 9794 (1986) *Building Businesses . . . not Barriers*

HC 19 1942/3 *Health and Welfare of Women in War Factories*

Home Office (1978) *Sex Equality*

House of Commons (1972/3) No. 333 'Special Report of the Select Committee on the Anti-Discrimination Bill'

House of Commons, *Hansard*, 4th 5th and 6th series

House of Commons Paper No. 63 1937/8 session

House of Lords (1972/3) No. 104 'Special Report on the Anti-Discrimination Bill'

House of Lords, *Hansard* 4th series

Public General Acts and Measures: Public General Acts
Regulations (Organisation for the Unemployed) Art.2 91.2 Statutory Rules
and Orders 1905, 1071. Unemployed Workmen Act 1905 Regulations
Act. V(i)(f)(g)
Report of the Central Advisory Committee for Education (The Plowden Report) Children and their Primary Schools, Vol. 1, 1967
Report of the Select Committee on Equal Compensation, 1942
Reports of the Unemployment Insurance Statutory Committee 1935 and 1936
Royal Commission on Equal Pay 1945
Royal Commission on Labour, 1893–4, *Minutes of Evidence*
Royal Commission on the Poor Laws, 1909, *Majority Report*
Royal Commission on the Poor Laws, 1909, *Minority Report*
Select Committee on Distress from Want of Employment. 1896
7th Report of the Expenditure Committee (1977) *The Job Creation Scheme*

Cabinet Papers

PRO (Public Records Office) Cab 65/20; Cab 65/29; Cab 65/220; Cab 2631

Newspapers

Board of Trade and Labour Gazette
Employment Gazette 1903–1995
Employment and Productivity Gazette
Guardian
Labour Gazette
Manchester Guardian, 1916
Ministry of Labour Gazette
Morning Post, 1908
Morning Star
Spare Rib, 1979
Sunday Times, 4 February 1973
The Times
Unison
The Vote 1925
The Woman Worker 1903–1921
Welfare Rights Bulletin, 1986
Women's Dreadnought, 1916
Women's Industrial News 1905–17

Index

THE
NORTHERN COLLEGE
LIBRARY

BARNSLEY

5877